New Worlds for All

The American Moment

Stanley I. Kutler
Series Editor

New Worlds for All

✦

*Indians, Europeans, and the
Remaking of Early America*

✦

Colin G. Calloway

The Johns Hopkins University Press

Baltimore and London

© 1997 The Johns Hopkins University Press
All rights reserved. Published 1997
Printed in the United States of America on acid-free recycled paper

Johns Hopkins Paperbacks edition, 1998
4 6 8 9 7 5 3

The Johns Hopkins University Press
2715 North Charles Street
Baltimore, Maryland 21218-4363
www.press.jhu.edu

Library of Congress Cataloging-in-Publication Data will be found at
the end of this book.

A catalog record for this book is available from the British Library.

ISBN 0-8018-5959-x (pbk.)

For Marcia, Graeme, and Meg

I am part of all that I have met.

—Alfred, Lord Tennyson, *Ulysses*

New World it is, for those who became its peoples remade it,
and in the process, they remade themselves.

—Sidney W. Mintz and Richard Price,
An Anthropological Approach to the Afro-American Past:
A Caribbean Perspective (Philadelphia, 1976)

Contents

Illustrations

Preface and Acknowledgments

IN 1491 THE WORLD stood on the brink of a new era. The old world, in both Europe and America, was about to *end*. Christopher Columbus's voyage the following year set in motion forces of change that altered the whole planet: Europe was never the same again after its so-called discovery of America; America was almost totally transformed. A prophecy attributed to a Spokan Indian on the Columbia Plateau toward the end of the eighteenth century, before contact with white Americans, echoed prophecies recorded among Indian peoples across the continent in its foreboding. "Soon," warned the prophet, "there will come from the rising sun a different kind of man from any you have yet seen, who will bring with them a book and will teach you everything, and after that the world will fall to pieces." In many ways, the worlds Indian peoples had created in North America over countless centuries did fall to pieces after European Christian missionaries and others came to their country. But the story did not end there. Indian people—those who survived the new wars, diseases, economic disruption, and societal disintegration generated by European invasion—picked up the pieces and set about rebuilding their world. They saved what they could from the old and used what they could that was new. The invaders, meanwhile, were also rebuilding their worlds, recreating what they could of their European past, but adding much that was new. This short book explores the new worlds that Indians and Europeans created together in early America and considers how conquest changed conquered people and conquerors alike.

The book is not a history of American Indians, though it involves Indian peoples and their experiences. Nor is it a narrative of Indian-white relations. It is a collection of essays, perhaps more accurately a series of impressions, that together suggest how things could not have been the way they were without the interaction of Indian and European peoples in America. The making or remaking of early America was not a "moment," characterized by a single dramatic and colorful event such as occurred at Jamestown or Plymouth Rock. It was an experience that lasted longer than the United States has existed as a nation, and it involved many different peoples adapting to many different situations. During those centuries, most of America was still Indian country, and even in areas of European settlement, Indians remained part of daily life. It was a world where Indian and European people lived, worked, worshiped, traveled, and traded together, as well as a world where, often, they feared, avoided, despised, and killed each other. The book is arranged topically rather than chronologically to provide readers with glimpses of what early America was like when and where Indians and Europeans came into sustained contact, and of how that contact changed things. The timeline at the front of the book should help orient readers accustomed to more chronological narratives and serve as a reference for key events.

This book attempts to avoid "ghettoizing" Indian people into some kind of exotic subcategory in American history and tries instead to integrate them as essential participants in the making of American history and the shaping of American societies. It is intended to prompt students and general readers to rethink their colonial past and their national roots, which are far less ethnically and culturally "neat" than they are often portrayed. Even so, this book tells only part of the story. It surveys and gives examples of Indian-European interactions throughout North America, but mentions only incidentally African-European and African-Indian interactions. Although colonial governments endeavored to keep Indians and Africans divided against each other, they frequently intermingled and sometimes intermarried. Such aspects of the cultural kaleidoscope of early America merit books in themselves.

I am grateful to Henry Y. K. Tom, executive editor, and to Stanley I. Kutler, American Moment series editor, for their invitation to write a book such as this, and to the National Endowment for the Humanities for a summer stipend, which allowed uninterrupted time to complete it. I began writing the book at the University of Wyoming and finished it at Dartmouth College. I am grateful to my colleagues at both institutions for their collegiality and support, especially Sergei Kan; Chris Jocks, who read chapter 4; and Allen Koop, who read chapter 2. Thanks to Linda Welch for patiently guiding my transition to a new computer system, and to the anonymous reviewer whose generous and constructive comments pointed out where the manuscript needed to be fine-tuned to produce a better book. Reed Detar skillfully reproduced many of the illustrations; Nancy Toth drew the maps; Phil Roberts prepared the index; and Barbara O'Neil Phillips did a nice job of copy editing. As usual, all errors are my own, and the book is dedicated to the people who remade *my* world.

Timeline

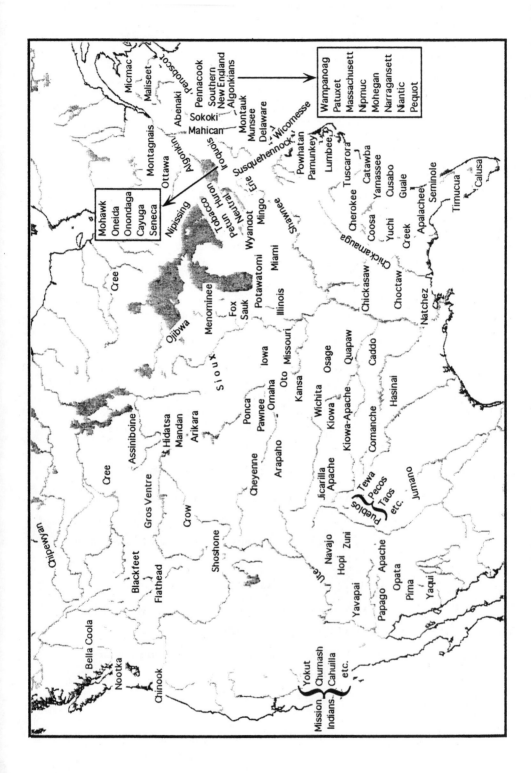

1616–19	Major epidemic (disease unknown) in New England
1620	Plymouth Colony established
1622	Powhatan Indians go to war against English in Virginia
1632–49	French Jesuit missionaries active in Huronia
1633–34	Smallpox epidemic throughout the Northeast
1636–37	Puritan war against the Pequots
1640s	Mayhew family missionaries active on Martha's Vineyard
1643	Governor Kiefft's War against the Indians of lower Hudson Valley and New York
1644	Second Powhatan war against English
1646–75	John Eliot's missionary work in New England
1649	Iroquois destroy Huron villages
1675–76	King Philip's War in New England
1680	Pueblo Revolt drives Spaniards from New Mexico
c.1680–c.1750	Plains Indians acquire horses
1681–82	René Robert Cavelier de La Salle travels down the Mississippi and claims the Mississippi Valley for Louis XIV as Louisiana
1689–97	King William's War
1692	Francisco de Vargas reconquers New Mexico
1700–1701	Iroquois establish peace with France and Britain
1701	John Lawson travels among Indian peoples of the Carolinas
1702–13	Queen Anne's War; Treaty of Utrecht, 1713
1703–4	English and Indian allies destroy Spanish mission system in northern Florida
1704	French and Indians raid Deerfield, Massachusetts

Map 1. Indian Peoples Mentioned in the Text: Approximate tribal locations at the time of their first sustained contact with Europeans

1715	Yamassee War against English colonists in South Carolina
1720–35	French wars against the Fox Indians in the western Great Lakes
1722	Tuscaroras migrate north from the Carolinas and join the Iroquois Confederacy; the Five Nations become the Six Nations
1738	Smallpox kills half the Cherokees
1741	Vitus Bering and Alexei Chirikov open Russian trade with native peoples of Gulf of Alaska
1744	Treaty of Lancaster between the Six Nations and Virginia, Pennsylvania, and Maryland
1744–48	King George's War between England and France
1754	Albany Congress between Six Nations and various English colonies; Benjamin Franklin's plan of colonial union
1755	French and Indians defeat Edward Braddock in Ohio; battle of Lake George
1756–63	Seven Years' War, also known as French and Indian war
1757	French and Indians capture Ft. William Henry, in New York
1759–61	War between Cherokees and English colonists
1763	Pontiac's Revolt Royal Proclamation establishes Appalachian Mountains as boundary to English settlement
1768	Treaty of Fort Stanwix: Iroquois cede lands south of Ohio River to Sir William Johnson
1769	First Franciscan mission established in California
1774	Lord Dunmore's War between Shawnees and Virginia
1776–78	Captain James Cook begins English trade with Northwest Coast peoples
1776–83	American Revolution
1778	Treaty of Fort Pitt between Delawares and U.S.; first treaty between U.S. and Indians

1779	General John Sullivan invades Iroquoia
1779–83	Massive smallpox epidemic from Mexico to Canada
1783	Peace of Paris: Britain recognizes the independence of its thirteen former colonies and transfers Indian lands to U.S.
1786	Governor Juan Bautista de Anza makes peace between New Mexico and Comanches
1790	Northwestern tribes defeat General Josiah Harmar in Ohio
1791	Northwestern tribes defeat General Arthur St. Clair in Ohio
1791–93	George Vancouver trades with Indian peoples on Pacific coast
1794	General Anthony Wayne defeats northwestern tribes at Fallen Timbers in Ohio
1795	Treaty of Greenville; northwestern tribes cede most of Ohio to U.S.
1799	Handsome Lake religion begins among the Senecas
1804–6	Expedition of Meriwether Lewis and William Clark from St. Louis to the Pacific

New Worlds for All

Introduction

.✳.

The Kaleidoscope of Early America

A T THE OUTBREAK of the American Revolution, the rebelling colonists solicited the support, or at least the neutrality, of the Indian tribes of the eastern woodlands in their war against Great Britain. Often, American agents invoked the shared experiences of white Americans and Indian Americans, pointing out that they were both native-born Americans facing a common threat at the hands of tyrannical Britons. "We are sprung from one common mother, we were all born in this big Island," American commissioners at Pittsburgh told visiting Mohawks, Senecas, Delawares, and Shawnees in 1776. Addressing Indian delegates in the Wabash country in 1778, Virginian George Rogers Clark declared that the "Big Knife [the Indian name for Virginians in particular, and Americans in general] are very much like the Red people." Like the Indians, and unlike the British, he said, the Americans did not know much about manufacturing, "and live chiefly by making corn, Hunting and Trade as you do." Speaking to the Indian tribes around Montreal on behalf of the Continental Congress, Ira Allen of Vermont made similar claims. He said he loved Indians, and hunted and fought as they did. In June 1776, when Congress in Philadelphia was debating independence, John Hancock told visiting Iroquois that the Americans and the Iroquois were "as one people, and have but one heart."

Most of this was just council-fire rhetoric. Clark, Allen, and most of the founding fathers were interested in Indian land, not in a shared Indian identity. But were the Americans on to something? Was there an Indian ingredient in the mixture of influences that made colonists incipient "Americans" by 1775? When George Rogers Clark and his ragtag army arrived at

Vincennes in 1779, the Spanish lieutenant governor in the area was shocked at how much they resembled Indians in their clothing and their appearance. Eight years later, another Spaniard described American backwoodsmen on Florida's northern frontier as differing from their Indian neighbors only in their skin color, language, and cunning. Did surface resemblances indicate a deeper and more pervasive Indian imprint on American culture and character?

In 1066, William the Bastard, duke of Normandy, invaded England to seize the throne from the Anglo-Saxon King Harold. Defeating and killing Harold in battle, William marched to London and took possession of the city, where he had himself crowned king. In the years that followed, the Normans imposed their government, system of justice, language, and culture on the conquered English people. What emerged, however, was an Anglo-Norman mixture, exemplified in the English language. The names for animals derive from the Anglo-Saxon words of the people who tended the livestock: sheep, cow, and pig; the names for the animals' meat derive from the words of the French-speaking Normans who dined on them: mutton, beef, and pork. Eventually, the Norman conquerors and their culture were absorbed by the conquered. Change occurred and England was never the same again, but it remained English. Such cultural confluences have been part of the give and take between conquered peoples and their conquerors for thousands of years throughout the world.

It would be unusual, then, if America, a country that prides itself and even stakes its identity on the multiplicity of peoples in its past and present makeup, did not illustrate the same phenomenon. After 1492, Europeans invaded America in ever-increasing numbers. Over the centuries, they built a new nation and a new society, and changed forever the American world they had invaded. But they became Americans.

The idea is not new. Many writers have pointed the way to an understanding of early America as a world of mixed and mixing peoples, with a substantial Indian presence. Frenchman Hector St. John de Crèvecoeur noted that America in the late eighteenth century demonstrated "that strange mixture of blood, which you will find in no other country." Moreau de Saint-Méry went so far as to assert that "the American is the perfect mean between the European and the Indian." More than a hundred years ago, Frederick Jackson Turner, in a famous study of the American frontier which has since been justly criticized and has fallen into disfavor, offered some of the same suggestions, although attributing change to environmental determinism rather than cultural interaction and employing language that today sounds dated and perhaps offensive:

> The frontier is the line of most rapid and effective Americanization. The wilderness masters the colonist. It finds him a European in dress, industries, tools, modes of travel, and thought. It takes him from the railroad car and puts him in the birch canoe. It strips off the garments of civilization and arrays him in the hunting shirt and the moccasin. It puts him in the log cabin of the Cherokee and Iroquois and runs an Indian palisade around him. Before long he has gone to planting Indian corn and plowing with a sharp stick; he shouts the war cry and takes the scalp in orthodox Indian fashion. In short, at the frontier the environment is at first too strong for the man. He must accept the conditions which it furnishes, or perish, and so he fits himself into the clearings and follows the Indian trails. Little by little he transforms the wilderness, but the outcome is not the old Europe. . . . The fact is, that here is a new product that is American.

In Turner's view of history, the wilderness and "free land" exerted powerful transforming influences on European colonists. But Turner's wilderness America was largely myth: European settlers often lived in reoccupied Indian towns, ate Indian foods, and dealt with Indian people on a regular basis. Human influences were as important as environmental ones in shaping the new America.

Anthropologist Jack Weatherford thinks that the "scramble of peoples and cultures in North America has created a cultural mixture that probably will not be repeated in world history until we encounter life on another planet." Historian Gary Nash points out that the continuous interaction of diverse cultural groups in colonial America produced "a conglomeration of cultural entities." People tend to construct their cultures in interaction with one another, not in isolation. Frank Shuffleton, considering the people of early America "a mixed race," defines ethnicity not as something static and constant but as "a dynamic relation between different cultural groups," who continually modify their understanding of themselves in light of shifting relationships with others. So, for example, English immigrants to New England tried to impose their culture on the Indian peoples living there, but "they were being ethnically transformed themselves in the process of confronting and being confronted by the people they found already on the ground." Europeans became Americans and Americans became different from Europeans "because they had to confront significantly different ethnic groups that they would eventually include, sometimes reluctantly, sometimes violently, as part of the meaning of America." In Shuffleton's view, the multiethnic character of America was well established long before the American Revolution.

The new societies that grew out of the interaction of peoples in early America were amalgams, combining Indian as well as European and African influences. Felix Cohen, author of the *Handbook of Indian Law*, wrote in 1952 that American historians had paid too much attention to military victories and territorial expansion and had failed to appreciate "that in agriculture, in government, in sport, in education and in our views of nature and our fellow men, it is the first Americans who have taken captive their battlefield conquerors." Cohen thought that the real epic of America was "the yet unfinished story of the Americanization of the white man."

Ethnohistorian James Axtell has written numerous lucid and suggestive essays and books in which he examines the contest and confluence of cultures in colonial North America. "Without the Indians," says Axtell, "America would not be America as we know it." In situations of culture contact, "one culture may predominate and teach more than it learns," but "the educational process is always mutual." And the Indian imprint on American society occurred most significantly in the formative, colonial era. Even Bernard Bailyn, a historian of the old school often criticized for ignoring women, ordinary people, and minorities in his view of the nation's past, recognizes that what he called the "mingling of primitivism and civilization" constituted "an essential ingredient of early American culture."

Europeans did not come to America to become Indians or even, in the early days, to become "Americans." They came, for the most part, to recreate in the New World the kind of communities they had left in the Old, with some improvements. By the eighteenth century, however, travelers and commentators regularly complained that the European settlers they encountered living on the frontier were "little better than" their Indian neighbors. They dressed, ate, hunted, grew corn, behaved, and even looked like Indians. According to German traveler Johann David Schoepf in the 1780s, they also acquired "similar ways of thinking." The complaints were not without foundation. As David Weber observes of Spanish experiences in North America, "However much they wished to conserve the familiar, Spaniards' scanty numbers and resources left them with no choice but to make concessions to their strange new environment and, on occasion, to learn from natives who understood local conditions better than they." Spanish colonists avoided changes that challenged their fundamental values, and they preserved the core of their culture intact, but they also wore Indian clothes, ate Indian foods, married Indian women, produced half-Indian children, and learned to speak Indian languages.

The nature and the degree of exchanges varied from region to region, and from time to time, according to the people who inhabited and invaded the area. Colonists from different regions of Europe developed varying relations with different Indian tribes, and did so in a variety of circumstances. Hispanic people in the Southwest and Frenchmen in Canada, the Great Lakes, and Louisiana generally intermingled more freely with Indian peoples than did English settlers on the Atlantic seaboard. A Franciscan friar in 1631 complained that Spaniards in New Mexico were "reared from childhood subject to the customs of [the] Indians," and the Indian imprint on society is visible today more clearly in New Mexico than in New England. In the Great Lakes region, in the seventeenth and early eighteenth centuries, Frenchmen and Algonkian Indians created what ethnohistorian Richard White calls "a middle ground," where the French and Indian worlds "melted at the edges and merged" and where it became unclear "whether a particular practice or way of doing things was French or Indian." According to cultural geographers Terry Jordan and Matti Kaups, interactions and cultural exchanges were greatest in "Midland America," where Swedish and Finnish settlers in the Delaware Valley established good relations with the local Indians and produced a mixed backwoods culture that later pioneers carried to large areas of America. The culture of immigrant Saro-Karelian Finns, joined to the indigenous culture of the Delaware Indians, "yielded all the essential ingredients of a syncretistic Midland American colonizing system." Subsequent generations of Scotch-Irish immigrants adopted the Finnish-Indian techniques of forest colonization they found in the Delaware Valley and pushed west and southwest. They added their own genetic and cultural input to early American backwoods culture and society, and only rarely replicated the patterns of peaceful coexistence forged by Finns and Delawares. New York's Mohawk Valley was the scene of bitter fighting during the American Revolution, but the eighteenth-century valley was more often a place where Indians and Europeans talked, traded, and intermarried, where some Indians drank tea and some Europeans tattooed their faces.

Many colonists from many places, at many times, interacted with Indian people, lived in Indian country, and adopted and adapted Indian ways. Writing in the middle of the eighteenth century, Swedish botanist Peter Kalm said that his countrymen who had come to America in the seventeenth century "were accused of being already half Indians when the English arrived," but noted, "we still see that the French, English, Germans, Dutch, and other Europeans, who have lived for several years in distant provinces, near and among the Indians, grow so like them in their behavior and thought that they can only be distinguished by the difference of their color."

Early America in the wake of European invasion became a cacophony of languages, peoples, and cultures. In this "kaleidoscope of human encounters," Indians and Europeans made what historian T. H. Breen calls "creative adaptations" to new places and new peoples. What emerged was something different, for both Indians and Europeans, from what had gone before. In his excellent history of the Catawba Indians, James Merrell has shown how invasions from Europe created a new world for Native peoples in North America. At first, European colonists had to fit into an Indian world and adapt to the Indians' ways of doing things. As the Europeans adapted to and then transformed America, however, eventually the Indians had to fit into a European world. "Like their new neighbors," writes Merrell, "Indians had to blend old and new ways that would permit them to survive in the present and prepare for the future without utterly forsaking the past." Both groups of peoples had to make adjustments, but not at the same time, place, or rate. By the end of the colonial era, Indians and Europeans alike had created new societies in America. The European societies displayed evidence of change; many Indian societies had changed beyond recognition.

However, the adjustments made by Europeans were not insignificant, and they were sometimes fundamental. European immigrants brought with them a cargo of germs, guns, goods, animals, religious zeal, land hunger, and cultural preconceptions that turned America into a new, and often nightmarish, world for Indian peoples. But those immigrants also brought with them personal belongings, inconsequential to anyone but themselves, mental pictures of friends and relatives they would not see again, private memories of sights, sounds, and smells in places where they had spent most if not all of their lives. Writing home from Pennsylvania in 1725, the son of Welsh immigrants recalled his parents talking about the world they had left: "Frequently during long winter evenings, would they in merry mood prolong their conversation about their native land till midnight; and even after they had retired to rest, they would sometimes fondly recall to each other's recollection some man, or hill, house, or rock." Such people did not leave "Europe"—the term had little meaning and less emotive appeal to most of them. They left a little and local world of regions, distinct dialects, familiar places, and human communities. Life would never be the same for them. Simply by leaving the place of their birth, they cut themselves off from ancient cycles of life and death and embraced a future unknown to their parents and ancestors.

That future involved building a new society and taking on a new identity. As early as the seventeenth century, New England Puritans worried that conquering the American wilderness and coming into contact with American Indians would alter the colonists' English culture and their sense of themselves as English people. Their American experience threatened to give the colonists a new identity—something deeply troubling to Puritan Englishmen in a new world. Originally, the term "American" referred to Indians, the first Americans. By the time of the Revolution, it designated England's former colonists who were creating a new nation. The colonists who dressed as Mohawk Indians to dump British tea into Boston Harbor in 1774 were not trying to disguise themselves. They were proclaiming a new, American identity.

Through it all, there were Indian people who, despite massive changes in the world around them, preserved intact their fundamental worldview and tribal values, just as there were Europeans who experienced little or no interaction with Indian people or for whom such interaction had little meaning and left no lasting impression. Nevertheless, many Indian people had to find new ways of surviving, of being Indian, in the new world created by the invasions from Europe, and many Europeans assimilated Indian elements into their new definition of themselves as Americans. By 1800, colonists in America had secured political, if not yet cultural and economic, independence from Great Britain. An "American" was now a citizen of the new country, the United States, not a Native American. The new Americans figuratively turned their faces away from Europe and toward "their" new country. The "backcountry" of the eighteenth century became the "frontier" of the nineteenth century. But it was all Indian country, and it left its imprint, however subtle, on the people who entered it and on the societies they built there.

One

❋

Imagining and Creating a New World

*E*ARLY EUROPEAN SAILORS, it was said, could smell the pine forests of North America long before they could see land. Even unseen, the land held abundance and promise. In *The Great Gatsby,* F. Scott Fitzgerald has Nick Carraway look out across Long Island Sound and reflect on how the old island must have appeared as "a fresh, green breast of the new world" to the first Dutch sailors three centuries earlier. "Its vanished trees . . . had once pandered to the last and greatest of all human dreams; for a transitory enchanted moment man must have held his breath in the presence of this continent, compelled into an aesthetic contemplation he neither understood nor desired, face to face for the last time in history with something commensurate to his capacity for wonder." Other breath-holdings surely occurred as European explorers encountered the Grand Canyon, the Great Lakes, the Mississippi River.

But the moments were transitory; Europeans came to America to build farms and towns out of the forests that beckoned them. They meant to create a new world, not leave intact the one they found here. As early as 1642, little more than thirty years after those first Dutch sailors had touched land, a Narragansett sachem named Miantonomi told the Montauk Indians of Long Island what they already knew: "Our fathers had plenty of deer and skins, our plains were full of deer, as also our woods, and of turkies, and our coves full of fish and fowl. But these English have gotten our land, they with scythes cut down the grass, and with axes fell the trees; their cows and horses eat the grass, and their hogs spoil our clam banks, and we shall all be starved." In the middle of the eighteenth century, French traveler Jean-

Bernard Bossu attributed similar sentiments to a Natchez Indian on the eve of that people's war against the French in the 1730s. "Before the French came into our lands," declared the Natchez, "we were happy with what we had, we walked boldly upon our paths, because then we were our own masters. But today we tread gropingly, fearing thorns. We walk like the slaves which we will soon be, since they already treat us as though we were." From New England to the lower Mississippi Valley, Indian people saw the world they had once known change rapidly and forever after Europeans arrived.

The "new world" existed in the imaginations of Europeans. Though old by 1492, America was, once, new to Indian peoples too. Native traditions trace tribal presences in their homelands back to a time beyond memory; many traditions tell how the people emerged out of the ground. Archaeologists and many other scholars prefer to explain the peopling of America as the result of migration from Asia across the Bering Strait via a thousand-mile-wide "land bridge" exposed during the last ice age (14,000–20,000 years ago), and penetration of the interior of the continent along ice-free corridors. There is no question, however, that Indian peoples were here thousands of years before Europeans set foot in, or even imagined, the "new world." The people of Taos Pueblo in New Mexico, seeking the return of the sacred Blue Lake in 1968, declared: "We have lived upon this land from days beyond history's records, far past any living memory deep into the time of legend. The story of my people and the story of this place are one single story. No man can think of us without also thinking of this place." In the hour of human presence in North America, Europeans arrive just minutes before the top of the hour; the United States begins its history as a nation just moments "before the bell."

Like later arrivals, Indians pioneered the land and built lives and communities here. Kiowa author N. Scott Momaday suggests that "when man set foot on the continent of North America he was surely an endangered species." However, humans possessed the ability to hunt, to manufacture tools and weapons, to make fire, to speak and think, to cooperate and maintain community. Over thousands of years, the first Americans fine-tuned these abilities and added other achievements. They developed a diverse array of lifestyles, according to the different environments they inhabited; a multiplicity of languages; and many different styles of architecture. Their subsistence strategies included greater or lesser degrees of farming, hunting, and gathering. Indian peoples' political systems ranged from theocracies and chiefdoms to egalitarian and fluid family band societies. They created art forms and craft specializations; extensive trade networks and elaborate rituals of exchange; and complex religions and sacred relationships. Temple mounds in the Ohio and Mississippi Valleys and the Southeast; intaglios, ancient irrigation systems, and abandoned cliff dwellings in the Southwest; legends and stories throughout the continent, all testified to the presence of the ancient ones, the ancestors of the many different Indian peoples who inhabited North America by the time of Columbus.

Columbus changed forever the history of the planet. But he did so by connecting two worlds of equal maturity, not by "discovering" a new one. Knowing this, some find it easy to dismiss European insistence on calling America the New World as nothing more than Eurocentric arrogance. Convinced that Europe was synonymous with civilization, colonizing Europeans failed to see anything of value in Indian civilizations. They regarded Indian peoples as "primitive" and viewed the land as virgin wilderness. Like other human beings, they were blind to much that lay before them and instead took in what they wanted to. In a very real sense, however, America did exist as a new world for Europeans. America was more than just a place; it was a second opportunity for humanity—a chance, after the bloodlettings and the pogroms, the plagues and the famines, the political and religious wars, the social and economic upheavals, for Europeans to get it right this time. In the beginning, the American dream was a European dream, and it exerted emotional and motivational power for generations.

Colonial promotional literature invented an image of America that never existed in fact, but even the real America impressed Europeans as a new and abundant land. It contained, to them, new peoples, new plants, new geography, new animal life, new climatic conditions, and unprecedented space. Knowledge about America prompted some European scholars to rethink their mental world; they had to expand their conceptions of geography, history, nature, and theology to embrace America. Attempting to understand this strange new world, writes historian David Weber, "required mental adjustments that engaged and defied the best European minds."

Early explorers endeavored to fit America into old concepts of world geography, which mandated that the "new" lands must be either islands or peninsulas off the Asian mainland. Gradually, Europeans realized that America was truly a new world. "I found that I was now come into a new world,"

wrote Swedish naturalist Peter Kalm after stepping off the boat in Philadelphia in 1748. "Whenever I looked to the ground I found everywhere such
plants as I had never seen before." He was, he admitted, "seized with terror
at the thought of ranging to many new and unknown parts of natural history."
The Europeans' struggle to adapt to such unfamiliar things dominated the
past five hundred years of American history; and, for most Europeans,
adapting meant controlling and subjugating.

Most Europeans who came to America endeavored to establish settlements, societies, and empires that mirrored or were modeled on those they
left behind. The names speak for themselves: New France, Nova Scotia,
New England, New Netherland, New Amsterdam, New York, New Hampshire, New Sweden, New Spain, New Mexico. Immigrants from particular
regions of Europe brought familiar names from home: English immigrants
created new towns with old names—York, Chester, Lancaster—while those
from Britain's borderlands dotted the Appalachian region with names like
Cumberland, Durham, Galloway, and Londonderry. Europeans imposed
new names and boundaries on the existing human geography of North
America, arbitrarily including, excluding, or dissecting numerous Indian
worlds in regions to which they assigned new cartographic and political
identities. Even *America* is a name of European invention, after the Italian
navigator Amerigo Vespucci.

European settlers sometimes did encounter empty lands as they penetrated North America. But "emptied" would be a more appropriate term,
since these population vacuums were usually the product of European diseases running ahead of contact. Pilgrims at Plymouth found cultivated fields,
which previous Indian inhabitants had cleared but then left after an epidemic
in 1617; Dutch settlers in New Netherland likewise thought abandoned Indian lands were "fit for use." The newcomers built on what they found. Often, European towns grew on the sites of Indian villages, taking advantage, as
had the previous inhabitants, of favorable locations and accessible resources.
Spanish colonists built a military post at Tucson, Arizona, on top of Native
American ruins dating from A.D. 800–900. New towns were given European
names to replace their ancient Indian names, and the pattern of settlement
rapidly obscured the Indian past and presence. In seventeenth-century New
England, for example, Agawam became Ipswich; Shawmut became Boston;
Naumeag, at the mouth of the Pequot River, became New London; and the

river itself became the Thames. In the Connecticut Valley, Norrwottuck, Pocumtuck, and Squakhaeg faded from history and cartography, to be replaced by Northampton, Deerfield, and Northfield, Massachusetts.

Names on a map reveal patterns of movement and accommodation as well as patterns of conquest. In the north of England, Anglo-Saxon town names exist alongside names of Roman and Scandinavian origin. Likewise, in New York, Iroquois place names survive alongside Dutch, German, and English names, and all four alongside names that are wholly "American." Farther west, in Ohio, for example, Indian names—Piqua, Chillicothe, Sandusky, Cuyahoga, and Coshocton—survive alongside place names of European origin—Schönbrunn, Athens, Milan, Dublin—as well as place names transplanted from the eastern colonies—New Haven, New Philadelphia.

Such renamings were part of the process of dispossessing Indian peoples and redrawing the map of North America. As the late British geographer Brian Harley explained, Indian peoples became "victims of a map." European cartographers replaced Indian with European names, described Indian country as wilderness, vacant land, or "terra incognita," and effectively excluded Indians from the new world they created on parchment and paper. Whereas Indian place names tended to convey the ecological characteristics of an area or how it was used, Europeans often named places after localities in Europe or after the new "owner." The land, said Harley, "had been effectively redescribed in the vocabulary of the conquerors." Settlers renamed the first rivers they came to on the East Coast—the Hudson, the James, the Charles, and so on—but many rivers, mountains, and lakes farther inland retained their original Indian names. According to Lakota scholar Vine Deloria Jr., "There remains a good deal more that is still wholly Indian in our landscape. Indeed the basic sacred geography of the Indian remains virtually untouched."

Those sacred places and other parts of the landscape that remain Indian represent only a fragment of the original tapestry. European colonists intended not only to take over the land; they also were determined to change it, to remake it into something more closely resembling the world they had left. They did not find a new world in America; they did set about creating one.

Indian peoples had made their mark on the natural world long before Europeans arrived, but their environmental imprint was negligible in comparison with what was to come. European invasion of America set in motion rapid and far-reaching ecological changes. European immigrants brought plants, animals, birds, and insects that mounted their own biological and zoological invasions and changed the natural world almost beyond recognition. All across the continent, tall native grasses and forests disappeared, swift streams slowed to a sluggish pace, and alien flora and fauna took hold. As historian Karen Kupperman explains, Old World seeds and animals colonized along with the human migrants: "Probably no European after the very first explorers ever saw an exclusively American meadow," she writes. "Birds and animals took up seeds carried in the holds of ships and in the guts of animals and spread them far beyond the frontier of contact."

The English and the Dutch imported European honeybees, the first arriving in Virginia in the early 1620s. Indians called them "English flies." Hector St. John de Crèvecoeur said that Indians viewed bees' arrival in the interior of the continent as a portent of the approach of white settlers. Europeans also imported blackflies, cockroaches, rats, and house mice. As early as 1609, when the colony was just two years old, settlers at Jamestown, Virginia, found "thousands of rats" from the English ships consuming their food, and they were forced to turn again to Indians for help in feeding themselves. English sparrows and starlings became ubiquitous in North America in the nineteenth century, competing for nesting spaces with indigenous species. Indians had dogs, but cats arrived aboard European ships. Virginia gentry imported red foxes for hunting, in an attempt to emulate the sporting life of English gentry. European cattle, pigs, and horses trampled Indian cornfields and drove away deer and other game on which Indian people depended. Indians complained to the colonists, but in time they, too, adapted the new livestock into their lives. Domesticated livestock altered the gender-based divisions of labor in Indian societies. Men had previously been responsible for hunting animals in the forests; women tended crops in the fields around the villages. Now animals became part of village life. Previously, hunters had prayed to the spirits of the animals they hunted; now animals could be regarded as a form of property. Sheep and goats became crucial components of Navajo and Pueblo economy. Horses revolutionized the lives of Indian peoples on the Great Plains, producing, for a brief period in the eighteenth and nineteenth centuries, the way of life that popular culture considers typical of all Indian peoples at all times. The mounted Indian hunting buffalo was a relatively recent phenomenon and a by-product of European invasion.

English colonists introduced rye, barley, wheat, oats, root crops, and various herbs and vegetables. They also, inadvertently, imported new weeds: dandelions, thistles, stinging nettles, chickweed, mayweed, nightshade, and plantain, which Indians called "Englishman's Foot," because it seemed to spring up wherever the newcomers "have troden, & was never known before the English came into this country." Bluegrass and white clover, initially brought from England as fodder and in the dung of the animals that ate them, spread quickly in areas where cattle grazed, and, mixed together, became known as "English grass." By the time pioneers crossed the Appalachians into Kentucky in the late eighteenth century, white clover and "Kentucky bluegrass" had already taken root there. Meanwhile, native grasses not accustomed to pastoralism began to disappear as cattle, sheep, and goats munched and trod their way into America. Spanish colonists who introduced European grazing animals into the arid and ecologically fragile lands of the Southwest generated chain reactions they could not have foreseen. Herds of sheep, cattle, and horses trampled grasses and compacted soils. They broke down vegetation, producing increased runoffs and gullying. In time, explains David Weber, "lush grasslands, dotted with trees and brimming with deer and other wildlife, began to diminish and, in some places, turned to desert." Omnivorous and adaptable pigs, first introduced to the Southeast by Spaniards in the sixteenth century, thrived in their new environment. They spread throughout America "like Vermaine upon the Earth." The swine not only fed immigrants but also had devastating effects on native flora and fauna and may have helped spread animal-borne Old World diseases. The introduction of alien cattle probably also spread anthrax, brucellosis, and other diseases to the buffalo herds of North America.

Europeans introduced species of animals new to America, and they also encountered species native to America but new to them. European travelers in the eastern woodlands usually commented on rattlesnakes, with revulsion. Bison, beaver, moose, raccoon, muskrat, cougars, alligators, various other snakes and reptiles, and numerous kinds of birds, all attracted the Europeans' attention, at the same time reinforcing European notions that America was both bountiful and a "wilderness."

Transforming that wilderness into a market and into "civilization" entailed systematic destruction of some native species. Fur traders did not set out to destroy the sources of their wealth, and European fur traders and Indians often had a common interest in restricting settlement in the lands they hunted. Nevertheless, the fur trade was the economic backbone of the

French empire in Canada and of many English colonies, and it had devastating effects on Indian country.

Before contact with Europeans, Indian people sometimes killed animals en masse: on the northern plains, they engaged in communal buffalo drives that stampeded herds over cliffs. Miami Indians on the Illinois prairies used fire to drive buffalo toward their hunters who, as Louis Hennepin observed in 1685, "sometimes kill two hundred in a day." After contact, many Indians became dependent on the manufactured goods the fur trade brought them, and hunted to meet the demands of European markets rather than the needs of their families. Indians thus began to participate in the systematic slaughter of animal populations with which they had formerly cultivated symbiotic and spiritual relationships and on which they had relied for much of their livelihood. One ethnohistorian has even suggested that Indians blamed offended wildlife spirits for bringing epidemic diseases and retaliated by waging war on fur-bearing animal populations. Between 1652 and 1658, Indian hunters brought in almost nine thousand beaver pelts to John Pynchon's trading post at Springfield, Massachusetts, as well as hundreds of moose, otter, fox, raccoon, mink, and other skins. In 1654 alone, Pynchon exported 3,723 pounds of beaver to England. French Jesuit missionary Sebastian Rasles noted in 1723 that the Indians with whom he lived in Maine "have so destroyed the game of their country that for ten years they have no longer either elks or deer. Bears and beavers have become very scarce." The Abenakis, he said, had scarcely anything on which to live but Indian corn, beans, and pumpkins. In 1792, the American naturalist Benjamin Smith Barton warned that beaver were on the verge of extinction in the Northeast.

The demise of beaver populations and the destruction of beaver dams had various and far-reaching impacts on local ecosystems. Carolyn Merchant lists some of the repercussions in New England:

> As beavers, along with their dams and ponds, disappeared from the New England states, so did other associated species. Fewer black ducks, ring-necked ducks, hooded mergansers, and goldeneyes returned to breed on beaver ponds in Maine. With beavers no longer able to maintain their dams, muskrat and otters were either flooded or frozen out by fluctuating pond levels. Mink and raccoon, both of which ate frogs, snakes, and suckers in beaver flowages, found less food to sustain their numbers when ponds shrank into marshes and finally became meadows. Larger animals that used the beaver ponds also were affected in subtle but negative ways. Moose and

deer had browsed on the leaves and roots of aquatic plants and escaped from flies by standing in cool water. Tree stumps cut down by the beaver for food and dams had sprouted tender stalks and leaves which fed deer, rabbit, and snowshoe hare. Black bears had wallowed in the moist earth on the edges of beaver flows. Trees felled by beaver provided the brush that had protected rabbit and the drumming logs for the springtime mating of the ruffed grouse. Red foxes who depended on these mammals for survival now found fewer to stalk.

Without beaver dams, streams flowed faster, altering fish habitats, and caused greater erosion. The result was more floods.

The deerskin trade was equally devastating in some areas of the country. Between 1699 and 1715, Charleston, South Carolina, exported to England an average of fifty-four thousand deerskins each year. Charleston and New Orleans each exported more than one hundred thousand pounds of deerskins annually in the 1750s. By 1705, Powhatan Indians in Virginia were killing large numbers of deer for trade: "They make all this Slaughter only for the sake of the Skins, leaving the Carcases to perish in the Woods," wrote Governor Robert Beverley. The Choctaw Indians of Mississippi had a mixed economy of farming and hunting that required them to maintain deer populations by restricting their hunting. By the eighteenth century, however, other peoples began to encroach on Choctaw deer herds. Escalating conflicts over hunting territories grew into war between Creeks and Choctaws in the 1760s. The Choctaws themselves became commercially dependent on European traders and widely addicted to European alcohol. After Britain defeated the French in 1763, there was less need for European powers to court Choctaw allegiance with gifts, and Choctaw people could secure manufactured goods and alcohol only by exchanging deerskins with English traders. Choctaw hunters depleted the deer herds in their own territories and began to cross the Mississippi to hunt. The depletion of the white-tailed deer population under pressure of European trade altered the Choctaw landscape and reduced the Choctaw economy to a shambles by the time of the American Revolution. Traveling in Florida on the eve of the Revolution, naturalist William Bartram noted that the Seminoles waged "eternal war against deer and bear" to obtain food, clothing, and other necessities and conveniences from the traders. Bartram felt that the Seminoles carried their hunting "to an unreasonable and perhaps criminal excess, since the white people have dazzled their senses with foreign superfluities."

Other animal populations suffered depletion. Colonists regarded the extermination of wildlife as a prelude to transforming wilderness into civilization. They waged war against wolves, offering bounties for their heads or ears and enlisting Indians in the campaign. In 1642, Plymouth Colony passed legislation requiring towns to set wolf traps and to check them every day. Bounties were also offered on wildcats, cougars, and other predators. Cougars were all but exterminated in southern Massachusetts and Connecticut by 1800. The killing of wolves and other predators may have helped deer survive the onslaught of commercial hunting. William Wood, writing in the 1630s, described flocks of hundreds of turkeys in New England; by 1672, according to traveler John Josselyn, English and Indian hunters had all but "destroyed the breed." By the early nineteenth century in Connecticut, wrote traveler Timothy Dwight, there were "hardly any wild animals remaining besides a few small species of no consequence." Passenger pigeons, which early settlers agreed flew overhead by the thousands and even millions and blocked out the sun, were extinct by the nineteenth century. Buffalo, once numerous east of the Mississippi, were driven out or exterminated: the last buffalo in Kentucky was killed early in the 1790s.

The pattern of animal destruction was not uniform, however. In areas where epidemic diseases wreaked havoc among human populations or where escalating warfare created a no-man's-land between tribal hunting territories, animal populations sometimes increased significantly. In time, such areas, regarded as a "hunters' paradise," attracted other Indians and settlers.

Indian peoples saw their world literally changing before their eyes as European invaders felled trees, cleared lands, built fences and farms, bridges and roads, and towns and villages. Indian farmers had created fields out of forests, which European colonists sometimes later occupied and planted as their own. But Indian villages relocated periodically, taking advantage of different resources and regions and allowing the natural environment a chance to recover. Settlers immediately set about subduing the "wilderness" and remaking the natural world into what historian William Cronon has described in New England as "a world of fields and fences." In doing so, they imposed unprecedented pressures on North American ecosystems and created permanent changes on the landscape.

Immigrants from Europe, where forests had been cleared and timber was in short supply, were impressed by the deep forests and abundant supplies of wood in eastern America. In England, homes were built wholly or partly from stone; fences formed from hedges or stone; in New England, both were made exclusively from wood. And there was an abundance of firewood. One colonist in Massachusetts in 1630 reckoned that "all Europe is not able to afford to make so many great Fires as New England. A poore Servant here that is to possesse but 50 Acres of Land, may afford to give more wood for Timber and Fire as good as the world, then many Noble Men in England can afford to doe." Indians in southern New England told Roger Williams they thought the colonists had come to America because they had no fuel at home. In the eyes of English settlers, forest equaled wilderness. By clearing the forests, colonists could, John Canup points out, "strike a blow for civilization" and keep themselves warm at the same time. William Cronon estimates that New Englanders consumed more than 260 million cords of firewood between 1630 and 1800. In the eighteenth century, as today, European visitors remarked on the incredible waste of fuel and thought Americans kept their homes unnecessarily warm.

Indians employed controlled fires to keep the forests free of undergrowth and attractive to game. Timothy Dwight noted that Indians set fires "to produce fresh and sweet pasture for the purpose of alluring the deer to the spots on which they had been kindled." The controlled use of fire to clear deadwood reduced the chance of rampant forest fires, such as the ones that swept Yellowstone Park in 1988, and produced a parklike quality in southern New England forests by the time English setters arrived. In addition, burning returned nutrients to the soil and thinned the forest canopy, allowing more sunlight to reach the ground, so that grasses and shrubs grew more luxuriantly. Indian burning practices maintained large grassy corridors like that of the Shenandoah Valley, which later served as major migration routes for European settlers.

European colonists transformed the forests, clearing huge swaths of the eastern woodlands. Swedish immigrants introduced the use of the axe to other settlers, and what became known as the "American axe" bit deep into American forests. Forests that had been too dense for Indians' stone tools succumbed to metal axes. New techniques of forestry, new crops, new animals, and new labor systems altered the composition of the forests. As settlers pushed Indians off the land, they converted some of the land to farming but left other areas covered in debris and neglected the forests. Tangled underbrush grew up, creating future fire hazards.

Lumbering became a major colonial industry, one that often employed Indian laborers in areas where traditional hunting economies had been all but eradicated. The Anglo-Dutch War (1654) and the Great Northern War between Russia and Sweden (1699–1721) disrupted Britain's Baltic sources of naval supplies. The British turned to America, and especially the white pine forests of New England, to provide masts, tar, and pitch. By 1715, America was supplying half of Britain's naval stores. Northern New England's tall white pines freed the British navy from dependence on Baltic sources and prompted significant technological changes (masts could now be created from one tree, instead of being pieced together from two or more Scotch fir).

But farming and lumbering wreaked havoc on the environment. According to French Canadian historian Denys Delâge, a single seventeenth-century warship "required over 2,000 oak trees, many of them from 100 to 150 years old and measuring more than fifty centimeters in diameter." English settlers borrowed from Indians the practice of clearing land and employed Indian burning techniques, such as the use of backfires. But they carried what they learned to new extremes: instead of burning the forest to remove undergrowth, they set fires to remove the forest itself. In the South, according to Timothy Silver, by the last quarter of the eighteenth century, "anyone traveling through the longleaf forests could witness the effects of naval production." In the North, in William Cronon's words, "New England lumbering used forests as if they would last forever." Swedish traveler Peter Kalm said much the same thing in 1749: "Their eyes are fixed upon the present gain, and they are blind to the future."

After victory in the French and Indian wars (1763) opened the territory between the Connecticut River and Lake Champlain to English settlers, British colonial authorities became concerned about their impact on lands once occupied by Abenaki Indians. Settlers cut down the oak and pine forests of the Champlain Valley, marketing their lumber, potash, and agricultural produce in Quebec. In 1768, Governor Guy Carleton of Quebec was ordered to take measures to protect the rich timber resources around Lake Champlain from destruction. The next year, the secretary of state for the colonies warned that unrestricted settlement was causing such destruction of forests in what is now Vermont that it posed a threat to the Royal Navy's supply of masts. By 1800, Timothy Dwight commented, the pioneers in the Green Mountains of Vermont "appear to have cut down their forest with an improvident hand; an evil but too common in most parts of the country." In coastal New Hampshire, Dwight reported that forests had not only been cut down, "but there appears little reason to hope that they will ever grow again." He was wrong: the "opening" of "new lands" in the West in the nineteenth century lured farmers away from northern New England's rocky soils and gave the forests a chance to recover; many areas of Vermont and New Hampshire are more heavily wooded today than they were in Dwight's time. Nevertheless, lumbering continued as a major industry in northern New England well into the twentieth century.

Clearing forests for farms and lumbering had unforeseen climatic repercussions. As a historian of New England's colonial timber economy explains, clear-cutting produces severe and sudden changes that affect the entire forest ecosystem: "Shade-loving plants die, food chains are interrupted, birds and animals migrate, and new microbes and insects invade. The relation of sun, land, vegetation, and fauna is drastically changed, and in the struggle for existence only those things that can adapt to the new environment will survive."

In the eighteenth century, people believed that clearing the land of trees changed the weather. What they were seeing were changes in how the landscape responded to the weather. Forests tended to keep the ground cooler and maintain a steadier climate. Deforestation meant lands became sunnier and hotter in the summer, less sheltered from wind, drier. Cleared lands were colder in the winter, but, exposed to sunlight, snow melted more rapidly, so that soil froze to greater depths than before. Spring runoffs began earlier in deforested regions, and flooding became more common. Timothy Dwight noted that the Connecticut River was "now fuller than it probably ever was before the country above was cleared of its forests, the snows in open ground melting much more suddenly and forming much greater freshets than in forested ground." There were six major floods in New England between 1720 and 1800. Extensive deforestation generated devastating spring floods in the Chesapeake in 1685, 1724, 1738, and 1752 and the worst flood in Chesapeake history in 1771.

Plowing with draft animals created even deeper ecological transformations. Indian fields seemed "messy" to Europeans: tree stumps remained; beans, squash, and pumpkins grew amid the corn. Europeans more often gave their fields over to intensive cultivation of a single crop. "Plowing," says William Cronon, "destroyed all native plant species to create an entirely new

The new landscape of the new world. Indians in birchbark canoes paddle (and ferry a European passenger) past a newly cleared and fenced farm. (From Patrick Campbell, *Travels in the Interior Inhabited Parts of North America in the Years 1791 and 1792*. Dartmouth College Library)

habitat populated mainly by domesticated species, and so in some sense represented the most complete ecological transformation of a New England landscape." Single-crop cultivation removed the nutrients that Indians had retained, and it hastened soil exhaustion. In some areas, the combination of deforestation, grazing animals, and plowing produced wind erosion. Floods produced further erosion.

The new crops Europeans introduced were not even safe from Old World diseases. A fungus known as "the blast," which devastated wheat and rye, made its appearance in New England early in the seventeenth century. Cronon describes how it came to America: "A European weed . . . had brought with it a European disease that made it exceedingly difficult for European farmers, keeping European animals, to raise a key European crop. The blasting of wheat was thus a kind of metaphor for the extent to which Old World ecological relationships had been reproduced in New England."

Indian settlement and subsistence patterns changed in response to changing economic and ecological conditions. Their hunting, farming, and fishing economies, which had formerly functioned by seasonal exploitation of diverse resources, became restricted as fur traders encouraged them to concentrate their activities and as settlers—and their livestock, fields, and fences—made inroads into what was once Indian country. Indian people confronted a new set of ecological challenges at the same time as they had to share their world with increasing numbers of human invaders. "The times are Exceedingly Alter'd," said Mohegan Indians, petitioning the Connecticut Assembly in 1789, "or rather we have Chang'd the good Times, Chiefly by the help of the White People." In times past, they remembered nostalgically, their forefathers had lived in peace and had plenty of everything. "But alas, it is not so now, all our Fishing, Hunting and Fowling is entirely gone."

Disrupted food sources and subsistence strategies produced famine and rendered Indian populations more vulnerable to new diseases. European traders came relatively late to the Northwest Pacific Coast—not until the second half of the eighteenth century did maritime merchants from Russia, Spain, Britain, and New England drop anchor to barter for sea otter pelts, which they then transported and sold at enormous profits in the markets of China—and coastal peoples at first were able to avoid dependence on them and to exploit the trading situation to their own advantage. Nevertheless, the reverberations of their involvement in the trade were quickly felt. The Indians devoted more energies to hunting sea otters, sometimes neglecting the fishing that had always provided food for the winter. Nootka Indians endured famine during the winter months in the 1790s. In the winter of 1799–1800, a group of Abenakis returned to the neighborhood of Troy and Potton, Vermont. They were reported to be "in a necessitous and almost starving condition, which probably arose from the moose and deer (which formerly abounded here) being destroyed by the settlers." With their world changed around them, and the sources of their traditional subsistence wiped out, these Abenakis tried to patch together a livelihood by making and selling baskets, birchbark containers, and trinkets. "They left in the spring and never returned," said the report.

The loss of land by war and treaty further diminished the Indian land base. One major development in the creation of a new world in America was that by which Indian land became European land, and later the territorial base of the United States. Competing European powers partitioned the continent, creating a patchwork of claims and jurisdictions and sometimes passing back and forth territory they claimed but where Indian people still lived.

Surveyors did much the same thing at the local level, marking the land off into uniform blocks of individual ownership. Europeans not only changed the landscape, they also introduced new concepts of ownership to North America. Indian peoples generally regarded land as something to be shared and utilized by the members of the community, although some groups had stronger rights to certain areas with, for instance, extended family hunting territories passing from generation to generation in some tribes. They soon learned that Europeans viewed land differently, as a commodity to be bought, sold, and owned exclusively. Many early land transactions contained the seeds of future conflict: Indians who believed they had given colonists the right to share their land, in return for gifts, found instead that they had sold the land "lock, stock, and barrel." Europeans not only claimed ownership of the land; they also claimed to own the animals that fed them.

Having acquired, or at least occupied, the land, Europeans set about building a new world on it. Popular history tells us that hardy pioneers carved out new lives for their families, transforming a wilderness into a landscape of farms and towns, and so indeed some did. However, the new America that Europeans created on Indian land was also built with Indian and African labor. African slaves cleared fields and cultivated tobacco, cotton, and rice in a world that was as new to them as it was to their European masters. Many Indian people also were attracted or coerced into transforming their own world. They worked as hunters, laborers, and porters in the fur and deerskin trades, they were drafted into service under Spanish labor systems, and they found employment in colonial towns and villages.

By 1800, the landscape of North America had changed in another significant way. There were far fewer Indian people. A country that John Winthrop described as "full of Indians" early in the seventeenth century, was now largely emptied of Indians. Those Indian people who survived, did so by adapting to a world that was very different from the one their forefathers had known and created. According to William Cronon, Indians "did not cease to be Indians, but became Indians with very different relationships to the ecosystems in which they lived." The people of European descent who occupied lands vacated by Indians built a new society in a land of abundance. Abundance also fostered wastefulness and thoughtless exploitation of natural resources, which people of other cultures still identify as characteristic of American people and which are hard habits to break as American society confronts the ecological consequences of past prodigality.

Two

.⁂.

Healing and Disease

*I*N THE WINTER of 1535–36, French explorer Jacques Cartier and his crew of 110 men were icebound in the St. Lawrence River near the modern-day city of Montreal. Their ships remained frozen in the ice from November to March. A disease we now recognize as scurvy broke out among the crew. Twenty-five men died, "and all the rest were so sicke, that wee thought they should never recover againe, only three or foure excepted." Then, just when Cartier feared they were doomed, "it pleased God to cast his pitiful eye upon us, and sent us the knowledge of remedie of our healthe and recoverie." The knowledge came from the local Indians. They showed the Frenchmen how to take the bark and leaves of a certain tree, which may have been white pine or hemlock, boil them down, and drink the decoction every other day. "According to them this tree cured every kind of disease." The French overcame their initial reluctance to drink the stuff and recovered rapidly. Almost two hundred years later, so the story goes, a British naval surgeon named James Lind read Cartier's account. Lind's experiments led him to conclude that lime juice was the best cure for scurvy, the scourge of British seamen in the eighteenth century. Limes, rich in vitamin C, became standard issue on British ships, and British sailors earned the nickname "limey."

The Indians who rescued Cartier's crew lived in Hochelaga, a town of about fifty bark longhouses and thirty-five hundred people. It stood at the foot of a mountain, which Cartier named Mont Royal, from which the modern city of Montreal derives its name. When the ice broke, Cartier returned down the St. Lawrence to Stadaconna, the Indian town located on the site of present-day Quebec City. The valley between these two major towns was lined with populous villages, extensive cornfields, and rich orchards. Some seventy years later, another Frenchman, Samuel de Champlain, traveled the same route. The towns were abandoned, the fields were overgrown, and the Indians were gone. Scholars still debate the mystery of their disappearance. Warfare between tribes north and south of the St. Lawrence seems to have been a major factor in creating a no-man's-zone, but epidemic diseases, introduced by Frenchmen like Jacques Cartier, undoubtedly took a deadly toll.

The events acted out on the St. Lawrence River in the sixteenth century were repeated across the continent and across the centuries as Indian and European patterns of sickness and healing converged. When Indians and Europeans met, they benefited from each other's medical knowledge and exchanged healing practices. Europeans also brought with them germs and viruses that erupted into epidemics of killer diseases among Indian populations. For Indian peoples, the new world often became a biological nightmare, in which impotent healers and distraught relatives watched helplessly as friends and loved ones succumbed to terrible plagues imported from Europe, as well as from Asia and Africa.

*

North American Indians did not inhabit a disease-free paradise prior to European invasion. The great epidemic diseases and crowd infections that ravaged Europe and Asia—smallpox, diphtheria, measles, bubonic and pneumonic plague, cholera, influenza, typhus, dysentery, yellow fever—were unknown in America. Indian peoples faced other, less devastating, problems. Bioarchaeological studies reveal evidence of malnutrition and anemia resulting from dietary stress, high levels of fetal and neonatal death and infant mortality, parasitic intestinal infections, dental problems, respiratory infections, spina bifida, osteomyelitis, nonpulmonary tuberculosis, and syphilis. Indian people also suffered their share of aches and pains, breaks and bruises, digestive upsets, arthritis, wounds, and snakebites. To deal with these things, Indian doctors employed a rich knowledge of the healing properties of plants and what today we would call therapeutic medicine. They combined knowledge of anatomy and medicinal botany with curative rituals and ceremonies.

Traditional Native American and contemporary Western ways of healing are not necessarily in conflict, and are often complementary, as evidenced when Navajo medicine men and Navajo oral traditions helped investigators from the Indian Health Service and the Centers for Disease Control identify deer mice as the source of the "mystery illness" that struck the Southwest in 1993. So too in early America, European and Indian cures could work together. Contrary to the popular modern stereotype that all Indians were and are attuned to plant life, all Europeans totally out of touch with nature, many early explorers and colonists possessed an extensive knowledge of plants and their properties, knowledge that modern urban Americans have lost. Europeans in the seventeenth century generally believed that for every sickness there were natural plant remedies, if one only knew where to find them. Indian healers, many of them women, knew where to find them, and Europeans were receptive to the cures they could provide.

Europeans who were dissatisfied with contemporary medical practices— purging, bleeding, and other drastic measures—often were inclined to see Indian healers as at least equal in ability to European physicians. Then as now, Western medicine offered a "disease cure" rather than a "health care" system. Many European observers spoke highly of Indian healers and re-garded Indian life as "more healthful" than their own. Dutchman Adriaen Van der Donck reported in the 1650s that the Indians in the Hudson Valley "know how to cure very dangerous and perilous wounds and sores by roots, leaves and other little things." From his travels in New Jersey and eastern Pennsylvania, Gabriel Thomas reckoned in 1698 that Indian healers were "as able Doctors and Surgeons as any in Europe." Englishman John Lawson, who traveled more than a thousand miles through Indian country in North and South Carolina in 1701, said the Indians displayed "extraordinary Skill and Success" in dealing with common ailments. He said they were "the best Physicians" for snakebites, and he saw them perform "admirable Cures . . . which would puzzle a great many graduate Practitioners." The cures he saw were "too many to repeat." Often, Indians went no more than a hundred yards from their homes to locate the remedy, and some of their chief physi-cians carried "their Compliment of Drugs continually about them, which are Roots, Barks, Berries, Nuts, &c. that are Strung upon a Thread." Lawson wondered why, in all the discoveries made by French and Spanish mission-aries, "none of them was so kind to the World, as to have kept a Catalogue of the Distempers they found the Savages capable of curing, and their Method of Cure, which might have been of some Advantage to our *Materia Medica* at home." Instead, he lamented, Europeans were "left in the dark" as to how the Indians effected their "great cures." Frenchmen Pierre de Charlevoix said the Indians of Canada possessed "secrets and remedies which are admirable." His countryman Jean-Bernard Bossu remarked that the Indians of Louisiana knew "a thousand medical plants good for purifying the blood." Their knowledge of plants' curative properties, said Bossu, constituted "rare and precious gifts which the Creator has not granted to everyone." Moravian missionary John Heckewelder, who lived and worked with Indians in Pennsylvania and Ohio in the eighteenth century, asserted that Indian physicians generally were "perhaps more free from fanciful theories than those of any nation on earth."

> Their science is entirely founded on observation, experience and the well tried efficacy of remedies. There are physicians of both sexes, who take considerable pains to acquire a correct knowledge of the properties and medical virtues of plants, roots and barks, for the benefit of their fellow-men. They are very careful to have at all times a full assortment of their medicines on hand, which they gather and collect at the proper seasons, sometimes fetching them from a distance of several days' journey from their homes, then they cure or dry them properly, tie them up in small bundles, and preserve them for use.

Indian people obtained through trade plants that did not grow locally: Pueblo communities traded plants, and they also obtained certain herbs from Jicarilla Apaches on the plains.

Like other forms of life, plants possessed power. Shamans and healers handled them with care and performed special rituals such as smoking and offering prayers as they collected, prepared, and administered herbal cures. Heckewelder dismissed such rituals as "superstitious practices," but, then as now, Native healing had a vital spiritual dimension as well as a physical one. Medicine men and women were people who had been given a special gift of power, often through a dream or a vision, and they demonstrated their spirituality in the healing ceremonies they performed. Coocoochee, a Mohawk medicine woman living on the Maumee River in the 1780s and 1790s, was esteemed for her skill in preparing and administering medicines and "for the power of her incantations which gave her insights into the future." Among the Hurons, shamans often were members of curing societies: they diagnosed illnesses, treated injuries, set broken bones, rendered spells powerless, and organized rituals to bring comfort to the sick. Missionaries—

the shamans' cultural equivalents and rivals—often were impressed by Indian knowledge and use of curative herbs, but they could not condone or tolerate medicine healers and their rituals. Jesuit Pierre Biard denounced Huron shamans as "sorcerers." They were "jugglers, liars and cheats," he said. "All their science consists of a knowledge of a few simple laxatives, or astringents, hot or cold applications, . . . leaving the rest to luck, nothing more." Europeans often displayed equally cynical attitudes toward their own physicians, but such hostility toward the spiritual dimension of native healing no doubt reinforced the Indians' determination to keep their practices secret from prying Europeans, who might offend the spirits.

Nevertheless, settlers not only used Indian remedies but sometimes did so in accordance with Indian customs and rituals. "In the days of our sickness," said Crèvecoeur, "we shall have recourse to their medical knowledge." European botanists compiled an impressive list of plants and cures employed by Indian healers, and Indian doctors compiled an impressive record in ministering to Europeans. As Cabeza de Vaca and his companions wandered across the American Southwest in the 1530s, they earned a reputation as healers, and Indian people brought their sick to them to be cured. De Vaca also experimented with Indian curing practices "with good results." John Lawson noted that "an *Indian* hath been often found to heal an *English*-man of a Malady . . . which the ablest of our *English* Pretenders in *America,* after repeated Applications, have deserted the Patient as incurable." Dr. Johann David Schoepf, a German physician, tended to be dismissive of Indian herbal medicines, but he nonetheless included many of them in the list of 335 plant remedies indigenous to the eastern United States which he published in 1787. The Reverend Manasseh Cutler, a contemporary of Schoepf, credited Indians for many of the 379 indigenous medicinal plants he described. English traveler John Lawson early in the eighteenth century and Italian visitor Luigi Castiglioni late in the century each recorded inventories of plants and described the curative uses to which Indian peoples put them. Indians used sassafras as a medicine, applying the leaves directly to wounds. Sassafras proved so effective that Europeans came to think of it as a kind of wonder drug, and as early as 1602-3 English ships sailed to Virginia and Massachusetts to trade with the Indians for it. New England Indians, and then their colonial neighbors, used the plant known as white or green hellebore as an emetic. Ginseng was popular as a medicine in Asia before Europeans found it in North America. Indians from southern Canada to Cherokee country used it. French Jesuits sent a shipment of ginseng from North America to China in 1718, and it became a valuable export for the colonies.

Castiglioni saw Indians treat wounds with the crushed bark of *Chionanthus;* use *Spirea* as a purgative like ipecac; apply the pulverized roots and leaves of *Dracontium* (known as skunk- or polecat-weed in the United States) after attacks of asthma; use a decoction of *Aralia spinosa* to treat rheumatic pains; apply the bark of witch hazel (*Hamamelis virginiana*) to tumors and inflammations and make a poultice from the inside bark as a remedy for burning eyes; relieve coughs with a decoction of *Adiantum,* which Canadian settlers learned to use for the same purpose; and use the resin from the buds of the tacamahac tree (*Populus balsamifera*) on the banks of the Connecticut River "for the treatment of various illnesses." Swedish traveler Peter Kalm said Indians used bayberry roots to soothe toothaches, and he gathered a variety of other remedies for toothaches and swelling. He maintained that Indians had "an infallible art" of curing venereal disease among Indians and whites as well. Seneca Indians in western New York collected petroleum from pools and applied it to relieve rheumatism and various aches and pains.

Like many other travelers, Castiglioni reported the various cures Indians had for venomous bites. Indian healers used snakeroots, some of which, like fernroot, produced a milky juice that could be taken internally while its leaves were applied to the bite. The plants mainly reduced pain and inflammation; Native healers kept their patients alive by sucking out the poison, or by preventing its spread with a tourniquet. John Lederer, a German surgeon exploring the Blue Ridge Mountains of Virginia in the summer of 1670, was "stung in my sleep by a Mountain-spider; and had not an Indian suckt out the poyson, I had died." John Lawson said Indians were the best physicians in the world for snakebites and "have perform'd several great Cures." Castiglioni explored the matter further and recorded how Native remedies gradually made their way into European medical knowledge:

> The Indians of North America used a root they call Senega or Sennaga to treat the bite of the rattlesnake, and they used to sell it reduced to a powder to the Europeans who settled there, wanting never to let them know what the plant was that produced this root. For many years efforts were made in vain to discover it and the roots of various plants were tried out, but they were all useless, or at least inferior to the Senega of the Indians. Finally, in

the year 1736 Dr. [John] Tennent, a Scottish physician, succeeded in discovering from information obtained from the Indians in Pennsylvania that the Senega root belonged to the *Polygala caule simplici erecto, foliis ovato-lanceolatus alternis, intergerrimis racerno terminali erecto* described by Gronovius.

Indians also had to deal with wounds. John Heckewelder maintained that an Indian surgeon could heal any wound a European doctor could, which may not have been saying much, given the state of European medicine at that time. He said that "every Indian warrior is more or less acquainted with the healing properties of roots and plants" for applying to wounds that might be sustained on the warpath. Jean-Bernard Bossu noted the care with which Choctaw Indians in Mississippi treated gunshot and arrow wounds. First, a medicine man sucked the wound and spat out the blood. Then he dressed the wound. "In their dressings," said Bossu, "they do not use lint or compresses. Instead, to make the wound suppurate, they blow into it powder made of a root. Another root powder is used to dry and heal the wound, and still other roots are used in a solution with which the wound is bathed to help prevent gangrene." The eighteenth century was a time of escalating warfare in the lower Mississippi Valley: Choctaw medicine men had ample opportunity to apply their skills.

Indian healers helped cure Europeans as well. European medical care was virtually nonexistent in seventeenth-century New Mexico—Franciscan friars carried rudimentary surgical equipment but generally lacked formal medical training. Rather than travel to a mission and entrust their recovery to a friar's uncertain skills, Hispanic settlers frequently turned to Indian neighbors and relatives for remedies, as well as for love potions and aphrodisiacs. That often led to their participating in the Native rituals that accompanied curing—and that attracted the attention of the Inquisition. Some Europeans, however, balked at the idea of seeking cures from Indians. According to one chronicler, English colonists in the late seventeenth century recognized that Indians were "Incomparable Physicians," but would not use them. Ministers had convinced the colonists that the Indians' healing skills were the work of the Devil.

However willing they might be to provide healing, Indians generally endeavored to keep their knowledge hidden. This did not prevent Europeans from trying to learn their secrets. English physicians and apothecaries in colonial Virginia apparently sent their apprentices into the woods to search out Indian herbal medicines. Castiglioni recommended that "efforts be made to obtain from the Indians the knowledge they have of the use of plants." John Lawson advocated intermarriage between Indians and Europeans, not least because "we should then have a true knowledge of all the Indian's Skill in Medicine and Surgery." When Crèvecoeur visited the Indian town of Oquaga on the Susquehanna River just before the American Revolution, he met colonists from Pennsylvania who had gone there in search of cures from the Indian healers. Crèvecoeur tried to get one healer drunk to make her reveal her secrets. Henry Tufts, a rather disreputable character, lived for three years or so among the Abenakis in western Maine about the same time, having gone to "the Great Indian Doctress," Molly Ockett, to find a cure for a knife wound in his thigh. Molly Ockett cared for him and cured him "with a large variety of roots, herbs, barks and other materials." Tufts had a hard time swallowing some of the potions, but, "having much faith in the skill of my physician," he forced them down. Tufts served as an apprentice to his healer, hoping to learn her medicinal secrets. Convinced she was holding out on him, Tufts, like Crèvecoeur, resorted to rum. He then returned home and used the knowledge he had acquired to pass himself off as a physician in the colonies. Molly Ockett continued as an itinerant physician, catering to Abenakis and settlers alike and becoming part of the folklore of western Maine. According to one legend, she healed a sick infant named Hannibal Hamlin, thereby saving the life of Abraham Lincoln's future vice-president.

Many Native botanical cures made their way into modern pharmacology, often via American folklore and a variety of home remedies. Like the Indians, Europeans did not completely embrace new things and new ideas; they borrowed selectively. Spanish settlers extended their pharmacopoeia with Native medicinal herbs—they used sassafras, tobacco, cactus fruit (as an antiscorbutic)—but did not change their theories about the causes and cures of disease or the practice of medicine. In David Weber's words, Spaniards "transplanted their medical practices intact from Iberia to the New World but extended them in anaemic form to the frontier, where all but the largest towns and military posts lacked doctors and hospitals."

In addition to herbal cures, Indian peoples incorporated sweat baths, purgatives, and rituals into their repertoire of healing. Whereas Western medicine tends to see illness as primarily physical and individualistic, many Indian cultures regarded (and still regard) it as a sign of imbalance in the spirit world, occurring when a person's spiritual being was out of harmony with other spirits, other people, the earth. "Being of good mind" was essential to one's spiritual and physical well-being and to maintaining harmonious relationships with others; communal energy and ritual were important ways of producing a good mind, restoring harmony between a patient and the community, and between the natural world and the spirit world. Illnesses that stemmed from violated taboos, witchcraft, or unfulfilled dreams and desires required ritualistic cures, such as were conducted by the False Face society among the Iroquois. Jesuit priests reported that the Hurons "recognize three kinds of diseases. Some are natural, and they cure these with natural remedies. Others, they believe, are caused by the soul of the sick person, which desires something; these they cure by obtaining for the soul what it desires. Finally, the others are diseases caused by a spell that some sorcerer has cast upon the sick person; these diseases are cured by withdrawing from the patient's body the spell that causes his sickness."

Huron views of disease were perhaps not too different from those of Europeans who still attributed illness to sin and witchcraft and sought cures in prayer and pilgrimages to holy shrines, but most Europeans dismissed the ritual and therapeutic aspects of Indian healing as primitive superstition. Nevertheless, some participated in shared health-preserving activities like sweat baths. Indians evidently bathed far more often than Europeans, and travelers commented on daily bathing. Sweat baths, in which water was poured on heated stones in a covered lodge, seem to have been universal in Indian America as a ritual for cleansing body and mind. Moravian missionary George Henry Loskiel said Indians resorted to sweat baths as "their general remedy for all disorders, small or great . . . and in many cases the cure is complete." Jean-Bernard Bossu observed sweat baths among the Choctaw Indians, who used "steam cabinets in which are boiled all sorts of medicinal and sweet smelling herbs. The vapor filled with the essence and salts of these herbs enters the patient's body through his pores and his nose and restores his strength." Bossu urged his countrymen to take a sweat bath at least three times a year. Missionary Gabriel Sagard was shocked to see Frenchmen in Canada share sweat baths with Indians. John Heckewelder related the story of a man who traveled from Detroit to a nearby Indian village in 1784 to take a sweat bath for an unspecified illness. The man enjoyed a complete recovery and declared it "was the best thing he had ever done in his life for the benefit of his health."

✳

Unfortunately, traditional Indian cures offered little protection against the new diseases that swept the land after Europeans arrived in North America. Separated from the Old World for thousands of years, the peoples of America escaped great epidemics like the Black Death, which killed perhaps a third of the population in fourteenth-century Europe. But they were living on borrowed time. Lack of exposure to bubonic plague, smallpox, and measles allowed Indian peoples no opportunity to build up immunological resistance to such diseases. From the moment Europeans set foot in America, hundreds of thousands of Indian people were doomed to die in one of the greatest biological catastrophes in human history.

Imported diseases accompanied Spanish conquistadors into Central and South America at the beginning of the sixteenth century, wreaking havoc among the great civilizations of Mexico, Peru, and Yucatán, and facilitating their conquest by the invaders. It was not long before the unseen killers were at work among the Indian populations of North America.

Established and well-traveled trade routes helped spread disease. Indians who came into contact with Europeans and their germs often contaminated peoples farther inland who had not yet seen a European; they in turn passed the disease on to more distant neighbors. It is likely that most Indian people who were struck down by European diseases like smallpox died without ever laying eyes on a European. In tracing the course of imported plagues among Indian populations in colonial America, many scholars describe them not as epidemics but as pandemics, meaning that the same disease occurred virtually everywhere.

As many as 350,000 people lived in Florida when the Spaniards first arrived, but the populations of the Calusa, Timucua, and other tribes plummeted after contact. Calusas who canoed to Cuba to trade may have brought smallpox back to the Florida mainland as early as the 1520s. When Hernando de Soto invaded the Southeast in 1539, the Spaniards found that disease had preceded them. In the Carolina upcountry, they found large towns abandoned and overgrown with grass where, said the Indians, "there had been a pest in the land two years before." In 1585, Sir Francis Drake's English crew, returning from plundering Spanish ships in the Cape Verde

Islands, brought a disease that was probably typhus to the Caribbean and Florida. Indians around St. Augustine died in great numbers, "and said amongste themselves, it was the Inglisshe God that made them die so faste." The population collapse continued in the seventeenth century. Governor Diego de Rebolledo reported in 1657 that the Guale and Timucua Indians were few "because they have been wiped out with the sickness of the plague and smallpox which have overtaken them in past years." Two years later the new governor of Florida said 10,000 Indians had died in a measles epidemic. According to one scholar, the Timucuans numbered as many as 150,000 people before contact; by the end of the seventeenth century, their population had been cut by 98 percent. The Apalachee Indians of northern Florida numbered 25,000–30,000 in the early seventeenth century; by the end of the century, less than 8,000 survived. Two and a half centuries after contact with the Spaniards, all of Florida's original Indian people were gone.

The pattern repeated itself elsewhere. In 1585, the English established a colony at Roanoke Island in Virginia. Almost immediately, local Indians began to fall ill and die. "The disease was so strange to them," wrote Thomas Hariot, "that they neither knew what it was, nor how to cure it." Across the continent, Pueblo Indians in New Mexico may have suffered from a huge smallpox epidemic that spread as far south as Chile and across much of North America in 1519–24. When they first encountered Europeans in 1539, the Pueblos numbered at least 130,000 and inhabited between 110 and 150 pueblos. By 1706, New Mexico's Pueblo population had dropped to 6,440 people in 18 pueblos. When de Soto's Spaniards passed through the area now known as Arkansas in 1541–43, the region was densely populated. Thousands of people lived in large towns, cultivating extensive cornfields along rich river valleys. One hundred thirty years later, these thriving communities were gone, victims of disease and possibly drought. When French explorers arrived in the mid-seventeenth century, they found Caddoes, Osages, and Quapaws living on the peripheries of the region, but central Arkansas was empty. Epidemic diseases continued their devastation. In 1698, Frenchmen found less than one hundred men in the Quapaw villages after a recent smallpox epidemic killed most of the people. "In the village are nothing but graves," the French chronicler reported.

Indian peoples in eastern Canada who had been in contact with French fur traders and fishermen since early in the sixteenth century experienced the deadly repercussions of such commerce. Jesuit Father Pierre Biard, working among the Micmacs and Maliseets of Nova Scotia in 1616, heard the Indians "complain that since the French mingle and carry on trade with them they are dying fast, and the population is thinning out. For they assert that before this association and intercourse all their countries were very populous and they tell how one by one different coasts, according as they traffic with us, have been reduced more by disease."

Deadly pestilence swept the coast of New England in 1616–17. Indians "died in heapes," and the Massachusett Indians around Plymouth Bay were virtually exterminated. As reported by Governor William Bradford, the Pilgrims found cleared fields and good soil, but few people, the Indians "being dead & abundantly wasted in the late great mortalitiy which fell in all these parts about three years over before the coming of the English, wherin thousands of them dyed, they not being able to burie one another; their sculs and bones were found in many places lying still above ground, where their houses & dwellings had been; a very sad spectacle to behold."

Smallpox was a fact of life—or death—for most of human history. An airborne disease, normally communicated by droplets or dust particles, it enters through the respiratory tract. People can become infected simply by breathing. Not surprisingly, it spread like wildfire through Indian populations. However, because early chroniclers sometimes confused smallpox with other diseases and because the contagions came so quickly, it is difficult to discern which disease was doing the killing at any particular time. By the seventeenth century, smallpox in Europe was a childhood disease: most adults, having been infected as children, had acquired lifelong immunity and were not contagious. The long transatlantic crossings further reduced the chances that European crews could transmit the disease to America. Not until children crossed the Atlantic did smallpox, and the other lethal childhood diseases that plagued Europe, take hold on Native American populations. The Spanish brought children to the Caribbean early, but not until the beginning of the seventeenth century did Dutch and English colonists bring their families to New York and New England. The arrival of sick European children sentenced thousands of Indian people to death.

Smallpox struck New England in 1633, devastating Indian communities on the Merrimack and Connecticut Rivers. Bradford reported how "it pleased God to visite these Indeans with a great sickness, and such a mortalitie that of a 1000 above 900. and a halfe of them dyed, and many of them did rott above ground for want of buriall." The epidemic reduced the Pequots in southern Connecticut from perhaps as many as thirteen thousand people to only three thousand, setting the stage for their defeat by the English in 1637, and it may have reduced the Mohawks in eastern New York from almost eight thousand to less than three thousand. Such mortality rates were not unusual when virulent new diseases cut through previously unexposed populations. Indians from the Hudson River told Adriaen Van der Donck in 1656 "that before the smallpox broke out amongst them, they were ten times as numerous as they are now." John Lawson estimated that in 1701 there was "not the sixth Savage living within two hundred Miles of all our Settlements, as there were fifty Years ago." A recent smallpox epidemic in the Carolina upcountry had "destroy'd whole towns."

At the beginning of the seventeenth century, the Huron Indians numbered as many as 30,000–40,000 people, living in perhaps twenty-eight villages on the northern shores of the Great Lakes in southern Ontario. The French identified them as crucial to their plans for North American empire. The Hurons were the key to extensive trade networks reaching far beyond the Great Lakes, and their villages could also serve as "jumping-off points" for Jesuit missionary enterprises among more distant tribes. French traders and missionaries arrived in Huronia, and it was not long before the new diseases were reaping a grim harvest among the Hurons. Their longhouses were transformed into death traps. The smallpox epidemic that ravaged New England in 1633 reached Huronia in 1634. Smallpox or measles was thinning Huron numbers in 1635–36. A Huron elder, blaming the epidemic on the Jesuits, said, "The plague has entered every lodge in the village, and has so reduced my family that today there are but two of us left, and who can say whether we two will survive." Influenza struck in 1636–37. Smallpox returned in 1639. Huron population was scythed in half between 1634 and 1640. In 1648–49, famine and the attacks of the Iroquois completed the deadly work the diseases had begun. The Hurons scattered, most of the survivors being absorbed by other tribes.

Smallpox continued throughout the eighteenth century. It killed half the Cherokees in 1738 and returned in 1760; the Catawbas of South Carolina lost half their number to the epidemic of 1759. In 1763, the British doled out blankets from the smallpox hospital at Fort Pitt to visiting Indians; smallpox erupted among the tribes of the Ohio Valley soon thereafter. Outbreaks of smallpox were reported among Indian populations in New Mexico in 1719, 1733, 1738, 1747, and 1749; in Texas recurrently between 1674 and 1802; and in California, where Indian neophytes congregated in Spanish mission villages made easy targets for new crowd-killing diseases.

The massive smallpox epidemic that ravaged western North America between 1779 and 1783 illustrates the speed with which the disease could spread its tentacles throughout Indian country. The epidemic seems to have broken out in Mexico, and it afflicted Indian peoples in Peru and Guatemala. Spreading north to Spanish settlements like San Antonio and Santa Fe, it was picked up by Indians who visited the area to trade for horses. It was then quickly transmitted north and west, through the Rockies and across the plains, slaughtering as it went. It spread into the Canadian forests, killed as many as 90 percent of the Chipewyans in the central subarctic, and by 1783 was killing Cree Indians around Hudson Bay.

Abundant sources of fish and other marine resources supported dense populations on the Northwest Coast before European maritime traders and explorers brought smallpox in the late eighteenth century. When English explorer George Vancouver sailed into Puget Sound in 1793, he met Indian people with pockmarked faces and found human skulls and bones scattered along the beach, a grim reminder of the ravages of an earlier epidemic. These northwestern populations declined dramatically over the next century.

Smallpox was probably the number-one killer of Indian people, but it was by no means the only fatal disease. Epidemics of measles, influenza, bubonic plague, diphtheria, typhus, scarlet fever, yellow fever, and other unidentified diseases also took their toll. Alcoholism added to the list of killer diseases imported from Europe. "A person who resides among them may easily observe the frightful decrease of their numbers from one period of ten years to another," said John Heckewelder, lamenting the impact of alcohol. "Our vices have destroyed them more than our swords."

Recurring epidemics allowed Indian populations no opportunity to bounce back from earlier losses. They cut down economic productivity, generating hunger and famine, which rendered those who survived one disease more vulnerable to affliction by the next. New diseases combined with falling birth rates, escalating warfare, alcoholism, and general social upheaval to turn Indian America into a graveyard. Decreased fecundity hindered population recovery. Nantucket, off the coast of Massachusetts, was once described as "an island full of Indians" and is estimated to have had a population of about 3,000 in the mid-seventeenth century. By 1763, there were 348 people. An epidemic of yellow fever that year left only twenty survivors. Some 3,000 Indians inhabited Martha's Vineyard in 1642; 313 survived in 1764. Mohawk population continued to decline to little more than 600 by the time of the Revolution. At the western door of the Iroquois confederacy, Seneca population remained stable, but this was largely because they adopted captives and immigrants from other communities ravaged by war and disease. The Illinois Indians of the Great Lakes region numbered more than ten thousand people in 1670; by 1800, no more than five hundred survived. On the banks of the Missouri in present-day Nebraska, the Omaha Indians numbered more than three thousand in the late 1700s; cholera and smallpox cut their population to less than three hundred by 1802. In years when Indian peoples needed all their resources to deal with Europeans and to cope with a world that was changing around them, their numbers were being steadily eroded by disease.

Survivors, many of them disfigured by pockmarks, faced the future bereft of loved ones and without the wisdom of elders to guide them. Societies woven together by ties of kinship and clan were torn apart. After disease struck Martha's Vineyard in 1645-46, one survivor lamented that all the elders who had taught and guided the people were dead, "and their wisdome is buried with them." In 1710, Indians near Charleston, South Carolina, told a settler they had forgotten most of their traditions because "their Old Men are dead." In some cases, power struggles followed the deaths of traditional leaders. Old certainties no longer applied, and long-established patterns of behavior must sometimes have seemed irrelevant. The impact of such losses on Indian minds and souls is incalculable.

Traditional healing practices proved powerless against the onslaught. Fasting, taking a sweat bath, and plunging into an icy river—a common Indian remedy for many ailments—aggravated rather than alleviated the effects of smallpox. Just as some Europeans looked to Indian skills and practices to deal with snakebites and ailments native to North America, so some Indian people looked to Europeans to provide relief from European sicknesses. Some believed that European witchcraft caused the new diseases; so it made sense to combat them with European power and medicine. Others, with their loved ones dying around them, were willing to try anything. Many Hurons accepted baptism from Jesuit priests, regarding it as a curative ritual and hoping it could save their children.

Despite instances of genocide and germ warfare against Indian populations, Europeans frequently provided what help and comfort they could.

Dead Indians were of no value to European missionaries seeking converts, European merchants seeking customers, or European ministers seeking allies. Hearing that Massasoit "their friend was sick and near unto death," Governor William Bradford and the Plymouth colonists "sente him such comfortable things as gave him great contente, and was a means of his recovery." French nuns ministered to sick Indians in seventeenth-century Quebec. Most Spanish missions in eighteenth-century California had dispensaries, medical supplies, and medical books, and some padres displayed genuine concern for the health of their mission populations. The state of medical knowledge was still rudimentary in the eighteenth century, but Europeans, motivated by self-interest as much as humanitarian concern, shared with Indians what medical advances there were. British Indian superintendent Sir William Johnson had the Mohawks inoculated against smallpox, and some Indians were vaccinated after Edward Jenner developed the cowpox vaccine in 1796. Many Indian people overcame their suspicion of the white man's medicine to accept the protection it could offer against the white man's diseases.

Nevertheless, the protection was too little and too late to stop demographic disaster. Not all Indian populations suffered 75 percent or 90 percent mortality rates—indeed, in some areas of the country Indian populations were on the rise in the eighteenth century—but the result was a world newly emptied of Indian inhabitants. Europeans arriving in Indian country in the wake of one or more epidemics made inaccurate estimates of precontact Indian population size on the basis of head counts of survivors. Seeing remnant populations, they gained a distorted impression of the size and sophistication of the societies that had once existed—and that distorted impression entered the history books. America, many believed, was an "empty wilderness," a "virgin land." If the country was empty, that was a recent development; it was depopulated rather than unpopulated. The new world of opportunity, which "free lands" opened for Europeans in North America, was in itself a by-product of European invasion.

Historians working to revise the old view of the European settlement of America as a story of progress and triumph have rightly stressed the biological cataclysm that followed European "discovery." But epidemic diseases also plagued European societies and shattered European families. France suffered epidemics and famine with appalling regularity throughout the seventeenth and eighteenth centuries. Recurrent outbreaks of plague devastated overcrowded London in the seventeenth century, sometimes, as in 1625, killing 25 percent of the population. In 1665, London experienced the horror of the Great Plague, which did not end until the Fire of London destroyed much of the city the following year. European immigrants to America did not entirely escape Old World diseases, and they succumbed to some new ones. Malaria wreaked havoc among Spanish expeditions in the sixteenth century. Early settlers at Jamestown, Virginia, suffered high death rates in unfamiliar environments. In 1740, Ephraim and Elizabeth Hartwell of Concord, Massachusetts, watched helplessly as all five of their young children died of the "throat distemper" that ravaged New England. Boston suffered recurrent outbreaks of smallpox in the seventeenth and eighteenth centuries. Yellow fever, imported from the Tropics, killed one out of every ten people in Philadelphia, then the capital of the United States, in 1793. But with less crowded communities, more sanitary conditions, improved diet, and greater economic opportunities, most colonists enjoyed a healthier life and longer life expectancy in their new world than did their contemporaries in Europe.

Though scholars disagree widely in their estimates, it is likely that in what is today the United States, Indian population stood at somewhere between 5 million and 10 million in 1492. By 1800, the figure had fallen to around 600,000. By contrast, the European population of the English colonies in America doubled every twenty-five years in the late eighteenth century. The first U.S. census in 1790 counted a total population of 3.9 million people. By 1800, North America had just under 5 million whites and about 1 million blacks. As James Axtell points out, the Indian people who survived in the eastern United States were being engulfed in a sea of white and black faces. The demographic complexion of the new world created by the interaction of Europeans, Indians, and Africans was very different in 1800 from what it had been three centuries before.

Nevertheless, the American population of 1800 combined Indian and European healing practices. Indians and Europeans alike employed "folk remedies" as well as doctors to cure diseases and injuries. The British lagged behind the Spaniards in establishing hospitals in the New World: Cortez built the first hospital in Mexico City for Indian and Spanish poor in 1521, and by the end of the seventeenth century, there were more than one hundred fifty hospitals in New Spain. In contrast, the first general hospital to care for the sick poor in the British colonies was established in Philadelphia in 1752; Massachusetts General Hospital, not until 1811. The first medical school was established at the University of Pennsylvania in 1765; Harvard Medical School, not until 1783. For most of the eighteenth century, American physicians who wanted a medical education had to go to Europe. With few trained physicians and few medical facilities available, people in rural and small-town communities turned in times of sickness to family, neighbors, clergymen, skilled women, and local healers. In many areas of the country, itinerant Indian physicians remained common well into the twentieth century, providing health care for America's poor, whether Indian, white, or black. Many Indian people preserved their belief in the efficacy of traditional medicine—both herbal and spiritual—even as they benefited from European medicine as practiced by white doctors. False Face societies and curing rituals continued among the Iroquois long after many Iroquois had embraced Christianity. Medicine was power, and Indian people needed to draw on all the power available to them as they struggled to survive in the disease-ridden land that was their new world.

Three

✦

The Stuff of Life

*I*N 1719, WILLIAM TAPP or Taptico, the last werowance (district chief) of the Wicomoco Indians of Chesapeake Bay, died. Three Englishmen compiled and appraised the inventory of his estate. Tapp owned goods and livestock valued at £100. His wardrobe consisted of English-style clothing—hats, vests, breeches, garters, and shoes. His house was furnished with chests, tables and chairs, and four feather beds, and there was an assortment of spoons, pewter plates, table linen, old books, and paper. The chief had lived in a manner comparable to that of neighboring English planters. But he also left fishhooks and line, a canoe, guns, and axes, indicating that he had continued to practice the traditional activities of an Algonkian male—fishing, hunting, and clearing the land. The presence of sheep, cattle, chickens, and a spinning wheel indicated that his wife, Elizabeth, had added spinning, knitting, and dairying to the traditional tasks of an Algonkian woman—preparing food, making pottery, and rearing children.

The clash of Indians and Europeans was a conflict between two ways of life; but even as the protagonists fought to preserve or impose their way of life, each way of life was undergoing substantial changes as a result of contact with the other. Nowhere in North America did Europeans and Indians fight each other all the time. They had to achieve ways of coexisting, however cautiously, and their daily interactions produced changes in their daily lives. As Indians and Europeans learned and borrowed from each other, they developed or adopted new diets and new ways of procuring food, new styles of architecture, new styles of clothing, and new ways of speaking, and they added new items to the things they used in their every-day lives.

.✦.

The diffusion of different items and different ways of living was nothing new in North America. Throughout history and throughout the world, nomadic hunting peoples and sedentary farming peoples have developed reciprocal trade relations, and such networks functioned in North America at the edges of different ecosystems, with Plains hunters, for example, trading with set-tled farming peoples on the banks of the Rio Grande or the Missouri River. Trade networks crisscrossed Indian America before Europeans arrived. Tur-quoise from New Mexico, copper from Lake Superior, pipestone from Min-nesota, marine shells from the coasts, flint, feathers, tobacco, hides, and different strains of corn made their way across vast distances. Ideas and influences followed the same trade routes, so that, for instance, pottery made by Mahicans, Munsees, and New England Algonkians came to reflect the ceramic styles of the Iroquois in New York, or vice versa. Some Indian peoples—the Ottawas of the Great Lakes and the Jumanos in the Southwest, for example—gained an early reputation as far-ranging traders, moving other peoples' goods to other people.

Indians' reasons for trade differed somewhat from Europeans'. Trade was a way of cementing alliances, preventing conflict, making and renewing friendships; it was an activity hedged around by social and ceremonial considerations. Existing trade networks and trading experiences provided a ready-made avenue for the incorporation of European traders and their items. When Jacques Cartier and his crew visited Hochelaga in 1535, the Indians were eager to trade: "These people came towards our boats in as friendly and familiar a manner as if we had been natives of the country, bringing us great store of fish and of whatever else they possessed, in order to obtain our wares, stretching forth their hands towards heaven and making many gestures and signs of joy."

Early French traders recognized the ceremonial aspects of trade and accommodated themselves to the customs of the country. When Samuel de Champlain opened trade with the Hurons early in the seventeenth century, he did so by following Huron rules of trade, giving generous gifts, which obligated Huron people to be more generous and encouraged them to return for more trade the next year. The French, says Denys Delâge, "had decoded the Amerindian system of exchange" and recognized that, over time, gifts given were sure to bring a good return. Rather than engage in hard bargaining for immediate profits, early French traders learned "the language of gifts" and gave them in ceremonies "that joined the parties in a pact of generosity." The more lavish the French were with their gifts of metal and manufactured goods, the more lavish the Hurons were with their gifts of furs. Traders in other regions and in later years also adopted the Native custom of ceremonial gift-giving as a way of initiating trade, although they were rarely as sensitive or as skilled as the French in employing Native trading practices to their advantage. Nevertheless, the flow of European manufactured goods into Indian country continued unabated.

Once an item passed from European to Indian hands, it did not necessarily stop there. It had entered a world of extensive contacts and intertribal communication that might carry it across half a continent and more. European goods reached Huron country by about 1580, before Hurons had ever met a European. When de Soto's conquistadors entered Cofitachiqui in South Carolina in 1540, they found a European dirk, two Castilian axes, and a rosary, which presumably had gotten there via Native trade routes from the coast or Mexico. An incised copper plate, unearthed in Georgia in 1984, illustrates the possibilities. An Aztec evidently made the plate as an adornment for a Bible or a box some time in the mid-sixteenth century. It made its way to northwestern Georgia, where it was traded to a Coosa Indian. Modifications made the plate a gorget, and it was finally buried with a child. As James B. Langford concludes, "The Coosawattee Plate provides a tangible and remarkable example of the crosscurrents of change sweeping through the Western Hemisphere in the sixteenth century. The history of the artifact parallels the history of the era: manufactured by a native of Mexico, influenced by the Christian religion of Europe, carried hundreds of miles to an unsettled frontier, traded for food or given as a gift, adapted for use by another culture, and finally buried with a child in a village soon thereafter abandoned." In such "small things forgotten" lie stories of people's lives and changing lifestyles.

Early explorers and chroniclers insisted that Indians regarded Europeans with awe and even attributed to them godlike qualities because of the impressive new technologies they possessed. But if Indians were awestruck at first, they soon got over it and started adapting the new items into their lives.

When Giovanni da Verrazzano, a Florentine sailing for the king of France, put in to Narragansett Bay in 1524, the Indians there evidently had not met Europeans before. They were not interested in trading for cloth or metal goods; they wanted blue beads, bells, and copper trinkets, objects similar to what they might have obtained in intertribal trade and that occupied a familiar place in their lives. As Verrazzano followed the coast northeast to Maine, however, he encountered Abenaki Indians, who clearly had had previous experiences with European sailors. They hid their women, "mooned" Verrazzano's crew, and refused to trade for anything but knives, fishhooks, and metal goods. By the 1620s, Montagnais Indians near the mouth of the St. Lawrence were using large quantities of metal tools and weapons and woolen clothing; they recognized the utility of the new items, but they hardly held European traders in awe. "The English have no sense," said one Montagnais. "They give us twenty knives like this for one Beaver skin." In the 1630s, William Wood observed that Indians in Massachusetts were at first amazed by European ships, plows, and windmills, but in time "the fresh supplies of new and strange objects hath lessened their admiration and quickened their inventions and desire of practicing such things as they see." When Nicholas Denys arrived in Acadia in 1638, the Indians there were already using portable iron kettles, metal axes, knives, and arrowheads.

European merchants funneled into Indian country an inventory of manufactured goods that included steel axes and knives, iron and copper kettles, spoons, metal hoes, ice chisels, fishhooks, gorgets, combs, scissors, awls, mirrors, needles, thread, thimbles, woolen clothing and blankets, linen shirts, jackets, hats, guns, and alcohol. In time, some Indian peoples' tastes extended to books and paper, spinning wheels, pewter and glassware, china, lace and silk, buckles, shoes, and feathered hats. Metal drills made possible the mass production of wampum. Glass beads from Italy, and even from Czechoslovakia, became a standard trade item. They flooded into Indian country by the thousands, supplanting or supplementing traditional sources of shells and porcupine quills in the manufacture of wampum belts and the decoration of clothing. Beadwork came to be regarded as a traditional craft in American Indian life. Woolens from Yorkshire, linen from Ireland, strouds (a cheaper cloth made from woolen rags) from the Midlands, guns from Birmingham, all became commonplace in Indian America. So pervasive was the influx of manufactured goods that, by the time of the American Revolution, Mohawks at Fort Hunter reportedly were living much better than most of their colonial neighbors. Some of their Oneida relatives lived in frame houses with chimneys and painted windows, ate with spoons from pewter plates, drank from teacups and punch bowls, combed their hair with ivory combs, used silk handkerchiefs, and wore white breeches. After the Revolution, the Mohawk chief Joseph Brant, who had a new home on the Grand River in Ontario, entertained visitors with dinner served on the finest tableware. Cherokee Indians used combs, scissors, pewter spoons, and a variety of metal tools and jewelry.

Indian peoples accepted European goods because they made life easier, more comfortable, warmer, and more pleasurable. Scissors and metal knives allowed Indian women to fashion traditional clothing from hides and skins with greater ease and precision. Metal pots were more durable and transportable than stone or bark ones, and they could be heated directly over a fire rather than having to drop heated stones into the contents. Steel hatchets surpassed stone axes. Guns possessed some advantages over bows and arrows. Indians also valued certain goods for aesthetic and spiritual reasons.

Archaeologists excavating eighteenth-century sites in the eastern United States often find it difficult to determine whether a settlement was Indian or European on the basis of the materials unearthed. Indian peoples quickly became tied into European trade networks, and by the eighteenth century they, like their colonial neighbors, were becoming part of an Atlantic economy and a growing consumer revolution that shaped their tastes, their lives, and the world they inhabited.

The new goods came with hidden costs—increasing violence, declining craft skills, and dependency on outsiders. As they became dependent on trade goods, some Indian communities found it difficult to preserve their lands and their independence. Many traditional lithic and ceramic technologies were abandoned in preference for European manufactures. The first European products reached the Senecas of western New York in the second half of the sixteenth century; by the end of that century, most Senecas had discarded stone axes and flint knives in favor of metal tools. In 1768, Eleazar Wheelock was disappointed in his efforts to find among the Iroquois an item of Native manufacture that was "without the least Mixture of foreign Merchandize"; he could find only a "small specimen." A Creek Indian named Handsome Fellow said in 1777: "We have been used so long to wrap up our Children as soon as they are born in Goods procured of the white

People that we cannot do without it." Anthropologist Oscar Lewis maintained that the Blackfeet could not remember how to make pottery a mere ten years after they first acquired iron pots from British traders.

Where Native pottery survived, it underwent changes. Spanish missionaries among the Hopis discouraged the use of pottery as burial offerings and encouraged potters to replace Native designs—which might involve association with animal spirits and other sources of power—with Christian designs such as flowers, Maltese crosses, and eight-point stars. Archaeological excavations at Spanish missions in Florida reveal Native-made copies of Spanish plates, pitchers, and tableware, although the pottery of mission Indians living in St. Augustine seems to have changed little over time. As Indian women married Spanish men, Native pottery, whether of traditional or Spanish design, or incorporating elements of both, became part of daily life in their households.

As European trade goods made their way into Indian country, a "pan-Indian" trade culture developed. However, it was not a simple substitution of Indian artifacts for European goods. Indians often took new items and refashioned them into traditional designs, or sought them for their symbolic and spiritual rather than their utilitarian value. European tools and implements became part of their everyday world in ways Europeans neither expected nor understood. East Coast Algonkians used the woolen stockings they got from Dutch traders in the seventeenth century as tobacco pouches, and they wore steel hatchet blades around their necks in place of stone ornaments. Europeans often thought Indians were gullible traders who would exchange beaver pelts for "beads and baubles," but in the world of eastern Algonkian people, colored glass beads and metal objects often possessed powerful symbolic and spiritual significance and were incorporated into ceremonial objects along with native crystal, shells, and copper. Invested with Indian meanings and put to Indian uses, trade items became, to a large extent, Indian goods of European manufacture.

Indians also made their own versions of European things. Spaniards appear to have introduced playing cards into the Southwest in 1598. Apache Indians later made their own decks of cards out of rawhide, copying and modifying the Spanish ones. Since the king, knight, and other figures on the Spanish cards meant nothing to the Apaches, they substituted their own designs, painting figures in Apache costume. Appreciating the value of hard

Spanish playing cards and, *below,* Apache playing cards adopted from them. (Courtesy Marc Simmons)

cash, Indians were not above making their own: two Apalachees living near St. Augustine were arrested in 1695 for counterfeiting Spanish coins out of tin.

European traders sometimes included in their inventory of trade goods for one tribe items manufactured by Indians of other tribes, with the result that some artifacts and customs of indigenous but particular tribal origin spread throughout Indian America. Indians were discriminating customers, and European manufacturers responded to their demands and accommodated their preferences to make goods specifically for the Indian trade: pipe tomahawks, muskets with large trigger guards for northern Indians wearing mittens, cloth of preferred colors as in the famous Hudson's Bay blankets, which became almost ubiquitous in northern regions of America.

Some Indian crafts, such as basket making, wood carving, and beadworking, were actually stimulated by European influences and demands. After Vitus Bering and Alexei Chirikov opened trade in sea otter pelts with the Natives on the Gulf of Alaska in 1741–42, Russian *promyshlenniki* (fur traders) developed a lucrative business selling the pelts in China. Spaniards,

Britons, and Americans soon got in on the act. In the second half of the eighteenth century, goods from factories half a world away poured into Indian communities on the Northwest Coast, producing increased wealth, more elaborate ceremonies, and an artistic florescence. When those tribes obtained steel chisels and other metal tools from maritime traders, they used the new tools to work wood on a scale never before possible and to develop new levels of artistry and intricacy. Huge totem poles—a symbol of "Indian-ness" in the popular imagination, but exclusive to the Northwest Coast, where they bore family and clan crests—proliferated. Unprecedented supplies of copper allowed more elaborate decorations and crests on dance masks. In the Northeast, Indians sometimes resorted to making baskets for sale to colonists as a way of earning a meager living after their traditional economies were disrupted. Working for a market and catering to the tastes of customers who might want baskets for decoration rather than use, they took basket-making skills to new heights and produced objects of great beauty.

Europeans also adapted items of Indian manufacture into their material culture. In addition to baskets and bowls peddled by Indian women in the settlements, frontiersmen employed Indian-style hatchets. Colonists traveled by Indian snowshoes, Indian toboggans, and Indian canoes. Birchbark canoes, manufactured from the bark of the paper birch, with ribs of white cedar and pitch from the balsam fir, were unmatched for travel in the rivers and lakes of northeastern forests. John McPhee, author of *The Survival of the Bark Canoe,* explains the impression these craft made on European sailors and the speed with which Europeans took to them:

> When white explorers first came to northeastern North America, they looked in wonder at such canoes—as well they might, for nothing like them existed in Europe. There was eloquence in the evidence they gave of the genius of humankind. The materials were simple, but the structure was not. An adroit technology had come down with the tribes from immemorial time, and now—in the sixteenth, the seventeenth century—here were bark canoes on big rivers and ocean bays curiously circling ships from another world. Long-boats were lowered, to be rowed by crews of four and upward. The sailors hauled at their oars. The Indians, two to a canoe, indolently whisked their narrow paddles and easily drew away. In their wake they left a stunning impression. Not only were they faster. They could see where they were going.
>
> White explorers got out of their ships and went thousands of miles in bark canoes. They travelled in them until the twentieth century, for bark ca-

noes were the craft of the north continent. Nothing else, indigenous or imported, could do what they could do.

Contemporary observers agreed that bark canoes were impressive craft. An anonymous Frenchman said the Indian canoes he saw on the Great Lakes in 1672 were "so light that one or two men at most carry them, and yet so made that some will hold six to eight persons with their belongings." Birchbark canoes enabled the French and the British to penetrate the north country. The fur trade, which introduced so many items of European manufacture into Indian country, depended itself on transportation by Indian canoe, often with Indian paddlers. Farther south, Indians used more cumbersome dugout canoes, but they were a vital means of travel. John Lawson noted how settlers in the Carolinas had adopted them from their Indian neighbors: "Many of the Women are very handy in Canoes, and will manage them with great Dexterity and Skill, which they become accustomed to in this watery Country."

✦

The European invasion of America produced a dietary revolution in the Old World. Potatoes, corn, tomatoes, squash, beans, pumpkins, and a host of other foods, hitherto unknown in Europe, enriched people's diets, improving their health and allowing them to live longer. Balances of power shifted north, away from the Mediterranean, as Prussia, Russia, and Britain fed their populations with potatoes, a plant that thrived despite short growing seasons. European population expanded dramatically, increasing the human pressure on an already overtaxed land base. Thousands, and eventually millions, of people left their overcrowded continent in search of more plentiful land in America. So dependent did the population of Ireland become on potatoes that when the crops failed year after year in the late 1840s and early 1850s, as many as 1 million people died, and another 1.8 million were propelled into emigration to America.

Diets also underwent substantial change within America where European crops and livestock altered Indian lifestyles, and European pioneers took to growing Indian corn and hunting in Indian fashion.

By the time Europeans came to America, Indian peoples were growing corn, usually supplemented with beans and squash, from the Rio Grande to the St. Lawrence. Introduced from Mexico, corn had spread north, and

"Costume of the Domiciliated Indians of North America," showing Indian adoption of elements of European material culture. (From George Heriot, *Travels through the Canadas,* 1807. Dartmouth College Library)

Indian peoples in New Mexico were growing a kind of corn by 3000 B.C. Elsewhere, Indian farmers developed new strains, like northern flint, suited to the soils and climate of their homelands. This maize or "Indian corn," which one scholar called "a marvel of Indian ingenuity," was said to be "the most remarkable plant breeding accomplishment of all time." It played a major role in Americanizing the diets of European settlers.

Many tribal stories attributed divine origins to corn. The Iroquois referred to corn, beans, and squash as the "sacred three sisters." Corn agriculture was an essential part of the landscape on the eastern edges of the Great Plains. Surrounding the earth-lodge villages of the Mandans, Hidatsas, and Arikaras on the banks of the upper Missouri River in North Dakota were cornfields. The surpluses of corn, beans, and other vegetables these peoples produced allowed them to develop a lively trade with buffalo-hunting peoples farther out on the plains. As part of their seasonal cycle of subsistence, the Pawnee Indians of east-central Nebraska hunted buffalo, but they also grew ten varieties of corn, one of them for purely religious purposes, not for consumption. They also grew eight kinds of beans, seven types of squash, and pumpkins. Corn was the staff of life for many Indian people before contact, and it became the staff of life for many European colonists.

Corn was higher in nutrition than most other grain crops, and it gave higher yields. John Lawson, who traveled in South Carolina and into the interior Indian country in 1701, was one of many colonists who sang the praises of corn. "The *Indian* Corn, or *Maiz,* proves the most useful Grain in the World," he wrote, "and had it not been for the Fruitfulness of this Species, it would have proved very difficult to have settled some of the Plantations in *America.*" It grew virtually anywhere. "It refuses no Grounds, unless the barren Sands, and when planted in good Ground, will repay the Planter seven or eight hundred fold."

One friar who accompanied Juan de Oñate's colonizing expedition into New Mexico in 1598 declared that "here, corn is God." Oñate and his followers established a system of tribute by which the local Pueblo Indians provided them with labor and food, especially corn. But Spanish aggression disrupted the traditional economy that produced the corn, and famine became a grim visitor in the next century. In Virginia in 1607, John Smith found countless stretches of open fields cultivated by Indians around Chesapeake Bay, some of them as large as 2,000 acres. Efforts by Smith and the Jamestown settlers to obtain corn by coercion produced hostilities with the Powhatan Indians. European colonists learned that the best way to get a secure supply of corn was to learn the Indian's corn culture themselves.

In New England, the Pilgrims at Plymouth benefited from Indian knowledge and food surpluses to survive their first hard years. The Pilgrims stole caches of corn before the Patuxet Indian Squanto came along and "directed them how to set their corne." Indians in southern New England traded agricultural surpluses to hunting peoples farther north; it was easy for them to share surplus food with English settlers in the initial years of contact, providing the basis for the "first Thanksgiving" so ingrained in the popular mythology about early America. Colonists also adapted Indian corn agriculture into their new way of life. "Many ways hath their advice and endeavor been advantageous to us," said one man, "they being our first instructors for the planting of their Indian corn, by teaching us to cull out the finest seed, to observe the fittest season, to keep distance for holes and fit measure for ills, to worm it, and weed it, and dress it as occasion requires."

After Indian men cleared the fields for planting, Indian women hoed the soil and planted the kernels in small hillocks formed by hand. They also planted beans and pumpkin seeds, which added nitrogen to the soil. The growing cornstalks served as beanpoles and also afforded shade to the pumpkin vines. Indian people taught the settlers how to harvest corn, how to grind it into meal, and how to preserve it through the year. Discussing the role of Indian corn in *Everyday Life in Early America,* David Freeman Hawke concludes that "the settlers adopted their corn culture entirely from the Indians. They planted when the Indians told them to—'when the white oak leaves reach the size of a mouse's ear'—and the way they told them, dropping several kernels in holes three or four feet apart, later 'hilling' the seedlings by scooping soil around them for support, then fertilizing them with herring which flooded up the streams to spawn during the late spring, though this last technique they may have brought from England." The Indians also showed them how to cook corn and beans together to make succotash, how to tap maple trees for sugar, and how to cook beans in earthen pots, to produce a dish that has since become known as Boston baked beans.

Corn fed colonists, and it provisioned colonial armies. From the Spanish invasions of the Southeast by Pánfilo de Narváez in 1528 and Hernando de Soto in 1539–43, to John Sullivan's invasion of Iroquois country in 1779, colonial expeditions relied on the corn they found in Indian fields and villages to feed the troops and keep the campaign alive. Colonists fed corn to their chickens, turkeys, and pigs, adding more meat to their diets than was common in Europe. They exported it to the Caribbean, where it fed slaves working on sugar plantations. Corn from America also stimulated population growth in Africa, the labor pool for America's plantations. Slaves and poor whites in the southern United States became so dependent on corn as a staple food that they succumbed to a new disease, a nutritional ailment called pellagra (something that Indians had avoided because their cooking methods, which included adding wood ashes to the food, enhanced the niacin in corn). Settlers planted European grains whenever they could, but corn agriculture became a way of life in much of pioneer America. Henry Adams, in his history of the United States during Thomas Jefferson's first administration, said simply that "Indian corn was the national crop."

European colonists tried to maintain their old diets. Virginia planters long preferred the roast beef of Old England to the abundant meats offered in America. Despite its American origins, the potato was not widely used in English colonies until north country Britons arrived in the eighteenth century and made the crop they had adopted at home an important part of the diet of backcountry settlers. The pattern by which newcomers adopted new foods was not straightforward, as David Hackett Fischer observes: "Native American plants such as potatoes and tomatoes rarely appeared on the best colonial tables until they had become fashionable in the mother country." Inevitably, though, settlers used what was available to create new varieties of old foods and drinks: cornmeal replaced oatmeal to produce "grits"; scotch whisky (distilled from barley) gave way to bourbon (made mainly from corn and rye).

Indian crops, combined with Euro-Indian farming techniques, produced prolific yields and an American backwoods farming culture that blended ethnic traditions. Finnish settlers in the Delaware Valley brought their own methods of cutting, clearing, settling, and fencing the land, but they adopted Indian practices of crop selection, hoeing, and mound cultivation. Colonial settlers also followed their Indian neighbors in gathering wild plants and berries, drawing on knowledge that Indian people had accumulated during centuries of living in the forests of eastern America. Berries, walnuts, pecans, hickory nuts, wild grapes, nettles, papaws, crab apples, and maple sugar supplemented the diets of European colonists, too.

Indians provided English colonists with another major crop, one culti-vated for inhaling rather than eating. After experimenting with several cash crops, colonists in Virginia finally settled on Indian tobacco as the most lucrative. The English found they preferred Caribbean to Virginian tobacco, and John Rolfe, who married Pocahontas, the daughter of Powhatan, im-ported seeds from the Caribbean and began turning tobacco into a large-scale commercial crop. The English experimented with a variety of pro-cedures until they hit upon the right one for mass production. In Jack Weatherford's view, "The final tobacco culture combined traditional aspects of both native American and European knowledge with some innovations developed in Virginia and neighboring tobacco colonies." With tobacco smoking a common and addictive social vice in seventeenth-century Europe, tobacco cultivation and export became the basis for the prosperity of colo-nial Virginia and many of its "first families." Tobacco smoking was also popular among European colonists in North America. Writing in the mid-eighteenth century, Swedish traveler Peter Kalm observed, "The French-men's whole smoking etiquette here in Canada, namely the preparation of the tobacco, the tobacco pouch, the pipe, the pipe-stem, etc. was derived from the natives, with the exception of the fire-steel and flint." Many Indians found that European curing processes made the new tobacco more desirable than their own varieties, and some stopped growing tobacco except for use in religious rituals.

Indians taught Europeans how to hunt and fish. As John Smith acknowledged, English settlers at first were out of their depth in America, unable to harvest the natural resources they found there: "Though there be fish in the sea, fowls in the air, and beasts in the woods, their bounds are so large, they so wild, and we so weak and ignorant, we cannot much trouble them." William Wood, who lived in the Massachusetts Bay area in the 1630s, said that the local Indians were "experienced in the knowledge of all baits, and diverse seasons; being not ignorant likewise of the removal of fishes, knowing when to fish in rivers, and when at rocks, when in bays, and when at seas." Traders on the Northwest Coast in the late eighteenth century relied on local Indians to supply them with fish, just as fur-trading posts and brigades across the continent relied on Indian hunters to provide them with fresh meat.

Finnish immigrants to New Sweden in the seventeenth century came from an area and a culture where hunting was still a way of life, and they brought their own hunting traditions and expertise. Most Europeans came from societies where hunting was a gentlemen's sport, and those who hunted for food often did so as poachers. Europeans had to adopt the Indians' hunting culture in order to survive in their new world. European hunters learned from Indians the use of animal skins as camouflage, decoys, various whistles and calls to attract the prey, and methods (such as deer runs) of taking animals. They borrowed from Indian woods lore to become familiar with animals and their habits and habitats, and they adopted Indian hunting gear. German gunsmiths in southeastern Pennsylvania developed the American long rifle, which became famous as the weapon of backwoods hunters like Daniel Boone, but most techniques those hunters employed had been learned from the Indians.

European missionaries and other groups intent on "civilizing" Indians urged them to give up hunting and concentrate on farming, and many Indians incorporated new crops, poultry, and livestock into their economies. Meanwhile, many European settlers who lived in the backcountry were becoming more dependent on hunting and less tied to agriculture. As hunters, they chose to live in less populated areas, moved over greater distances, and lived more like their Indian neighbors. Seventeenth-century Puritans had feared the wilderness; by the mid-eighteenth century, backcountry settlers were living and hunting in it, much as the Indians did. Eastern elites and European travelers who ventured into the American backcountry commonly remarked with repulsion the extent to which frontiersmen and their families resembled Indians in their way of life. Missionary David McClure said that backcountry Virginians were "generally white Savages, and subsist by hunting, and live like the Indians." What they were witnessing was the emergence of a new way of life, a new frontier culture that drew on Indian and European traditions and centered on hunting as a means of subsistence. In this way, says Jack Weatherford, "the Indians Americanized the settlers." Many conflicts between Indians and backcountry settlers, notes Daniel Boone's biographer John Faragher, occurred "not because they were so alien to each other but because they were so much alike" and competed for the same forest resources.

But the transformation was not complete. Backcountry hunters did not usually adopt the Indian hunting ethic that required respectful treatment of the prey and restraint in the kill. Wasteful and disrespectful hunting practices on the part of Euro-American hunters remained a constant source of friction between Natives and newcomers, even as market pressures began to undermine the Indians' own hunting ethics.

Indian diets also changed considerably with the introduction of European crops and domestic animals. De Soto's conquistadors brought hundreds of pigs to the Southeast. Indian villages soon had their share of chickens, pigs, and cattle. The Cherokees were eating pork by the middle of the eighteenth century. When English explorers reached the interior of Georgia and the Carolinas, they found peaches growing wild in the woods and assumed they were an indigenous fruit. In fact, peaches had been introduced in Florida by Spanish or French colonists. The Indians developed a taste for them and traded and transplanted them farther north. When William Bartram visited Indian villages in northern Florida and Georgia on the eve of the American Revolution, he noted that the surrounding fields "were plentifully stored with Corn, Citruels, Pumkins, Squashes, Beans, Peas, Potatoes, Peaches, Figs, Oranges, &c." The Spaniards also introduced watermelons to Mesoamerica. Indian people quickly adopted them and traded them from one group to another ahead of the Spanish advance northward. Oñate found Pueblo people growing watermelons by the time he got to the Rio Grande in the 1590s; the French explorer René Robert Cavelier de La Salle saw them

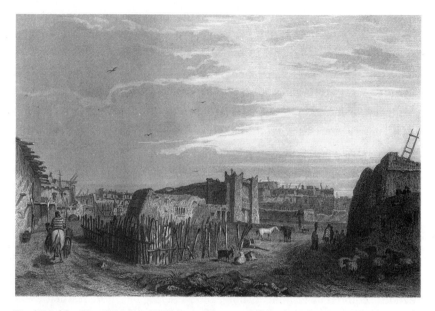

Zuni Pueblo, New Mexico. Franciscan friars established a mission at Zuni in 1629. In addition to new religious teachings and the new architecture of the mission chapel nestled among traditional pueblo structures, the Spaniards introduced new crops, horses, sheep, and goats into the daily lives of Zuni people. (Engraving of a drawing by Seth Eastman, from a sketch by Richard H. Kern, 1851. From Henry Rowe Schoolcraft, *Information Respecting the History, Condition and Prospects of the Indian Tribes of the United States,* 6 vols. [1851–57], vol. 4. Dartmouth College Library)

among the Caddoes in eastern Texas in 1682. La Salle also saw peach trees in Quapaw villages in Arkansas. Spaniards brought fruit trees and grain cereals from Europe, and they brought tomatoes and chilies from Mexico to the Pueblos on the Rio Grande, adding permanent ingredients to New Mexican cuisine.

Pueblo Indians in New Mexico and the Hopi Indians in Arizona kept corn as the center of their subsistence base, but took on domesticated plants and livestock introduced by the Spaniards. By the eighteenth century, sheep were replacing deer and antelope as food items, wool replaced cotton as the most popular textile, cowhide and sheepskin replaced deerskin for moccasins and other leather goods. Hopi people also learned knitting and blacksmithing from the Spaniards. Spanish missionaries in the 1770s remarked on the large herds of cattle, horses, and sheep grazing around Hopi villages.

Apaches and Navajos raided Spanish and Pueblo livestock, but in time the Navajos became shepherds themselves, and they had large flocks of sheep by the end of the eighteenth century.

Dietary changes proved a mixed blessing. Spanish missionaries enforced agriculture as a key component of "civilization," and mission agriculture eventually produced food surpluses that were less vulnerable to seasonal and annual fluctuations than were traditional Native resources. However, the wide variety of foods enjoyed by Indian peoples before contact tended to be replaced by a steady diet of wheat, corn, and beans, supplemented occasionally with fruit and vegetables in season. Mission Indians could expect three meals a day, but it was a diet very high in carbohydrates. The monotonous diet was also deficient in high-quality proteins, vitamins A and C, and riboflavin. These deficiencies made Indian neophytes, especially women and children, more susceptible to disease. Indians in California, Georgia, and Florida in the seventeenth century experienced a shift from a rich variety of foods acquired by hunting, fishing, and gathering to a more restricted and less nutritious diet at the missions, and their health suffered accordingly.

European contact changed how Indian people procured their food, just as contact with Indians changed how Europeans procured theirs. Spaniards introduced horses into the Southwest, and Indian peoples quickly recognized the new animals as a tremendous asset. Horses spread north on to the Great Plains in the late seventeenth and eighteenth centuries, opening a new world of mobility for the Indian inhabitants and changing the way they harvested the enormous herds of buffalo. Instead of hunting on foot and by dangerous buffalo drives, Plains Indians became efficient mounted hunters. A sophisticated horse-buffalo complex evolved that brought Plains peoples unprecedented prosperity and became ingrained as the core of their way of life. New groups of people moved on to the plains to take advantage of new opportunities, embrace the new way of life there, and acquire new identities as Plains Indians. Their increasing efficiency and their numbers subjected the buffalo herds to new pressures even before white hide-hunters entered the area.

✦

When Europeans came to America, they brought with them styles of architecture and ideas about the kinds of houses they wanted to build in their new world. They took scant notice of Indian architecture, regarding Indian homes as impermanent dwellings. Despite the thousands of years in which Indian people had been building homes and societies in America, Europeans saw little evidence of the civilizations that had risen and fallen here. When William of Normandy conquered England in 1066, London had a population of between ten and fifteen thousand people. In that same year, at least as many people, and perhaps twice as many, inhabited the Indian metropolis at Cahokia, near what is now East St. Louis. Founded in about A.D. 600 and occupied for almost seven hundred years, Cahokia was the largest urban center north of the Rio Grande, a planned city with one hundred earthen mounds and a city center of six square miles. But no European saw Cahokia at its height: the city went into decline and was gone long before Europeans came to America. London, on the other hand, mushroomed, to include almost two hundred thousand people in the city and its suburbs by 1600.

Indian towns existed throughout the Southeast when the Spaniards invaded in the sixteenth century, and there were Indian towns at Chaco Canyon and other sites in the Southwest long before Europeans arrived. Even after war and disease had taken their toll, Indian villages were often far larger and far more impressive than the nascent settlements European colonists inhabited. But Europeans, then as now, did not think of Indians as living in "towns."

As Jack Weatherford observes, "North American history did not speak" to the invaders from Europe. The continent seemed silent to them "because the civilizations of North America did not always speak in loud stone." Often, they spoke—and built—in earth, wood, and fiber. In time, Indian people across America were living in European-style houses. But in a country where land and wood were plentiful, housing styles became modified, so that the houses Indians adopted from Europeans were different from those found in Europe. Moreover, settlers who met immigrants from other parts of Europe in a new, shared environment sometimes adopted other styles from the Old World. New Englanders stuck to clapboard houses, but Scotch-Irish settlers in Pennsylvania and elsewhere built log cabins, which Scandinavians had introduced to North America.

Contrary to popular opinion, all Indian peoples did not inhabit tepees or wigwams. They had many different styles of architecture, suited to their particular needs and appropriate to their specific environments. Constructed from the available raw materials and following time-honored techniques,

Indian lodgings—whether the longhouses and wigwams of the Northeast, the earth lodges and tepees of the Great Plains, the plank houses of the Northwest Coast, or the pueblos of the Southeast—served to shelter the people, keeping them warm in winter and cool in summer. Indian architecture made arrangements of space that catered to peoples' social, ceremonial, and subsistence needs. Algonkian wigwams were typically versatile and movable: Giovanni da Verrazzano said that the Indians he met on Long Island in 1524 "change their habitations from place to place as circumstances of situation and season may require." When people moved they often carried elm or bark coverings, portable roofing that they laid over the sapling frames they had left standing at familiar campsites. Iroquoian longhouses of 100 feet and more in length, constructed from sheets of bark laid over such frames, were multifamily dwellings where people related by clan through their mother's line lived year-round. Southeastern Indian towns often contained council houses, ball fields, and ceremonial plazas.

European observers varied in their opinions of Indian housing, but some recognized its utility. Daniel Gookin, an astute observer of the Indians in Massachusetts in the seventeenth century, said, "I have often lodged in their wigwams, and found them as warm as the best English houses." Jesuit missionary Joseph François Lafitau said the Iroquois were "the most comfortably lodged of all America." When William Bartram visited a Yuchi community on the Chattahoochee River in Georgia before the American Revolution, he described it as "the largest, most compact and best situated Indian town I ever saw; the habitations are large and neatly built; the walls of the houses are constructed of a wooden frame, then lathed and plastered inside and out with a reddish well-tempered clay or mortar, which gives them the appearance of red brick walls, and these houses are neatly covered or roofed with cypress bark or shingles of that tree."

Indians were not always impressed by the Europeans' houses. A Micmac chief in the seventeenth century asked French visitors why men who were five or six feet tall needed houses sixty to eighty feet high: "Do we not have in our dwellings all the conveniences and advantages that you have in yours, such as reposing, drinking and sleeping, eating and amusing ourselves with our friends . . . ?"

Colonists borrowed from Indian housing techniques, if only temporarily, as they adjusted to their new environment. At Salem, in Massachusetts Bay Colony early in the seventeenth century, a settler adapted a local Indian wigwam, adding a door at one end and a fireplace at the other. However, when European colonists resorted to Indian-style housing, it usually was a makeshift measure until they could build a more substantial and permanent home. More often, Europeans employed American materials and American labor in constructing European-style buildings. Hispanic women learned from Pueblo women how to plaster adobe houses. Indian converts built many of the Spanish missions, and Spaniards set up *encomienda* and *repartimiento* systems, requiring Indian towns to provide teams of laborers. Pueblo Indian workers built Santa Fe, New Mexico; Florida Indians spent fifteen years building Fort San Marcos in St. Augustine. "The infrastructure of Spain's fledgling empire in North America was built with repartimiento labor in both New Mexico and Florida," concludes David Weber.

More often, it was Indian architecture that changed in response to European influences. Indians modified and adapted their dwellings for centuries before Europeans arrived, and Pueblo Indians in the Southwest continued to live in their settled, multistoried towns long after, but by the eighteenth century in the eastern woodlands, changes in Indian housing were widespread and permanent. Europeans brought new building materials and tools—iron nails and hinges, hammers and saws. They also generated dramatic changes in Indian societies and demographic changes in Indian country, which often resulted in fewer people living in communities farther apart. Iroquois peoples in New York began to live in single-family log cabins rather than in the communal longhouses that traditionally sheltered many families of the same clan. Iroquois villages that formerly were surrounded by palisades now tended to be scattered. Cherokee towns in Tennessee and the Carolinas followed a similar pattern of dispersal as people began to farm family plots, European-style, rather than tend communal fields shared by the whole village. Peter Kalm, who visited the Hurons at Lorette on the St. Lawrence River in the mid-eighteenth century, said that the Indians no longer lived in huts but had "built all their houses after the French fashion." The log cabin, built with notched-log construction and first introduced by Finnish and Swedish settlers into the Delaware Valley in the mid-seventeenth century, became almost the standard lodging of American backwoods pioneers and was also extensively adopted by Indian communities.

Single-family homes proliferated and communal lodgings like longhouses decreased, which altered social uses of space. Relations between people changed, and the bonds within and between clans, families, and communities sometimes weakened. In times of severe social stress, changing living arrangements surely had far-reaching repercussions. Many Indians grew up in what, in the context of their societies, constituted "broken homes."

✦

When Don Juan de Oñate and a wagon train of colonists set out to establish the first Spanish settlement in the Southwest, they brought with them the clothes they had been accustomed to wearing in Mexico. The men had velvet suits with high collars and lace cuffs, sateen caps, and richly embossed and stitched leather shoes from Cordova in Spain. The women had full silk dresses decorated with gold piping and lace trim, wore dainty and brightly colored slippers, and covered their heads with fringed and embroidered shawls imported from Manila. Such clothing had no place on the Rio Grande frontier. "Before long," notes historian Marc Simmons, "the colonists packed away their finery and took to dressing like the Indians." Velvet suits and silk dresses gave place to clothes made of gamuza (chamois) or buckskin, the softly tanned hide of deer and antelope. Buckskin remained the standard clothing of New Mexicans, whether Indian or Hispanic, until

A Creek log cabin in the late eighteenth century, showing the adoption of European building styles first introduced to North America by Scandinavian settlers.
(Smithsonian Institution, National Anthropological Archives, photo no. 1169-A)

the Santa Fe Trail opened in 1821, which meant large quantities of cheap American cloth appeared in the New Mexican market, and it did not disappear until the second half of the nineteenth century when railroads brought cheap cloth from New England mills.

The Spanish experience in New Mexico was mirrored by other Europeans in other parts of the country. Europeans of status sometimes insisted on wearing their European clothing, however impractical, as a mark of their "civilization" in a land of "savagery" and "wilderness." In Europe, clothes symbolized one's position in society. In Indian country, however, practicality usually outweighed social status, and most colonists who ventured there found it made sense to wear Indian clothing or a version thereof. High-ranking Spaniards might try to preserve a style of dress appropriate to their status, but common Hispanics replaced worn-out shoes and boots with Indian moccasins or moccasinlike shoes. Peter Kalm said that French colonists who traveled in Canada "generally dressed like the natives." Backcountry settlers in eighteenth-century America wore moccasins, leggings, and hunting shirts. Men from the British borderlands were long accustomed to wearing such shirts and leggings, but in America they added moccasins and breechcloths. Young men in backcountry Virginia reportedly were proud of their "Indian-like dress" and wore it to church, where the sight of leggings, breechcloths, and bare thighs caused quite a stir among young women in the congregation. During the Cherokee War (1759-61), young Carolina men borrowed from the clothing styles of British soldiers and Cherokee warriors. Colonial militia serving alongside British regulars during the French and Indian wars often wore hunting shirts as a mark of identity, to distinguish them from the redcoats. When George Rogers Clark and his Virginians arrived at Kaskaskia during their invasion of the Illinois country in the Revolution, they were dressed Indian style, "in hunting shirts and breech cloth." Members of the British Indian department often wore a mixture of Indian and European clothing, and it was not uncommon for British and Frenchmen to dress completely in Indian attire when on campaign with Indian allies.

Wearing Indian clothing was more than a matter of comfort and practicality for Europeans in Indian country: dressing in "the Indian fashion" made a statement and increased their cultural mobility. In the same way, Indians who donned ruffled shirts and three-cornered hats often were announcing their role as cultural mediators and their ability to deal with Euro-

The Mohawk sachem Hendrick, or Theyanoguin, was a member of the Wolf clan and a convert to Christianity. He visited London in 1710 and 1740, and he died fighting alongside the British at the battle of Lake George (1755). In this etching, he wears an English hat, coat, waistcoat, and shirt given to him by George II. He also holds a wampum string and bears facial tattoos. (Collection of the New-York Historical Society)

Sir John Caldwell, a lieutenant colonel in the Eighth Regiment of Foot, served at Detroit during the Revolution and returned to England with a collection of Indian artifacts. In this portrait by an unknown artist, he wears an Indian headdress, breechcloth, leggings, and moccasins, and Indian jewelry in his ears and nose. (King's Regiment Collection. Courtesy The Board of Trustees of the National Museums & Galleries on Merseyside)

peans. As European colonists living in or near Indian country pulled on Indian moccasins, leggings, and hunting shirts, Indian people living near colonial settlements acquired shirts and jackets, trousers and shoes. Cloth shirts and pants were more comfortable than garments fashioned from hide. Indians attributed their own meanings and values to the articles of clothing they adopted, and they sometimes wore European clothes in very non-European ways—shirts hanging loose, hats on backwards or sideways, jackets unbuttoned, trousers cut off at the thighs and worn as leggings—attracting the ridicule of European visitors. Like Europeans in Indian country, Indians who had contact with Europeans often mingled European and Indian clothing. In 1602, Captain Bartholomew Gosnold met six Micmac Indians in "a Basque shallop with mast and sail" off the coast of Maine. One Indian wore "a waistcoat and breeches of black serge, made after our sea fashion, hose, and shoes on his feet." An early French observer noted how Indians in that region readily utilized European clothing: "In Summer, they often wear our capes, and in Winter our bed-blankets, which they improve with trimming and wear double. They are also quite willing to make use of our hats, shoes, caps, woolens and shirts, and of our linen to clean their infants, for we trade them all these commodities for their furs."

Alexander Hamilton, a Scottish physician traveling in New England in the 1740s, met two "French Mohawks," presumably from Caughnawaga, on the road outside Boston. The Indians were on horseback, "dressed *à la mode Français* with laced hats, full trimmed coats, and ruffled shirts," but behind one of them sat "a pritty woman all bedaubed with wampum." At Lake Champlain, Peter Kalm met Abenaki women who were wearing Frenchwomen's waists and jackets; their funnel-shaped caps trimmed with white beads may also have derived from styles worn by early European sailors. Kalm noted that Indian men in Canada wore French jackets and shirts but preferred leggings to trousers. "Even those who are Christians have always refused to wear breeches, despite the most earnest entreaties of the missionaries," Pierre Pouchot, a French officer in the Seven Years' War, said of his Indian allies.

In other times and places, Indian people adopted European clothing almost completely. An observer said that the members of one of John Eliot's Indian congregations wore English clothing—"You should scarce know them from English people." Other Indians in Massachusetts dressed so like their neighbors that they were "very often mistaken for English." By the first decade of the eighteenth century, Indians on Martha's Vineyard were "generally clothed as the English are." In Rhode Island, Alexander Hamilton visited the Niantic leader Ninigret or "King George," who had built himself a huge mansion and whose wife "dressed like an English woman" in silks, hoops, and stays. In 1759, traveler Andrew Burnaby said Indians in Virginia "commonly dress like the Virginians" and were sometimes mistaken for lower-class whites. When Italian traveler and botanist Luigi Castiglioni visited the Penobscots on Indian Island in Maine in 1785, he noted, "Their attire is no longer the ancient one, made of skins, but European dresses and shirts, and uniforms of French and English soldiers."

Europeans, and later white Americans, often assumed that if Indian people adopted the outward trappings of "civilization" they would become like white people; wearing European-style clothing and using manufactured goods would ease their spiritual transformation into Christians. However, Indians, like Europeans, took what they wanted from their new neighbors to make their lives easier, more comfortable, more productive. European clothes and metal goods did not transform Indians into Europeans any more than Indian leggings and moccasins made colonists into Indians. The battle for spirits and souls went deeper than such surface adjustments.

Four

✦

A World of Dreams and Bibles

WHEN EUROPEANS FIRST encountered Indian peoples, they saw no churches and little they recognized as organized worship. They met shamans and witnessed dances but dismissed Native American belief systems as primitive superstition or devil worship; Indian ceremonies struck them as heathen rituals. In the eyes of the Christian invaders, Indians had no real religion; converting them to Christianity would be a simple matter of filling a dark void with the light of the Gospel. Indian people, for their part, must have been mystified by the odd behavior of European "holy men," who came into their villages carrying Bibles and preaching about sin and damnation but who surely committed daily acts of sacrilege by failing to observe the rituals and proper behavior that maintained relationships between humans and spirits in the Indian world. Indian peoples responded to spirits and believed in the power of dreams to foretell the future and guide their lives. Father Jacques Frémin said the Senecas had "only one single divinity . . . the dream"; Jean de Brébeuf said dreams were "the principal God of the Hurons." Christians, too, believed in visions, but missionaries insisted that Indian people follow the injunctions of the Bible, not the messages in their dreams. In the new religious climate created by European invasion, many Indian people read the Bible and attended church services, but many continued to dream as well.

The soldiers of Christ were entering a world of deeply held religious beliefs every bit as complex and sophisticated as their own, but one they would rarely fathom or even try to understand. Native religions did not possess a specific theology; nor did they require that "believers" give verbal confessions of faith and live in obedience to a set of religious tenets stipulated by the church. Nevertheless, religion and ritual permeated the everyday lives of Indian peoples. European missionaries, convinced that there was only one true religion and it was theirs, tended to see things as black or white, good or evil. Indians who converted to Christianity must demonstrate unquestioning faith; Indians who resisted were clinging to heathen ways. For Christian missionaries, conversion was a simple matter: Indian people who had been living in darkness and sin would receive the light and accept salvation. It proved to be not that simple.

The introduction of Christianity into Indian America brought thousands of Indian people into a new religious world, which included priests and ministers, churches and missions, bells and Bibles, candles and crucifixes, hymns and sacraments, new codes of conduct, new concepts of heaven and hell. Such strange new words and rituals, and the zeal of the missionaries who introduced them, generated a variety of interactions and responses, which created significant religious change and inspired some new religious movements. Indian religions tended to be much less exclusive and intolerant than Christianity, and Indian people often explored, considered, and incorporated elements of its teaching. Sometimes, Indians converted to Christianity and abandoned old beliefs. Often, old and new beliefs continued to exist side by side. Sometimes, Christianity itself changed as Indian people adopted it. They reshaped it to fit their notions of the world, eventually making it into an Indian as well as a European religion. Some Indians even used Christianity, and the missionaries who taught it to them, as a way of resisting white culture, of remaining Indian.

The Great Seal of Massachusetts Bay Colony bore the figure of an Indian saying, "Come over and help us," a heathen plea for the blessings of Christianity. Real Indians were usually much less eager to have Christians come to their country and "save" them. For many Indian people, Christians did not dispel darkness; they created it. The newcomers infected their bodies, stole their land, killed their game, and threatened to sever sacred relationships that had kept the world in balance for thousands of years. European invaders not only changed the world Indian people inhabited, they also demanded that Indian people see it in very different terms and cast aside spiritual certainties that had sustained them from time immemorial.

The historical reputation of Christian missionaries has declined considerably in recent years. There was a time when, relying primarily on records written by missionaries and sharing their assumption that Christianity was synonymous with civilization, historians portrayed them as many missionaries thought of themselves. Courageous and selfless servants of Christ dedicated their lives to doing God's work and saving heathen souls. Indians gave up pagan ways, found contentment in their new lives, and experienced the joy that comes with the promise of everlasting life. Indian converts lived in peace and harmony with their priest or padre in idyllic mission communities within the sound of church bells.

Today, we are more inclined to question the missionaries' assumptions, finding their arrogance repellent and despising them as agents of cultural genocide. Indian people were wrenched from their homes and concentrated into mission villages, where they died of new diseases or had their traditional beliefs beaten out of them. Missionaries exploited their labor, stole their lands, and subjected them to sexual abuse. Oppression and chaos, not peace and harmony, characterized life in the missions. Christianity was a weapon of conquest, not a path to salvation.

Depending on time and place, circumstance and individual experience, one could provide examples to support any or all views of missionaries and their work. Indians were deeply spiritual people, but Europeans in those times, whatever we think of their assumptions and actions, were also spiritual, the products of powerful religious movements that enjoined them to go out and convert others.

For some Indian people, the missionaries brought them a new religion that changed their lives on earth and gave them reason to believe in eternal life in the hereafter. These individuals renounced their old ways and embraced the new, worked hard to make their mission villages into model Christian communities, and found meaning and hope in the church. Kateri Tekakwitha, a Mohawk girl (her father was a Mohawk; her mother, an adopted Algonkin), lost her immediate family in a smallpox epidemic when she was four years old. She herself survived the disease, but it disfigured her face and weakened her eyes. As she grew up she converted to Christianity. Fleeing to the Jesuit mission at Caughnawaga (or Kahnawake), she devoted herself to a life of chastity, prayer, and penitence. After she died at twenty-four in 1680, pilgrims began to visit her shrine. The Catholic Church declared her venerable in 1943, beatified her in 1980, and considered recognizing her as a saint. The Pennacook chief Wanalancet resisted Puritan missionary John Eliot for four years, but in 1674, when he was in his fifties or sixties, he was won over. "I have, all my days, used to pass in an old canoe," he explained, "and now you exhort me to change and leave my old canoe, and embark in a new canoe, to which I have hitherto been unwilling; but now I yield myself up to your advice, and enter into a new canoe, and do engage to pray to God hereafter." Some of Wanalancet's people deserted him; others preferred to listen to French Jesuit missionaries. Like the Mahican and Housatonic Indians who decided to move to the new mission town at Stock-bridge, Massachusetts, in the 1730s, Wanalancet recognized that conversion to Christianity meant radical changes and carried weighty consequences.

Many more Indians kept the missionaries at arm's length, weighing their words but evading their evangelism by various strategies of passive resistance. "However much they are preached at," wrote a French officer in the Seven Years' War, "they listen very calmly & without ill-will, but they always return to their usual refrain, that they are not sufficiently intelligent to believe and follow what they are told, that their forefathers lived like them & that they adopt their way of life." The Indian custom of listening politely while missionaries regaled them with the word of God led many priests to misinterpret silence as tacit agreement and to see conversions where none occurred.

Other people did not listen quietly. They fought tooth and nail against the alien religion that threatened their world, resisting every effort to separate them from their cultural and spiritual roots, and saw missionaries as malevolent forces. The Reverend Samuel Kirkland encountered one Seneca in the 1760s who was of the "fixed opinion that my continuance there would be distructive to the nation, & finally over throw all the traditions & usages of their Forefathers & that there would not be a warrior remaining in their nation in the course of a few years." Another Seneca took a shot at the persistent missionary. Shamans tended to denounce missionaries and their words, but often in a losing battle. Missionaries trying to discredit the traditional spiritual leaders in an Indian community could point with effect to the shamans' failure to predict the arrival of new diseases, to cure the sick, or to give meaning to the chaos.

Thousands of Indian people, however, selected a middle path of their own making. They heard the missionaries' message, asked questions, and found areas of common ground between old and new beliefs. According to David Weber, many of the Indians whom Spain claimed as converts "simply added Jesus, Mary, and Christian saints to their rich pantheons and welcomed the Franciscans into their communities as additional shamans." In a new world of suffering and uncertainty, people listened to preachers who assured them that terrestrial pain was temporary, life in paradise an eternity. Why not pray to the Christians' God? They had nothing to lose, so long as they did not abandon their own prayers, rituals, and beliefs. A crucifix added to a medicine bundle would surely enhance the power of a traditional spiritual artifact. Missionaries were rarely able to eradicate Indian religious beliefs, which they never really understood. Nor did they appreciate the depth of Indian spirituality.

The collision and confluence of religious beliefs in North America did not occur in a vacuum. Indian people were dying of new diseases, succumbing to the inroads of alcohol, losing their economic independence, fighting new wars with deadly new weapons, struggling to hold on to their lands, and watching the physical world change around them. Converts most commonly came from communities that were falling apart. Christianity promised relief from the pain and suffering, but religious change also added to the turmoil.

Indian people and Christian missionaries shared areas of understanding. Both, for instance, attributed "natural" events to "supernatural" phenomena, although most Indian peoples saw no such arbitrary distinction between the two. At the same time, however, they saw their place in the world in radically different ways. For Christians, man was at the top of the hierarchy of creation and Europe at the pinnacle of civilization. Indian people shared their world with animals, plants, and their spirits. Where Europeans saw a religious void, Indian people had daily rituals and cycles of ceremonies that sustained life, propitiated spirits, and offered thanks, which helped maintain balance and order in the universe and gave meaning to the world. Missionaries who insisted that Indian people stop practicing such ceremonies were asking them to invite disaster.

Indian hunters often relied on the power of their dreams to help them locate their prey and foretell the kill. Hunting was a ceremonial activity as much as an economic necessity, since only if the proper rituals were observed would the animals consent to let themselves be taken, or agree to return. Traveling in the Carolina backcountry in 1701, John Lawson reported how the Indians he met carefully preserved and then burned the bones of the animals they killed, believing "that if they omitted that Custom, the Game would leave their Country, and they should not be able to maintain themselves by their Hunting." At a time when Indian people were becoming increasingly dependent on European trade goods, and commercial hunting to satisfy the demands of the European fur and deerskin trades threatened to undermine such ritual observances, European missionaries tried to sever Indians' ties to the animal world and to separate them from the world of dreams. For northern hunting peoples such as the Montagnais and Algonkins in eastern Canada, whose lives depended on maintaining good relations with the other-than-human persons in their world, following Christian teachings was tempting disaster. An Algonkin Indian told Jesuit missionary Paul Le Jeune in the 1630s that there was a time when "my dreams were true; when I had seen Moose or Beavers in sleep, I would take some." But then missionaries came and demanded they pray instead. "Now, our dreams and our prophecies are no longer true,—prayer has spoiled everything for us." Prayer had replaced many of the Algonkins' customs, said the Indian, and "we shall all die because we give them up."

But they did not all die. Even as their hunting economy began to collapse, Montagnais and Algonkin people found they could use prayer in traditional ways: they prayed to Jesus for assistance in hunting animals. Nevertheless, as Carolyn Merchant points out, Christianity was altering the symbolic superstructure of the Indians' economy: "An ethic of moral obligation between human and God replaced the ethic of reciprocity between human and animal." God was above nature; the new religious teachings required no respect for animals and the natural world. Old hunting rituals continued, "but they ceased to function as a restraining environmental ethic." The way was open for Indian peoples to become commercial hunters, responding to the lure of the marketplace rather than listening to the spirits of the animals.

Farther west, on the northern shores of the Great Lakes in Ontario, Huron people also found ways to accommodate Christianity. The Hurons were trading partners of the French, and Jesuit priests were eager to carry the word of God to the Huron villages and establish a base for future missions. The Hurons were a people in crisis in the 1630s. Recurrent epidemics of disease cut Huron population in half between 1634 and 1640, but the mortality rate among children was much higher. Many Hurons blamed the Jesuits for the disaster: "With the Faith, the scourge of God came into the country," wrote Jesuit Father François Joseph Bressani, "and, in proportion as the one increased, the other smote them more severely." The Hurons believed that the Jesuits were sorcerers who, like shamans, could use their power for good or evil. But the need to maintain trading alliances with the

French prevented them from exacting vengeance on the missionaries; indeed, the French would not sell guns to non-Christians in the first half of the seventeenth century, and many Hurons accepted baptism to secure firearms. Meanwhile, as traditional curing practices and ceremonies proved ineffective against the new killer diseases, Huron villages filled with the sick and dying. People looked in desperation for new answers or at least for some source of hope, and parents brought their children to the Jesuit fathers for baptism. The Jesuits recorded only twenty-two Huron baptisms in 1635, but baptisms increased dramatically as the Huron population plummeted. By 1646 there were more than five hundred; by 1648 about twenty-seven hundred Hurons, one fifth of the population, had been baptized. Between 1632 and 1672, the Jesuits claimed to have baptized more than sixteen thousand Indians, some twelve thousand in Huronia alone. Many of these "converts" saw baptism as a ritual that might cure or protect their infants in this world, not as a full-fledged acceptance of Christianity that would save their souls in the next.

However, there was little protection for Hurons in this dangerous new world. Weakened by disease and famine, and possibly in their own eyes by a religion that undermined the male's role as warrior and hunter, the Hurons succumbed to massive attacks by the Iroquois in 1649. Only the Tahontaenrat Hurons survived as a group; the rest of the people scattered throughout the Great Lakes region. Many of them became incorporated into the villages of their Iroquois enemies; some survived at the mission town of Lorette on the St. Lawrence.

In New England, meanwhile, Indian peoples encountered a different brand of Christianity as English missionaries introduced them to the tenets of Puritanism. Puritan missionaries demanded what amounted to cultural suicide from their Indian converts, insisting that they live like their English neighbors if they intended to practice the Christian religion. Nevertheless, many Indian people accepted conversion as they sought spiritual meaning in an increasingly chaotic world. Thomas Mayhew Jr. began preaching to the Wampanoag Indians on Martha's Vineyard in the 1640s but with relatively little success. Then, epidemic diseases swept the island in 1643 and 1645. The shamans, the traditional spiritual leaders and healers, were unable to cure the sick. Scores of Indian people looked to Christianity to provide new explanations, if not new cures, and to fill a void left by the decline of traditional communal rituals. The Indians built their own church community and passed the Gospel from generation to generation.

But the Indian converts on Martha's Vineyard did not become English or cease being Indian. Some Indians who worshiped in Christian churches continued to live in wigwams. They made Christianity an Indian religion. Indian men served as preachers, pastors, and deacons; Indian women found that Christianity honored their traditional roles, offered them the opportunity to learn to read and write, and provided solace and support as their island society threatened to unravel amid alcoholism and violence. Christian Indians took Christian names, but they continued to be called by their Indian ones. A deacon named Paul, for instance, kept his Wampanoag name, Mashquattuhkooit. In time, some Christian Indian families began to use given names and surnames, in the European style. But the surnames were based on traditional names—the descendants of Hiacoomes, the first Indian convert on Martha's Vineyard, became known by the surname Coomes.

As historian James Ronda explains, Indian people on Martha's Vineyard "shaped Christian forms to serve native public and familial needs. The communal functions once undertaken at powwow ceremonies were now carried on in worship services, thanksgiving feasts, and home devotions." Sermons, prayers, and psalms helped fill the spiritual space left by loss of traditional rituals. "Indian Christianity became its own tradition, nourishing the lives of native believers." Bombarded by changes that threatened their very existence, Indians on Martha's Vineyard do not appear to have succumbed to an alien religion. Instead, they used Christianity as a source of strength, blending old and new ways to create a culture that was both Christian and Indian. In this way, Indians often reinterpreted Christian messages and adapted Christian rituals to create Indian Christianity or Christianized versions of their traditional religions.

On the mainland, John Eliot hoped to prevent any such "compromises." Eliot came to America in 1631, began to learn the Massachusett Indian language in 1643, and started preaching three years later. He compiled a dictionary and grammar of Massachusett and by 1663, with the assistance of Indian translators, had translated the entire Bible into Massachusett. For Eliot, enabling Indians to read the Bible was a vital first step on the road to "civilization." Eliot also established a total of fourteen "praying towns," model Christian communities where Indian converts lived quarantined from the negative influences of unconverted relatives or unsavory English characters. He laid down harsh penalties for Indians who disobeyed his rules. Men must work hard; women must learn to spin and weave. They must wear their hair English-style, stop using bear's grease as protection against mosquitoes, and give up plural wives. Discarded wives and children presumably suffered misery and poverty so that their now-monogamous ex-husbands and fathers could live Christian lives. Eliot's program promoted social revolution and cultural disintegration.

Not surprisingly, many Indian people refused to accept such an assault on their way of life. Indian communities that had not yet experienced devastation proved more resistant to Puritan teachings. At their height, Eliot's praying towns held only about eleven hundred people, and the extent of individual conversions among these people, and how many accepted Eliot's complete program of social change, remains uncertain. At Natick, Eliot's showpiece praying-town, some Indian converts were given a Christian funeral service, but were interred in traditional fashion with wampum, beads, and other earthly items. As Daniel Mandell notes, "The desire to maintain an Indian community in an English/Christian world extended even to the grave."

John Eliot recorded the kinds of questions Indian people asked, as a way of preparing Indian missionaries for the challenges they would meet among their own people: "Can a good man sin sometimes?" "If a man commits a sin without knowing it's a sin, what will God say?" "God made hell in one of the six days. Why did God make hell before Adam sinned?" Most Indians refused to defer to the Bible as a guide for life, and they found ideas of sin and guilt, heaven and hell to be alien and even repugnant. An Indian convert from Natick who returned to his relatives with the word of God met a polite but firm rebuff: "Our forefathers . . . taught us nothing about our Soul, and God, and Heaven, and Hell, and Joy, and Torment in the Life to come. . . . We are well as we are, and desire not to be troubled by these wise new sayings."

For those who did accept Christianity, conversion may have meant something different from what it meant to Eliot. Massachusett Indians believed in a creator, but their world was inhabited by countless *manitowuk*, spirits who directed the course of their daily lives. Adding God or Christ did not necessarily disrupt their worldview. Puritans thought in dualistic terms of a power struggle between God and Evil, God and the Devil; but New England Algonkian peoples believed that anything of great power was manitou; spirits possessed (and were) manitou; so might humans, animals, trees, and even some inanimate objects. Christ could be manitou, and missionaries, like shamans, might possess manitou.

Some people may have embraced Christianity as a way of fending off annihilation as the world crumbled about them. Missions offered Indian people a haven from some of the turmoil and provided them knowledge and skills to deal with the strange new world that was being created. Learning to read was a way of acquiring knowledge about the English as well as about God; it could be used to understand treaties, laws, and deeds in addition to the Bible. It may also have carried status and involved ritual and spiritual qualities of which Eliot would not have been aware. Some women may have been attracted to Christianity because it redefined gender roles or simply because they wanted to learn to spin. For all these people, conversion to Christianity had meaning; but that was not necessarily the same meaning that it had for Eliot.

However complete their conversion, the inhabitants of the praying towns could not find shelter from the storms around them. During King Philip's War (1675–76), Indians from Natick supported the English, but the colonists viewed all Indians with fear and suspicion. Praying-town residents were rounded up and incarcerated on Deer Island in Boston Harbor. Eliot's mission program fell to pieces. Only four praying towns were rebuilt after the war. Reservations were to be the new homes for New England's defeated Indian people. Natick, once the "flagship" of Eliot's program, declined to 166 inhabitants by 1750, and to 22 by the 1790s. Many Indian people had converted to Christianity, perhaps as a strategy of survival, perhaps as a way of revitalizing their societies and giving new meaning to their lives in a time of crisis. Many more kept intact the core of traditional beliefs, and it was a good thing they had.

Like Eliot in New England, Spanish missionaries in the South labored to save Indian souls with an assault on Indian culture that severed kinship relations, restricted sexual practices, altered settlement patterns, and promoted new divisions of labor. Jesuit Father Juan Rogel declared in 1570: "If we are to gather fruit, the Indians must join in and live in settlements and cultivate the soil." Spanish missionaries regarded resettling Indian people as peasants living in sedentary communities as a prerequisite to Christianity. Under the Spanish mission system, Indian people built the missions, raised and tended the crops and stock that fed the mission community, and performed the routine services that sustained the mission. But the reality the missions achieved rarely matched the goal they pursued. The Spanish missions also produced massive population decline, food shortages, increased demands for labor, and violence.

At its height in the mid-seventeenth century, the Spanish mission system in the colony of La Florida included seventy friars in forty missions stretching from St. Augustine to the coast of South Carolina in the north and the Apalachicola River near present-day Tallahassee in the west. The Franciscans boasted that more than twenty-five thousand Christianized Indians lived in La Florida. The mission system aimed to convert Indian people into a Catholic labor force that would support the colony. Friars burned "idols," attempted to stamp out traditional ball games and other "un-Christian" practices, and tried to regulate the daily lives of mission Indians. Mission Indians were baptized, married, and buried according to Catholic rites. But Indians resented and resisted Franciscan efforts. Guale Indians rebelled against their missionaries in 1597; Christian Apalachees revolted in 1638 and 1647; Timucuans, in 1656. British and Indian raids from the north at the beginning of the eighteenth century effectively brought the mission system to an end. The net result of Spanish missionary efforts in the area was abandoned missions, fragmented communities, and refugee converts huddled around St. Augustine.

Following Juan de Oñate's colonizing expedition into New Mexico in 1598, Spanish Franciscan missionaries established themselves in almost every pueblo along the Rio Grande. The Spanish Crown saw missions as a line of defense, protecting the colony from Indian enemies and European rivals. The Pueblos may have seen them in somewhat similar terms: the missions could stand against Apache enemies and against potentially aggressive Spanish soldiers and colonists. But Spanish priests not only invaded kivas (underground ceremonial chambers), they desecrated kachina masks and tried to suppress Native rituals and sexual practices. Many Pueblos refused to accept a new faith that threatened their social and spiritual order; others continued to practice their ancestral ways behind closed doors or, more accurately, in underground kivas. Some fled west to the Hopis and other more distant Pueblos; others retaliated in periodic outbreaks of violence. Drought, falling populations, and increasing Navajo and Apache raids indicated that the new religion was not a source of powerful spiritual protection, and that people should return to their ancient ways, if they ever had left them. In 1680, Popé, a Tewa medicine man from San Juan, synchronized an uprising of the different Pueblos that drove out the Spaniards for a dozen years. The Indians killed and mutilated many of the friars who had been trying to stamp out their religion and desecrated the alien paraphernalia of Catholicism.

The Spaniards returned, but they had learned from the experience. Where their predecessors had tried to eradicate all Native rituals, friars now more often turned a blind eye to such practices—a shift, as historian John Kessel describes it, "from crusading intolerance to pragmatic accommodation." Indian people meanwhile became resigned to the Spaniards and adopted more subtle tactics of resistance. When Diego de Vargas returned on his campaign of reconquest in 1692, Luis, a Picuri Pueblo leader, appeared before him dressed in animal skins and wearing a band of palm shell around his head; but he also wore a rosary round his neck and carried a silver cross, an Agnus Dei, and a cloth printed with the image of Our Lady of Guadeloupe. A century of contact with Spanish missionaries had left its imprint. Many Pueblos accepted the outward forms of Hispanic Christianity while keeping the friars away from clan, kiva, and kachina, the things that constituted the core of their religion and their Pueblo identity. Many Pueblos became nominally Catholic, attending mass and observing Christian holidays, but they continued to practice traditional rituals and kept their worldview intact. What Henry Bowden describes as a "double standard of external acquiescence and internal resistance" assured Christianity a peripheral status in Pueblo society. Spaniards often built churches on top of sites that Indian people regarded as sacred, in a deliberate attempt to desecrate Native religious spaces and replace Native belief with Christian worship. But such policies were probably not effective, since Native prayers and beliefs centered on sacredness of place rather than of building.

The Hopis were more insulated than other Pueblos from Spanish crusading. Their villages sat atop isolated mesas in northern Arizona, and they were better able to keep Spanish priests at arm's length. Hopi religious leaders not only resisted those Spanish missionaries who made the trek to their villages, they even on occasion debated and denounced the padres in public confrontations. A visiting Franciscan lamented that the Hopi religion in 1775 was "the same as before they heard about the Gospel." When Franciscan fathers Francisco Atanasio Domínguez and Silvestre Vélez de Escalante visited the Hopi villages on Second Mesa in November 1776, they communicated with the councilmen "partly by signs and partly in Navajo." The friars began to preach, and the Hopis at first maintained they could not understand. When the fathers pressed them, the Hopis made it clear "that they wanted to be our friends but not Christians." The frustrated Franciscans held out threats of eternal damnation and assurances "that if they submitted they would enjoy continual and sure recourse to Spanish arms against all infidels who should war against them, as did the rest of the Christian pueblos of New Mexico," but the Hopis adamantly refused to give up the ways of their ancestors. The Franciscans withdrew "quite crestfallen" at such "obstinacy." Five years later, General Teodoro de Croix reported that Hopi priests were "inexorable in their purpose of remaining heathen, preserving these customs, and remaining in their desolated pueblos." Because Spaniards traveling the long distances to the Hopis had to pass through Zuni villages, the Hopis usually received advance warning of their coming, and Hopi leaders presented a united front. Sometimes they gave the appearance of acquiescence: they told the Spaniards what they wanted to hear, waited for them to leave, then went about their lives as before. The Hopis decided which, if any, parts of Spanish culture they would accept.

The Franciscan friar Junípero Serra brought Catholicism to the Indians of California in 1769. Traveling north to the San Francisco Bay area, his expedition established the first Catholic mission at San Diego. Other missions followed until a chain of twenty-one missions stretched more than 650 miles. By 1800, Indian neophytes—as the converts were called—numbered some twenty thousand, testimony to the disintegration of Native societies under the hammerblows of new diseases as much as to the power of Christianity. But the fact that Indian neophytes adopted Christian symbols and stories did not necessarily mean they accepted conversion on Spanish terms. They may have seen in the pageantry and paraphernalia of Catholic services new sources of spiritual power which they could acquire without jeopardizing their old beliefs. Spanish missionaries congregated Indian peoples into new communities and used Indian labor to support the mission system while they themselves labored to save Indian souls. The friars segregated unmarried men and women into separate dormitories at night to enforce Catholic moral codes, imposed strict labor regimens, and resorted to whipping, branding, and solitary confinement to keep the Indians on the path to "civilization and salvation." Jean François de La Pérouse, a French sea captain and scientist who visited the mission at Monterey in 1786 during a voyage around the world noted: "Sins which are left in Europe to Divine justice, are here punished by irons and stocks," and he compared the mission to a slave plantation. Felipe de Nove, governor of California, said in 1780 that the Indians were "worse than slaves" under the Franciscans. Indian populations plummeted. Many Indians ran away from the missions; others turned to violence: several hundred Indians launched an unsuccessful attack on the San Diego mission in 1775.

Missionary efforts elsewhere met with limited success, although not always for the same reasons. Moravian missionaries won many converts among the Delaware Indians in Pennsylvania and Ohio in the eighteenth century, and some Delawares clearly embraced the Christian way of life that missionaries such as John Heckewelder and David Zeisberger brought them. But the Moravians and their converts were building peaceful mission havens in what was fast becoming a war zone. The colonial and revolutionary wars that raged in the Ohio Valley in the second half of the century disrupted the missionaries' work, dislocating their communities, and brought disaster to the converts. In 1782, American militiamen butchered ninety-six pacifist and unarmed Moravian Indians in their village at Gnadenhütten. The Moravians and their converts migrated to Canada in the years after the American Revolution.

Missionaries left their imprint everywhere they went. Indian people knelt in chapels, reciting liturgies in Latin, praying and singing hymns in English, French, Spanish, Iroquoian, Algonkian, and Uto-Aztecan. However selective they might be in what they accepted from Christian teachings, Indian people found that Christianity brought far-reaching changes in their world, if not necessarily in their worldviews. Powhatan Indians in Virginia came to believe that when they died, instead of going to a single afterlife for all as their ancestors had, those who had led wicked lives went to a place of endless torment and flames. Eighteenth-century travelers observed Indians attending Christian services and commented that Indian people appeared to be living model Christian lives. Alexander Hamilton sat next to Indians in a Boston church listening to an Irish preacher. Traveling west of Albany, he came to a Mohawk town where Dutch-style wooden and brick houses and traditional longhouses clustered around a church, where the preacher spoke to the Indians in their own language, "for the bulk of the Mohocks up this way are Christians." Richard Smith, visiting the Iroquois town of Oquaga on the upper Susquehanna River in 1769, saw one hundred Indians, men, women,

Mohawk Indians in church. Frontispiece from the Mohawk *Book of Common Prayer*, 1787. (Dartmouth College Library)

and children, called to Sunday morning service by a horn blown three times. The Indians sang psalms and read from the Scriptures; the service "was conducted with regularity and solemnity." An Indian priest officiated and an Indian clerk, the Oneida chief Good Peter, translated the psalms into Oneida. Englishman Nicholas Cresswell visited the Delaware Moravian mission town at Schönbrunn in Ohio on the eve of the American Revolution. The Indians held service in a meetinghouse, which had a bell and glass windows, listened to their parson's words through an interpreter, and sang hymns in Delaware. The service was conducted with "the greatest regularity, order, and decorum, I ever saw in any place of Worship in my life," wrote Cresswell in his journal.

Missionaries intended that Indian converts should play their part in spreading the new religion—indeed, they had little choice. The missionaries, in James Axtell's words, "were on their own, forced to rely on their wits, tongues and personal charisma to earn the Indians' respect and to purvey their alien brand of spirituality." Sixteen friars spearheaded the Franciscan effort to spread the Gospel to the Pueblos in 1616. There were never more than half a dozen Jesuit missionaries working among the thirty thousand Yaquis in Sonora throughout the seventeenth century. The priests relied on Yaqui converts to spread the Gospel, accepting that those Yaquis would attach their own meanings to Christian concepts and put their own interpretations on the missionaries' teachings. The missionaries had "to use persuasion and then let the persuaded Yaquis take it from there." The result was thousands of Yaqui baptisms and a new kind of Christianity that was distinctly Yaqui in many ways. Recollect and Jesuit missionaries in seventeenth-century New France followed the example of Capuchin missionaries in South America and sent some Indian boys to France, where they were educated to serve as missionaries on their return to Indian country, but the program had little success.

John Eliot founded an Indian college at Harvard in 1654 to house Indian students who would train as ministers. Only six students attended and only one graduated; he died of tuberculosis the following year. Harvard's Indian college closed its doors in 1692 and was pulled down six years later. However, some Indians did become ministers—there were 133 Native preachers in New England before the Revolution. Eliot trained and ordained Daniel Tokkohwomput as his successor. Several graduates from Eleazar Wheelock's Indian school served as missionaries. Samson Occom (1723-92) was a

Mohegan Indian from Connecticut who grew up as his people's way of life fell apart. Like many other Indian people in southern New England, he became a Christian during the Great Awakening, the revival of evangelical religion that swept the American colonies in the 1730s and 1740s. A student at Wheelock's Charity School in Lebanon, Connecticut, Occom, despite ill health, pursued the goal of ministering to the spiritual needs of Indian people. He left school in 1747 and received a Presbyterian license to preach, settling at Montauk on Long Island, as minister to the Indian congregation there. He held services three times each Sunday, taught school, performed marriages, and conducted funerals like any white preacher, but he also lived in Indian wigwams and filled some of the sachem's traditional roles, providing leadership and extending hospitality. Given little respect and less pay by New England's missionary authorities, Occom nevertheless stuck to his calling and in the early 1760s made lengthy visits to the Oneidas of New York. In 1766, he traveled to England on a fund-raising tour for Wheelock's Indian school and raised £12,000, an enormous sum of money in those days. In 1769, Wheelock founded Dartmouth College in Hanover, New Hampshire, ostensibly with the intention of educating Indians. But Occom became bitter and disillusioned in later life. Few Indian students attended Dartmouth—Occom said the college resembled Alba Mater (White Mother) rather than Alma Mater—and the funds Occom had raised were diverted to other purposes. Occom returned to Mohegan and lived as an itinerant minister to various Indian groups in southern New England.

Occom wrote hymns that became part of the hymnody of nineteenth-century America. Another of Wheelock's students, the Mohawk Joseph Brant, worked with the Reverend John Stuart, the Anglican missionary at Fort Hunter, to translate the Gospel into Mohawk.

Converted and unconverted Indians alike noted differences between Christianity as preached and as practiced. Indians commonly countered missionary arguments by declaring, "We are better Christians than you." Those, like Occom, who converted during the Great Awakening found fault with the established church. Many Narragansetts converted to Christianity in the 1740s, embracing a religious movement that challenged the intellectual elitism of Puritanism. It more closely resembled their traditional religion, emphasizing visions, the spoken rather than the written word, and religious leadership based on a "calling" rather than on formal education. The Narragansetts built their own church and had Narragansett ministers. Samuel Niles, the first Narragansett minister, said that his people regarded educated ministers as "Thieves, Robbers, Pirates, etc. . . . . They steal the word. God told the Prophets the words they Spoke: and these Ministers Steal that Word." Indians who adhered to traditional beliefs were often equally suspicious of those who presumed to teach them to live like Christians. "Learn yourself to understand the word of God, before you undertake to teach and govern others," Iroquois leaders told Wheelock in 1772.

Indians spread Christianity in less direct ways than operating as missionaries. Iroquois Indians who converted to Catholicism in the seventeenth century formed new mission communities at places like Caughnawaga near Montreal. In the early years of the nineteenth century, Iroquois from Caughnawaga migrated to the Rocky Mountain region to work in the fur trade as trappers and guides. Some of them intermarried with local Indian women and brought their Indian Catholicism to the tribes there.

Though many Indian people looked to Christianity for help in times of crisis, Christianity often generated additional crises and tensions in Indian communities. Rituals such as the Green Corn Ceremony united Indian communities, bringing people together in seasonal ceremonies of prayer, thanksgiving, and world renewal; Christian missionaries prohibited their converts from participating in such "pagan rituals," thereby severing ties of community and identity. Missionaries also attempted to set up new patterns of work and behavior between the sexes. In gender-egalitarian societies like the Hurons and the Montagnais, where women enjoyed an influence unknown in Europe, French missionaries tried to subordinate women, to reorder Indian society along more "civilized" lines.

Some communities split between traditional and Christian factions. The Hurons were bitterly factionalized by the time the Iroquois attacked them in 1648–49. Delawares who converted to the Moravian faith lived in separate villages from their unconverted relatives and sometimes experienced ridicule and resentment from them. Formerly viewed with respect by other Iroquois, Oneida headmen by 1772 felt "despised by our brethren, on account of our christian profession." Some opportunistic Indian leaders embraced Christianity to add spiritual sanction in their political challenge to established leaders. At Natick in the seventeenth century, Waban used Christianity as a core around which to organize a faction challenging the leadership of Cushamekin, which rested on more traditional spiritual foundations. Men like Waban employed the missionaries as allies to serve their own political interests.

Some communities split even further as factions formed around different

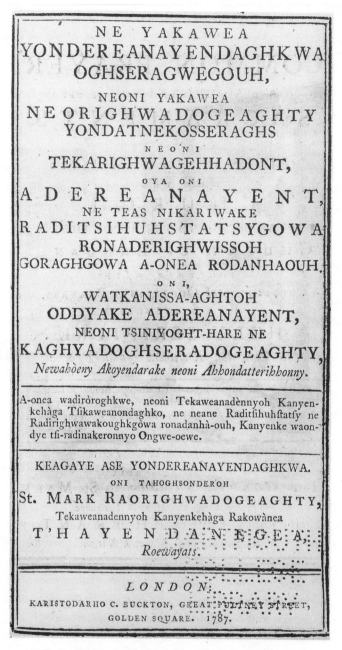

NE YAKAWEA
YONDEREANAYENDAGHKWA
OGHSERAGWEGOUH,

NEONI YAKAWEA
NE ORIGHWADOGEAGHTY
YONDATNEKOSSERAGHS

NEONI
TEKARIGHWAGEHHADONT,

OYA ONI
ADEREANAYENT,

NE TEAS NIKARIWAKE
RADITSIHUHSTATSYGOWA
RONADERIGHWISSOH
GORAGHGOWA A-ONEA RODANHAOUH,

ONI,
WATKANISSA-AGHTOH
ODDYAKE ADEREANAYENT,

NEONI TSINIYOGHT-HARE NE
KAGHYADOGHSERADOGEAGHTY,
Newahòeny Akoyendarake neoni Ahhondatterihhonny.

A-onea wadiròroghkwe, neoni Tekaweanadènnyoh Kanyenkehàga Tſikaweanondaghko, ne neane Raditſihuhſtatſy ne
Radirighwawakoughkgòwa ronadanhà-ouh, Kanyenke waon-
dye tſi-radinakeronnyo Ongwe-oewe.

KEAGAYE ASE YONDEREANAYENDAGHKWA.
ONI TAHOGHSONDEROH
St. MARK RAORIGHWADOGEAGHTY,
Tekaweanadennyoh Kanyenkehàga Rakowànea
T'HAYENDANEGEA,
Roewàyats.

LONDON:
KARISTODARHO C. BUCKTON, GREAT PULTNEY STREET,
GOLDEN SQUARE. 1787.

Title pages of *The Book of Common Prayer . . . to which is added The Gospel according to St. Mark, Translated into the Mohawk Language, by Capt*[n]. *Joseph Brant* (London, 1787). Other editions of *The Book of Common Prayer* were printed in Mohawk only; this one has English on the opposite pages so that "hereby the

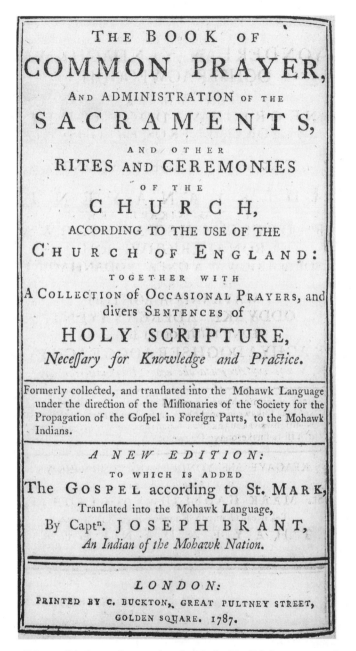

THE BOOK OF
COMMON PRAYER,
AND ADMINISTRATION OF THE
SACRAMENTS,
AND OTHER
RITES AND CEREMONIES
OF THE
CHURCH,
ACCORDING TO THE USE OF THE
CHURCH OF ENGLAND:
TOGETHER WITH
A COLLECTION of OCCASIONAL PRAYERS, and divers SENTENCES of
HOLY SCRIPTURE,
Neceſſary for Knowledge and Practice.

Formerly collected, and tranſlated into the Mohawk Language under the direction of the Miſſionaries of the Society for the Propagation of the Goſpel in Foreign Parts, to the Mohawk Indians.

A NEW EDITION:
TO WHICH IS ADDED
The GOSPEL according to St. MARK,
Tranſlated into the Mohawk Language,
By Captn. JOSEPH BRANT,
An Indian of the Mohawk Nation.

LONDON:
PRINTED BY C. BUCKTON, GREAT PULTNEY STREET,
GOLDEN SQUARE. 1787.

Indians will insensibly be made acquainted with the English language; and such White People in their vicinity as chuse to learn Mohawk, will hence derive much assistance." (Dartmouth College Library) denominations. In about 1700, the Christian Wampanoag community at Gay Head on Martha's Vineyard split into Baptist and Congregational churches. Most Mohawks became nominal Anglicans in the early eighteenth century; their relatives who accepted the Catholic faith moved away to form new communities near the French at St. Regis (present-day Akwesasne) and Caughnawaga. The surface harmony Richard Smith witnessed at Oquaga in 1769 concealed widening divisions between Anglican and Presbyterian factions within the community.

All across America, Christian and Indian peoples and elements mingled. In Quebec and northern New England, Abenaki Indians took French saints' names as surnames, wore crucifixes around their necks, spoke French, prayed to Catholic saints, and even hung wampum belts on Catholic statues. As did Spanish officers in the Southwest, French officers in the Northeast acted as godparents at baptisms of Abenaki children. Sebastian Rasles said the Abenakis' faith was "the bond that unites them to the French," and Abenakis themselves rejected English missionary efforts, asserting their loyalty to the French: "We have promised to be true to God in our Religion, and it is this we profess to stand by." But Abenakis also kept traditional rituals alive. When French priests frowned on dancing to drums, they danced to rattles instead.

The missionary experience also left an imprint on some missionaries, however. Men who went into Indian country to convert the "heathen" sometimes found themselves slowly being converted to an Indian way of life they were dedicated to destroy. Living and working among Indian people for years could produce new levels of tolerance among previously intolerant missionaries; the zeal to convert "savages" and save their souls sometimes became tempered by an appreciation of common humanity and a desire to do some good in this life. French Jesuits who made their homes in Indian villages had to adapt to Indian ways, and some of them became almost totally immersed in Indian culture. They shared Indian lodges with extended families and dogs, ate Indian food, endured hunger and cold when the Indians did, paddled Indian canoes, snowshoed through the forests, learned Indian languages, received Indian names, and in some cases joined the Indians in their struggle against English expansion.

As they did in China and Paraguay, Jesuit missionaries modified their practices to accommodate the culture of the native peoples whom they hoped to make into Catholics. They realized that their best strategy lay in first winning acceptance and support in the communities where they lived and preached, building on common ground and avoiding head-on confrontations with Native practices that did not clash openly with Christian teachings. They adapted their messages to suit Indian styles of oratory, looking for parallels in Indian belief systems and behaving as much as possible according to Native protocol. When Father Nau wanted to establish a mission among the Iroquois in 1735, he recognized that he would need to conform to Iroquois ways: he accepted adoption into the Bear clan, because, he explained, "a missionary would not be an acceptable person in the village were he not a member of the tribe."

Missionaries sought to discredit traditional spiritual leaders, yet took over many of their functions in Indian society—they dispensed advice, spoke in council, shared what they had, and ministered to the sick. Sebastian Rasles lived almost thirty years among the Abenaki Indians at Norridgewock in Maine. He dedicated himself to converting the Indians to Christianity and changing their way of life forever. It was, he wrote, "necessary to conform to their manners and customs, to the end that I might gain their confidence and win them to Jesus Christ." Yet, in a letter to his brother the year before he died, Rasles confided that the conversion process had been mutual: "As for what concerns me personally, I assure you that I see, that I hear, that I speak, only as a savage." The English hated Rasles, feared that he used his influence among the Indians to incite attacks on English settlements, and put a price on his head. In 1724, they raided Norridgewock, burned the village, killed Rasles, and mutilated his body.

David Brainerd, a young Presbyterian minister preaching to Indians along the Susquehanna River in the 1740s, found that their responses prompted him to question and reevaluate his mission. Munsee Indians rejected Christianity as a corrupting influence and told Brainerd they preferred to "live as their fathers lived and go where their fathers were when they died." Delawares in western Pennsylvania seemed equally unreceptive. The blank stares of the Indians whose souls he had set out to save drove Brainerd into a critical period of soul searching, reassessing his goals and even wondering about his God. More receptive Indian audiences brought a renewed commitment before Brainerd's early death from tuberculosis, but the Indians he met clearly molded the young missionary's character and influenced "everything from his evangelistic method to his psychological health." On the other side of the continent, in the 1770s, a Spanish priest named Francisco Garcés traveled far and wide among the Indians of the desert Southwest, visiting Mojaves, Yavapais, Havasupais, and others. He would sit with Indians for hours, shared their food and lifestyle, and, in the opinion of a fellow Franciscan, appeared "to be but an Indian himself." Not all Indians accepted Garcés, however: he was killed by Yumas in 1781.

Indian people who converted to Christianity did not necessarily assimilate European ways of life. For some people, Christianity proved to be a revitalizing force, providing a broader spiritual basis on which to cope with crisis, rebuild fragmented communities, and maintain group identity. Often a disruptive force in Indian communities, Christianity also on occasion linked refugees, converts, and individuals from shattered societies into new communities, offering a common identity as Christian Indians. Membership in Christian communities—even Indian ones—sometimes also offered refuge from surrounding racism and a haven from the alcohol-induced chaos that tore some traditional villages apart. In some communities—the Narragansetts, for instance—the church became a tribal institution and even a symbol of tribal identity. Christianity offered new sources of spiritual strength and community resilience as people struggled to live as Indians in what was rapidly becoming a white man's world. An Indian congregation could still be an Indian community.

As James Axtell explains, the direction of religious change in North America was "decidedly unilinear," largely because Indian religions, unlike Christianity, were tolerant of other faiths. Indian religions were always on the defensive, and any changes that occurred in colonial religion "were minor and self-generated," not in response to Native pressures to convert. Nevertheless, being on the defensive did not totally rob Indians of the initiative. Frequently, they used elements of Christianity for their own purposes: "By accepting the Christian priest as the functional equivalent of a native shaman and by giving traditional meanings to Christian rites, dogmas, and deities," writes Axtell, "the Indians ensured the survival of native culture by taking on the protective coloration of the invaders' culture."

Periodically, new religious movements developed in Indian country, and messiahs preached a return to traditional ways of life. By the second half of the eighteenth century, as Gregory Dowd has argued, Indian peoples in the eastern woodlands who fought to preserve their remaining lands from European and American expansion also struggled to recover their world by restoring and reviving traditional rituals. Some messiahs and prophets preached total rejection of the white man and his ways. Indian people could become whole again only if they denounced alcohol, trade goods, and Christianity. Others offered a more flexible approach. In 1799, a Seneca Indian named Handsome Lake, who had given in to alcoholism and despair as his world crumbled around him, experienced a vision. He renounced alcohol and began to preach a program of social reform and cultural rejuvenation, urging his people to abandon what was evil but take what was best from white culture. He also offered them a religion that blended elements of Christian teaching, possibly picked up from neighboring Quakers, with traditional rituals such as the Green Corn Ceremony and the Midwinter Ceremony. Handsome Lake revived and restructured traditional religion for a new world. The Longhouse religion, as it became known, thrived and spread and continues today.

Time and again in North America, Christian missionaries established a foothold in Indian communities during a crisis, reaped a harvest of converts, and then were pushed back or held at arm's length as Indian people kept or revived ancient beliefs. Indian people learned that the best way to preserve their religious beliefs was to hide them from evangelizing Europeans, a strategy that, ironically, often convinced outsiders that the Indians' religion had died out. The result often lay somewhere between total acceptance and total rejection. In southwestern pueblos, kivas still exist alongside Catholic churches, and Indian people often participate in Christian as well as traditional ceremonies. At Gay Head and Mashpee, in Massachusetts, where Indians became Christians as early as the seventeenth century, Native folk beliefs about ghosts, witches, and spirits survived into the twentieth century. In such instances, Christianity did not eradicate old beliefs; rather, it supplemented and even strengthened them, providing a new, broader spiritual basis. The new world that emerged was one in which Christian and traditional beliefs alike, sometimes separately and sometimes together, guided and gave meaning to people's lives.

Five

.✶.

New World Warfare and a New World of War

WHEN THE FRENCH first penetrated the St. Lawrence Valley in the sixteenth century, they met Indian warriors who went into battle wearing wooden and leather body armor and who fought standing in ranks, from which they hurled projectiles and insults against their enemies. To men accustomed to the bloodbaths of Europe, the Indians' conflicts appeared small-scale, ritualized, and not particularly bloody. In 1609, Algonkin and Montagnais Indians from the St. Lawrence Valley were paddling Samuel de Champlain and his French companions across Lake Champlain when they encountered a large party of some two hundred Iroquois, no doubt Mohawks, from the west side of the lake. The Iroquois beached their canoes and set about building a defensive barricade. They then dispatched emissaries to ask if their enemies wished to fight. "They said that as soon as the sun should rise, they would attack us," said Champlain, "and to this our Indians agreed." The Indians sang and danced all night in ritual preparation for war and, come morning, formed ranks ready to do battle. Three Iroquois chiefs, clearly distinguished by their headdresses, advanced before their warriors. At this point, Champlain and two French companions, concealed in the undergrowth and having primed their guns, took careful aim and shot down the three chiefs. Astonished, the Iroquois fled into the woods with the Algonkins and Montagnais hot on their heels.

This brief battle changed the face of war in northeastern America in a pattern that was repeated across the continent. Guns rendered wooden armor and shields obsolete and made fighting in ranks suicidal. Indian warriors quickly adopted hit-and-run guerrilla tactics, in which mobile war parties, armed with guns, fought from cover. The Iroquois cultivated trade relations with the Dutch and then the English on the Hudson River to obtain firearms and soon were warring against neighboring tribes in an effort to maintain their arsenals.

The confrontation of different nations and cultures in North America produced a new world of warfare such as Indian peoples had never seen. It also introduced Indians and Europeans to new ways of fighting that changed forever how Indians, Europeans, and later Americans waged their wars. Indians experienced new weapons and tactics of mass destruction; Europeans learned to emulate Indian hit-and-run tactics. The "Indian way of war" was not something that had been handed down without change across generations. Indians passed on to the colonists lessons they themselves had learned from conflicts with Europeans and from wars fought with European guns. Military historians disagree about whether the conflicts in early America fostered a uniquely "American way of war," but there is no question that those conflicts presented Indians and Europeans with new challenges and left lasting impressions on their societies.

✦

The first formal military encounter between Indians and Europeans in what is now the United States occurred at the battle of Hawikuh on July 7, 1540. It illustrated the collision of differing concepts of warfare and the disparities in the military cultures of the protagonists. The Spanish expedition of Francisco Vásquez de Coronado was pushing north in search of the rumored "seven cities of gold" when they sighted the town of Hawikuh, near today's border between Arizona and New Mexico. Hawikuh was a typical Zuni pueblo, a multistoried mud and adobe structure, hardly a glistening citadel, but the conquistadors resolved to take possession of it. The Zunis scattered a line of sacred cornmeal between the Spaniards and their town, symbolically closing the road. The Spaniards either misinterpreted or ignored the gesture, and with a cry of "Santiago!" the Spanish cavalry charged across the line. The Zunis fought furiously for perhaps an hour, coming, wrote Coronado, "almost to the heels of our horses to fire their arrows." Coronado himself was knocked unconscious by a rock hurled from the terraces of the pueblo. However, arrows and rocks were no match for armored cavalry, firearms, and Spanish steel. The hungry Spaniards soon occupied Hawikuh and threw open its storehouses of corn and beans.

Coronado's troops occupied Hawikuh until November 1540 and dispatched scouting parties to the Hopis in Arizona, to the Grand Canyon, and on to the southern plains. Meanwhile, Spanish soldiers among the southern Tewa Pueblos at Tigeux commandeered food and clothing and raped Indian women. When the Indians resisted, the Spaniards retaliated in fury, slaughtering hundreds of Indians. They burned one hundred warriors at the stake.

The Spaniards who invaded America in the sixteenth century were products of a culture of violence that had been forged in their homeland by centuries of conflict between Christians and Muslims. In 711, Moors from North Africa had conquered the Iberian Peninsula. Beginning in the eleventh century under the leadership of legendary El Cid, Spaniards gradually pushed the invaders back. In 1492, the year of Columbus's voyage, the *reconquista* was complete. Spanish warriors, raised from generation to generation to fight Moorish foes, now had to look for new enemies and new lands to conquer. They brought to America the legacy of eight centuries of conflict against "heathen" peoples in the Old World. They were not likely to fight with any less brutality against the "heathens" they encountered in their new world.

The Spanish soldiers who invaded the southeastern United States under Hernando de Soto from 1539 to 1543 encountered powerful chiefdoms that could field massed ranks of warriors who fought according to planned and coordinated strategy, and who engaged the Spaniards in pitched battles. The ability to wage organized warfare did not carry over into systematic conquest, and the Indians also made small-scale guerrilla raids against their Spanish foes. The Spanish-Inca chronicler Garcilaso de la Vega described the warfare of the peoples de Soto encountered as consisting mainly of "ambushes and subtlety" and only rarely of pitched battles. Casualties were generally light, he said. On occasion, when the battles were more heated, the Indians "went so far as to burn towns and devastate fields, but as soon as the conquerors had inflicted the desired damage, they regathered in their own lands without attempting to take possession of the land of others."

The brutality of the Spanish invasion echoed the slaughter the conquistadors had carried out during the conquest of Mexico twenty years earlier. New diseases wreaked silent havoc, and Spanish troops hit the Indian civilizations of the Southeast with an intensity from which they would never recover. De Soto, a veteran of the campaigns in Panama, Nicaragua, and Peru, and a man, according to chronicler Rodrigo Rangal, "very much given to hunting and killing Indians," led a well-equipped and disciplined army and did not hesitate to apply scorched-earth policies and terror tactics to demoralize numerically superior enemies. Spanish soldiers burned villages, ransacked temples, and unleashed huge dogs trained for combat. The Spaniards' reputation traveled before them: "To me," said one chief to de Soto, in words attributed to him by Garcilaso de la Vega, "you are professional vagabonds who wander from place to place, gaining your livelihood by robbing, sacking, and murdering people who give you no offense."

Spanish brutality elicited desperate responses. Apalachee Indians in northern Florida burned their own village rather than see it fall to the Spanish. Even Spanish veterans of the Mexican and Peruvian slaughters were shocked by the "incredible ferocity" of the day-long battle of Mabila in October 1540. The Indians drove the Spaniards out of the town time and again. Exhausted Spanish soldiers "went to drink at a pond, nearby, tinged with the blood of the killed, and returned to the contest." Eventually, the Spaniards captured the town and set fire to it, but the inhabitants fought on. Women and children picked up abandoned weapons and joined the fray, fighting to the death. Some hanged themselves rather than fall into Spanish hands; others threw themselves into the fire. Several thousand Indians died. "One could not walk through the street for the dead bodies," recalled a chronicler. The Spaniards rested three weeks in the area, recovering from their wounds, "and burned over much of the country."

By the end of the sixteenth century, the powerful chiefdoms of the Southeast had collapsed under the hammerblows of imported disease and Spanish invasion. Never again did European invaders confront massed Indian armies such as challenged de Soto's entrada. Indian peoples had learned to avoid pitched battles with armies of determined European gunmen. Melting away before the invaders, then turning to strike when time and terrain were suitable, proved far more effective methods of resistance. With their numbers terribly reduced, Indian tribes also learned to avoid going to war against Europeans without first aligning other Europeans as allies, but that way of helping to preserve tribal independence often only bought time and caused increased dependence.

The first English settlers at Jamestown, Virginia, in 1607, reported how the Powhatan Indians painted and dressed themselves for battle, engaged in elaborate rituals of singing and dancing, and then formed ranks before steadily advancing in a half-moon formation. In 1607, several hundred

Powhatan warriors launched a frontal assault on James Fort. The colonists beat them back with musket fire from the fort and cannon shot from their ships. But the Indians also employed guerrilla tactics, "creeping on all foure, from the Hills, like Beares, with their Bows in their mouths." As southeastern Indians had learned from bitter experience in conflict with the Spaniards, so Virginia Indian warriors resorted more often to stealth and surprise, and only rarely to massed charges, in their conflicts with the English. The Powhatans, having overcome their initial fear of the noise and smoke produced by guns, made every effort to acquire firearms and modified their tactics so as to use the new weapons most effectively. The colonists tried to keep guns from the Indians, but the Powhatans increased their arsenal, which they turned against both English and Indian enemies.

European musketeers could not match Indian archers in rate of fire or accuracy. Powerful bows and arrows remained the weapon of choice for many warriors even after firearms became available. The longbows of Florida Indians were formidable. Cabeza de Vaca said that Spanish armor "did no good against arrows" fired from such bows, and de Soto's soldiers feared and respected Indian archers who "were born and bred in the midst of bows and arrows." Indians continued to use, and sometimes preferred, bows and arrows for both hunting and warfare. Nevertheless, Indians could not afford to be without guns if they hoped to survive in a world of increasing violence. Guns had an undoubted psychological impact. They altered the look, sound, and smell of battle. Their smoke and noise replaced the twang of bowstrings and the hum of arrows; spears, arrows, and war clubs could be dodged or deflected, but soft lead bullets that flattened on impact produced horrible wounds as they smashed bones and tore through bodies. Some Indians who invoked their war medicine to bring them success in battle and protect them as they faced death believed that it could negate the power of firearms—convinced of their invulnerability, they exposed themselves to the white man's bullets. Others were perhaps impressed by the spiritual power of their European adversaries' weapons of destruction.

Governor William Bradford of Plymouth Colony noted that the Wampanoag Indians were eager for firearms by the 1620s: "They became mad (as it were) after them and would not stick to give any price they could attain to for them," he wrote. The New England colonies passed laws to try to keep guns out of Indian hands. But by the time of King Philip's War, Indians in New England had obtained plenty of firearms from French, Dutch, and illegal traders. Indians not only fought with flintlocks, they were also skilled in their use and knew how to repair them, make gunflints, and cast bullets.

Puritan Roger Williams of Rhode Island said that wars between Indians in New England were "farre less bloudy, and devouring then the cruell Warres of *Europe*"; a professional soldier maintained that Indians fought "more for pastime, than to conquer," and reckoned they "might fight seven years and not kill seven men." Indians, of course, had reasons for fighting that differed from those of Europeans. Warriors went to war to avenge the deaths of relatives, to gain prestige and plunder, and to take captives who might be adopted or ritually tortured. Their wars tended to be small in scale, limited in extent, and seasonal in duration. New England Indians soon experienced a very different kind of warfare.

European warfare as imported to North America was the product of thousands of years of tactical evolution and technological innovation. Like Indians, Europeans had had to alter their ways of fighting after the introduction of gunpowder. The English adjusted their warfare to new conditions when they invaded Ireland during Queen Elizabeth's reign late in the sixteenth century. Sir Humphrey Gilbert found an answer to the problem of dealing with elusive foes who fought back with guerrilla tactics in the use of "counter-insurgency terrorism." Gilbert "killed manne, woman and child, and spoiled, wasted and burned, by the grounde, all that he might; leavying nothing of the enemies in saffetie, which he could possiblie waste or consume." Torn by religious conflict and dynastic rivalry, seventeenth-century Europe enjoyed only four years of complete peace. During the Thirty Years' War (1618–48), rival armies crisscrossed the continent, burning food supplies and pillaging cities. Thousands of Swiss towns and villages were destroyed, and 7.5 million Germans, about one third of the population, perished before the war was over.

Immigrants from war-torn Europe quickly applied their Old World military experiences, and the terror tactics they had developed there, to New World enemies. Racial war in America produced new levels of savagery among all the participants. From the first conflicts with the Indians of the Chesapeake, English and other European nations targeted Indian villages and food supplies as the way to win wars against people who would not stand and fight.

In 1636, escalating tensions broke out in open war between the Puritans and the powerful Pequot Indians of southern Connecticut. During an interlude in an early skirmish, Pequot warriors called out to their English adversaries, asking if it was true that the English killed women and children. The English gave them their answer the next year. An English army marched to the main Pequot village on the Mystic River, surrounded it, and put the Indians' houses to the torch. As the Pequots fled the firestorm the English soldiers shot them down. "Those that scaped the fire were slaine with the sword," wrote Governor William Bradford. "Some hewed to peeces, others run throw with their rapiers, so as they were quickly despatchte, and very few escaped." Somewhere between three hundred and seven hundred Pequots perished. Narragansett Indians who were present as allies of the English "stood rounde aboute," said Bradford, "and left the whole execution to the English." When it was all over, they said they "greatly admired the manner of Englishmen's fight," but were shocked because "it is too furious and slays too many men." Bradford admitted that it was "a fearful sight to see them thus frying in the fryer, and the streams of blood quenching the same, and horrible was the stinck & sente thereof," but he felt that the victory was "a sweete sacrifice." The English gave thanks to God for delivering their enemies into their hands and set about hunting down the rest of the Pequots, killing the men and selling the women and children into slavery.

John Underhill, one of the English commanders in the Pequot assault, got the chance to apply his talents again in Governor Kiefft's War between the Dutch and the Indians of the Hudson Valley in the early 1640s. Launching a night attack on an Indian village, Underhill surrounded it with musketeers and torched the buildings to flush out the inhabitants. Several hundred Indians died in the attack; as many as one thousand died in Kiefft's War.

The Narragansetts got a taste of the Pequots' medicine during King Philip's War. Harboring refugees from other tribes, the Narragansetts had, in English eyes, aligned themselves with the anti-English confederation led by Metacomet. In December 1675, an English army assaulted and burned the Narragansett village in the Great Swamp Fight in Rhode Island, killing hundreds of people. They also destroyed a blacksmith's forge—the Narragansetts were by this time repairing their own guns.

Even the French, noted for their relatively amicable relations with Indian peoples, burned Iroquois villages in the late seventeenth century and launched campaigns of genocidal intent against Fox, Natchez, and Chickasaw communities in the early eighteenth century. In historian Ian K. Steele's words, Indians "learned the hard way that they must defend nothing, not even a stockaded settlement or cornfields." Only by guerrilla warfare could they fend off European campaigns.

Guns became increasingly vital in conflicts with other Indians. Economically motivated warfare, to secure trade and to obtain firearms and metal weapons, supplemented and sometimes replaced traditional reasons for going to war with other tribes. The arms race raised intertribal hostilities to new levels of intensity, which combined with deadly new diseases to devastate Indian populations. Captive taking was a traditional part of the culture of war in many Indian societies, and Iroquois warriors regularly brought captives back to their villages for ritual torture or for adoption into the community, in either case assuaging the grief of relatives who had lost loved ones. Now, Iroquois warriors went to war both to acquire captives and to maintain access to hunting grounds. In 1649, Iroquois war parties smashed the confederacy of their Huron trade rivals, laying waste to Huronia and adopting many survivors. In subsequent years, the Iroquois overran the neighboring Petuns, Neutrals, and Eries. By the 1660s, they were fighting Indian peoples from the St. Lawrence to Virginia, from New England to the Great Lakes.

Access to firearms gave Indians an advantage over less well armed neighbors, but in the shifting world of intertribal and interethnic trade and diplomacy, such an advantage often proved short-lived. Westo Indians in the Carolinas obtained guns from Virginia and South Carolina by the 1670s and turned them on the Yamassees, Creeks, Cherokees, Catawbas, and Cusabos, taking captives to sell to English slave traders, who paid for them with guns. In 1680, war broke out between the English colonists and the Westos. The English now increased their arms trade to other Indians, who seized the opportunity to help defeat the Westos.

The arrival of Europeans sometimes transformed captive taking into slave raiding. De Soto's conquistadors "brought along iron chains and human collars to link Indians into human baggage trains" during their invasion of the Southeast. Spanish slaving expeditions raided into Texas as early as the 1560s, and Juan de Oñate sentenced the adult males of Acoma to slavery after the Spaniards recaptured the mesa-top city in 1599. The English sold Indians into slavery in the West Indies after the Pequot War and King Philip's War. Indian peoples, desperate for metal weapons and firearms, sometimes went to war to take captives whom they could then barter as slaves. Indians raided deep into the southern interior for slaves to trade to the English at Charleston. Choctaws, Chickasaws, and other tribes engaged in slave raids

A Huron warrior equipped for ritualized and
defensive conflict in the early seventeenth century.
(From a map by Samuel de Champlain. Dartmouth College
Library)

French depiction of an Iroquois warrior equipped with traditional war club, steel axe, and musket for warfare in the eighteenth century. (National Archives of Canada, C-3165)

on both banks of the lower Mississippi in the late seventeenth and early eighteenth centuries. Hundreds of people, captured in intertribal clashes and dragged east, were shipped out of Charleston to a brief living death on plantations in the West Indies. In 1704, Colonel James Moore of South Carolina led a joint Indian-English assault on northern Florida. They destroyed fourteen Spanish mission towns and took as slaves one thousand men, women, and children. In the Southwest, the Spanish mining frontier needed slave labor and prompted Indian raids for captives: Utes conducted extensive raids against neighboring peoples; Apaches and Comanches took members of other tribes to barter in New Mexico for horses and metal weapons. Spaniards shipped Apache war captives to slavery in Cuba. In the Northeast and the Great Lakes region, Indians sought captives to trade to the French. On the plains, Pawnee Indians were taken captive and sold so often that "Panis" became synonymous with "slave" in French colonies.

Schooled in Old World tactics and concepts of battlefield honor, Europeans looked with contempt on the Indians' "skulking way of war," but they soon learned to fear it and eventually emulated it. Indians' marksmanship often proved to be superior to that of their English adversaries. The English colonists clung to matchlocks and shooting in formation, as practiced on European battlefields or as rehearsed on village greens during militia training, but Indian warriors, accustomed to taking aim at a single human or animal rather than laying down a barrage of fire, quickly recognized the superiority of flintlock muskets for accurate shooting. Indian war parties moved stealthily, attacked with speed and ferocity, and then melted away into the forests; in the words of a French officer, they "approach like foxes, fight like lions and disappear like birds." New England colonists in 1665 accused the Indians of acting "more like wolves than men," of "fighting in a secret skulking manner, lying in ambushment, thickets and swamps by the way side, and so killing people in a base and ignoble manner." Ten years later, however, New England colonists resorted to such tactics themselves to defeat the Indian confederation led by Metacomet. Captain Benjamin Church in particular employed Indian tactics and Indian allies against Indian enemies. Church had lived among the Indians, and he put what he had learned to good use. He ordered his men to follow "the Indian custom to March thin and scatter," rather than plod through the forest in columns. He taught them to avoid lighting fires, to refrain from shooting in volleys, and to "creep . . . on their bellies" and get as close as possible to the enemy before taking aim.

In August 1676, Church's men tracked Metacomet and shot him down in a swamp, presumably "in a base and ignoble manner." The Puritan missionary John Eliot reflected on the transformation in English tactics since the Pequot War: "In our first war with the Indians, God pleased to show us the vanity of our military skill, in managing our arms, after the European mode. Now we are glad to learn the skulking way of war . . . what God's end is in teaching us such a way of discipline I know not."

When the Yamassee War broke out in South Carolina in 1715, colonial authorities there feared they had no answer to Indian tactics. The Indians seemed capable of raiding English settlements at will, "Lying Sculking in the Bushes and Swamps that we know not where to find them nor could follow them if we did So that we may as well go to War with Wolfs and Bears."

As elsewhere, the colonists applied European tactics of mass destruction and economic warfare where possible, Indian-style guerrilla warfare where necessary, and used Indian allies where available. They also operated on the assumption, new to North America, that wars should stop only after the enemy was entirely defeated. Indian warriors generally let up after scoring a victory; Europeans in sustained campaigns drove the Indians back to their villages and destroyed their homes. Warfare in North America ceased to be a seasonal activity fought for limited objectives. More often, it became a series of systematic operations until the job was finished.

It would be wrong to think of ferocity in war as a European import. Archaeological evidence suggests that warfare was both commonplace and brutal long before Europeans arrived. Indians evidently killed noncombatants on occasion and, like their European counterparts, indulged in ritual tortures. Elaborate rituals already surrounded scalping when Europeans first recorded it. Collecting war trophies—in some cultures, the heads or the ears of the vanquished enemy—was common elsewhere in the world, and to many Indian peoples it had important spiritual significance. Europeans institutionalized it by offering scalp bounties, for the hair of men, women, and children, and the practice spread across much of North America. Colonial soldiers lifted scalps as readily as did Indian warriors. By the eighteenth century, scalping was done equally by Indians and Europeans in North America. During the Revolution, George Rogers Clark accused his British rival, Governor Henry Hamilton of Detroit, of buying scalps, but he himself lifted hair: at the siege of Vincennes in 1779, Clark tomahawked and scalped several Indian prisoners in full sight of the garrison and then tossed their bodies into the river. In the late eighteenth century, Spaniards offered bounties on pairs of Apache ears.

Indian and European forms of warfare merged in other ways. Colonial legislatures required supplies of moccasins for their soldiers because "without Indian shoes, they can't perform their duty." French soldiers invaded Iroquois country in the dead of winter, using Indian snowshoes. Soldiers learned to fire their weapons in new positions, lying prone and from forest cover rather than in a rank of comrades. European equipment was Americanized to suit the terrain in which it was to be used. Soldiers modified or discarded armor and uniforms. Heavy weapons and swords gave way to lighter and more practical muskets and hatchets. "One doesn't wear a sword in this country," wrote La Salle, "as it is an enormous encumbrance when walking in the woods, and useless against the hatchets normally carried there." An Indian, he said, could bury his hatchet in an enemy's skull from thirty paces.

Indians enlisted as allies of Europeans from almost the earliest conflicts in North America. When Spaniards invaded New Mexico in the sixteenth century, they defeated the Pueblo Indians in sieges and pitched battles. But Diego de Vargas recruited Pueblo allies to complete his reconquest of New Mexico after the Pueblo Revolt of 1680, and in the eighteenth century, Pueblos and Spaniards fought side by side against Apache, Comanche, Ute, and Navajo enemies. The Spanish garrison at Tucson included three companies of Opata Indians in the second half of the eighteenth century. Northern Pima Indians, who revolted against Spanish colonial rule in 1751, participated in Spanish expeditions against the Apaches in 1779. The Spaniards came to rely on Pimas and Papagos for assistance against the Apaches; the Pimas and the Papagos in turn acquired direct experience of the Spanish army, military organization, and tactics, producing what some scholars have seen as a notable "European militarization of Northern Piman culture."

As France and England battled for hegemony in North America in the eighteenth century they each employed Indian scouts and allies. England employed Mohawks, Mohegans, and Mahicans in its wars on the northern frontiers; Indians sometimes composed as much as one seventh or even a quarter of New England colonial armies. French officers and agents "sang the war song" and recruited allies in Indian villages from the St. Lawrence Valley, the Great Lakes, the Ohio, and the Mississippi. Battling to save France's crumbling North American empire in the 1750s, the marquis de

Montcalm counted in his army Algonkins, Hurons, Nipissings, Abenakis, Penobscots, Maliseets, Ottawas, Chippewas, Menominees, Mississaugas, Potawatomis, Delawares, Shawnees, Sauks, Foxes, and Iroquois from various tribes. The French depended on them: "It is necessary," wrote Montcalm's aide-de-camp Louis Antoine de Bougainville, "to inform them of all the plans, to consult with them, and often to follow what they propose. In the midst of the woods of America one can no more do without them than without cavalry in open country."

Indian tribes in turn sought European allies in their struggles against other Europeans and other Indians. Many of the so-called Indian wars in early America were not clear-cut conflicts between Indian warriors and white soldiers and settlers; they pitched Indians and colonists against other Indians and colonists. More than simply wars for empire, the Anglo-French conflicts became occasions for interethnic, intertribal, and intercolonial violence. The Indians who fought in the Seven Years' War (1756–63) participated in what was essentially the first world war; their efforts mattered in a contest that was also being waged in India, Africa, Europe, and the West Indies, and their lives were affected by the outcomes of battles on the other side of the globe.

Europeans paid their Indian allies, provided them guns and ammunition, and also offered them the opportunity to strike peoples with whom they were already at war. Enlisting as soldiers in colonial armies offered escape from a world that was falling apart and income in times of wrenching disruption of Indian economies. Moreover, as historian Richard Johnson explains, it was a way to continue being Indian: unlike whaling, domestic service, or another subordinate role in the colonial economy, "it allowed young men to earn their manhood in traditional ways frowned upon by a surrounding white society." For similar reasons, Plains and Apache Indians in the late nineteenth century served the United States as scouts, allies, and Indian police.

The cost was high. Indian men died in large numbers in battle or in disease-ridden camps. A census of the Christian Indian town of Natick, Massachusetts, in 1749, a year after King George's War, showed that one fifth of the women were widows. Natick suffered further losses in the Seven Years' War: the town had twenty-five families in 1754; ten years later, only thirty-seven Indians remained. Many men died on campaign; "others returned home and brought contagious sickness with them," wrote Stephen

In 1609, Samuel de Champlain and two French musketeers firing from cover shoot down Iroquois warriors who have formed ranks to fight ritualized warfare, compelling the Iroquois to develop new ways of fighting. (From *The Voyages of Samuel de Champlain,* 1613. Dartmouth College Library)

One hundred forty-six years later, Indian warriors and their French allies fire from cover into the ranks of General Edward Braddock's British regulars, inflicting a defeat that emphasized the need for European troops to adopt "Indian" tactics in North American conflicts. (State Historical Society of Wisconsin, negative WHi [X3] 29984)

Badger, the town's minister. "It spread very fast and carried off some whole families." The Indian town of Mashpee, on Cape Cod, suffered similar losses. Wounded and sick Indian veterans often had to sell land in order to make ends meet and pay medical bills.

Indians and Europeans who fought alongside each other as well as against each other continually refined their strategies to deal with their enemies' ways of war. Europeans showed Indians that survival depended on securing and using guns; Indians taught Europeans that success in American warfare demanded adapting to the American environment. The result, in historian Ian Steele's apt phrase, was "a confusing medley" of regular and guerrilla warfare. In 1755, General Edward Braddock led an army of British redcoats to a stunning defeat on the Monongahela River in Ohio at the hands of a force of 72 French regulars, 146 Canadian militia, and more than 600 Indians, led by Daniel de Beaujeu, who apparently went into battle, and to his death, bare-chested and in buckskins like his Indian allies. Colliding with the enemy, the British regulars stood and attempted to fight while Indian warriors concealed in the forest poured deadly fire into their ranks. Braddock was killed and his army routed. After the battle, an Iroquois chief, the Oneida Scarouady, laid the blame for the disaster squarely on Braddock's shoulders. The British commander had refused to listen to reason and to fight Indian-style. "We often endeavored to advise him, and to tell him of the danger he was in with his soldiers," Scarouady said, but Braddock was arrogant and treated his Indian allies with contempt. They left him to his fate. Braddock's defeat convinced General John Forbes that if the British were to prevail in a war for empire waged in America, "we must comply and learn the Art of War, from Enemy Indians."

The battle of Lake George, fought that same year between Sir William Johnson, colonial militia, and Mohawk allies on one side, and Baron Dieskau's French army and Indian allies on the other, and in which the Mohawk chief Hendrick died, illustrated the mingling of regular and irregular warfare that conflict in Indian country produced. Steele points out the many ironies of the situation: "A frontier trader and adopted Mohawk chief, who had absolutely no conventional military experience, struggled to conduct his campaign like a regular officer. A European-trained French general, in North America for only three months, adopted Amerindian ambush techniques successfully. A veteran Mohawk warrior was among forty who died after failing to scout adequately. American volunteers and Mohawks defended a makeshift breastwork against attack by bayonet wielding French regulars, rather than scattering to fight a guerilla war in the woods."

The fall of Fort William Henry, at the southern tip of Lake George, in 1757, and the massacre of its garrison by France's Indian allies, revealed remaining distinctions in the nature of warfare as practiced by European officers and Indian warriors. "The capitulation is violated and all Europe will oblige us to justify ourselves," wrote Bougainville. "I make war for plunder, scalps, and prisoners," explained one warrior to the French. "You are satisfied with a fort, and you let your enemy and mine live."

Indians who fought in the Seven Years' War got a taste of European-style conflicts, where artillery pounded fortified positions and disciplined regulars carried the day. After Braddock's rout in 1755, the tragedy at Fort William Henry, and James Abercromby's suicidal assault on Fort Ticonderoga in 1758, Britain managed to turn the tide of the war. More and more British regulars were dispatched to the forests of North America. "Now war is established here on the European basis," wrote Bougainville in 1758 after the siege and slaughter at Ticonderoga. "Projects for the campaign, for armies, for artillery, for sieges, for battles. It is no longer a matter of making a raid, but of conquering or being conquered. What a revolution! What a change!" British victory was finally secured by "conventional" means—army defeating army, laying siege to cities, and capturing key strategic objectives.

Nevertheless, British officers and soldiers also adapted to forest fighting, to avoid the repetition of Braddock-like disasters, and operated more effectively as light infantry. "The art of War is much changed and improved here," wrote one officer in 1758. "The Highlanders have put on breeches. . . . Swords and sashes are degraded, and many have taken up the Hatchet and wear Tomahawks." Capable commanders learned how to campaign in North American forests. The British developed more efficient transportation and supply services, established chains of frontier forts, and employed light infantry trained to fight in backwoods warfare. Specialized ranger companies, like that formed by Robert Rogers of New Hampshire during the Seven Years' War, incorporated Indian tactics in their fighting and Indian elements in their clothing. Throughout the first half of the eighteenth century, Abenaki Indians, allied with the French in Canada, had kept English soldiers and settlers at bay in Vermont and New Hampshire, raiding the frontier settlements and then slipping away through heavily wooded terrain to their home villages in the North. English militia companies pursued them with indifferent success. In 1759, however, Rogers' Rangers struck deep into

Abenaki country and burned the village of Odanak or St. Francis on the south side of the St. Lawrence, even though the heavy casualties sustained on the retreat home rendered this a pyrrhic victory for Rogers. Rangers, Indian allies, light infantry, boatmen, and foresters smoothed the way across forest terrain, enabling British regulars to confront and defeat the enemy in more European-style conflicts—such as occurred when General James Wolfe turned his artillery on the city of Quebec and defeated Montcalm on the Plains of Abraham. The British capture of Quebec in 1759 and Montreal in 1760 completed the defeat of the French.

To defeat Indian people who would not stand and fight, Europeans consistently burned their crops and villages. The French burned Iroquois towns, cornfields, and orchards several times in the late seventeenth century. In the 1730s, they and their Indian allies launched campaigns of annihilation against Fox villages in Wisconsin and Illinois. They employed Choctaw allies to destroy Chickasaw towns and crops in Mississippi. In the eighteenth century, European professional soldiers waged wars over territory and imperial successions, but in this "age of reason" and perhaps in reaction to the bloodlettings of the previous century, they were supposed to act with restraint toward civilian populations on the European continent. Those standards of waging war did not apply, however, when the enemy were "uncivilized" peoples such as Highland Scots or Indians. British troops invaded Cherokee country in 1760–61 with orders to "destroy every house, every cornfield, every orchard, and every vegetable plot." Indians learned to pull back in the face of such invasions, giving up their fields and villages rather than losing warriors in a last-ditch defense, and harassing the enemy as they retreated. But the loss of food and homes was often devastating.

Colonial militias learned the lessons of North American forest warfare better than the British army, even though British troops in the eighteenth century also had experience of guerrilla wars in Scotland and Flanders. European professional soldiers generally took the leading role in fighting the enemy's regular troops, leaving colonial militiamen and Indian allies to battle the enemy's militia and Indian allies, and colonists were more likely to experience and adopt the Indians' way of fighting. British regulars in North America wore their regimental uniforms, designed to keep up morale and to serve military purposes on the battlefields of Europe, but which made them easy targets for enemy marksmen. Colonial troops often wore a mixture of Indian and European clothing and accoutrements.

British attempts to govern and finance the empire they had won from the

French in 1763, and to restrict the movement of settlers on to Indian lands, alienated many colonists—especially those, like George Washington, who had substantial investments in western lands. When the American colonies revolted against the British Empire in 1775, many Indians tried to remain neutral, but they were drawn inevitably into the conflict. George Morgan, American Indian agent at Fort Pitt, said, "They have long been taught by contending Nations to be bought & sold." Most tribes sided with the Crown as their best hope of protecting their lands, but some—Oneidas, Tuscaroras, Catawbas, and Stockbridges—supported the Americans.

The British and their Indian allies raided American frontier settlements during the Revolution, as the French and their Indian allies had raided New England settlements in previous conflicts. For their part, the Americans applied well-tried European tactics of total warfare in fighting Indians during the Revolution, and they applied American ways of war, developed over generations of fighting Indians, against British redcoats. American armies burned Cherokee and Iroquois villages late in the season, when the corn was either already harvested or dry in the fields and highly flammable. When General John Sullivan invaded Iroquois country in 1779, his army burned forty towns and spent whole days destroying cornfields and orchards. With no time to raise new crops, the Indians faced starvation in the coming winter.

According to military historian John Ferling, by the time of the Revolution, the colonists "saw themselves as a hybrid of the European and the American, and they fashioned their culture and their conduct of war accordingly." George Washington lost more pitched battles than he won, but he employed hit-and-run tactics in wearing down a superior enemy force. American rifle companies fought in hunting shirts and moccasins, wielded hatchets, and fired from cover into British ranks. As James Axtell observes, beating the British would have been virtually impossible "without stratagems and equipment gained from the Indians." In some ways, the American victory in the Revolution stemmed from the lessons they had learned in past Indian wars, and from the sense of unity men from different colonies had developed in fighting common Indian enemies.

The devastating losses they suffered, of both land and people, prompted Indians to forge multitribal resistance movements in the late eighteenth century. In 1763, the tribes of the Great Lakes and the Ohio Valley united against the British in a war that became known as Pontiac's Revolt, for the Ottawa war chief who played a prominent role. After the Revolution, confronted with American claims that the Indians of the Old Northwest had forfeited their lands to the United States by right of conquest, Mohawk Joseph Brant, the Miami chief Little Turtle, the Shawnee Blue Jacket, and other tribal leaders patched together a confederacy that held American expansion in check for almost a decade, fighting to restore the Ohio River as the barrier to settlement. The Americans demonstrated that they had not fully learned the lessons of Braddock's defeat. In 1791, northwestern Indians ambushed an army led by General Arthur St. Clair, and they inflicted a crushing defeat and nine hundred casualties. It took the United States three years to build a new army. General Anthony Wayne trained his men in the harsh realities of Indian fighting, advanced into Indian country using scouts and flankers, and threw up defensive works at every camp. The Indians called him the "general who never sleeps." Meanwhile, growing divisions plagued the Indian confederacy. In August 1794, as Wayne approached, the warriors began their ritual preparations for battle, fasting in anticipation of the fight. But Wayne did not attack, and many Indians dispersed in search of food. Then Wayne attacked. On the advance of disciplined legions trained to fight an Indian war, yet employing a European-style bayonet charge against an Indian force already weakened by internal disunity and ritual observances, hung the outcome of the war for Ohio. Wayne's victory was decisive.

All this warfare had far-reaching effects on the Indian societies caught up in it. Indians compared their position between contending powers to being trapped between the blades of a pair of scissors, which cut what lay between them as they closed but did no damage to each other. Villages were burned, crops ruined, and people went hungry. Wars disrupted ancient cycles of planting, harvesting, fishing, hunting, and gathering. Like colonial militias and unlike British regulars, Indian males were part-time warriors. Men who were away at war could not clear fields for planting, hunt for meat, or protect their families against enemy raids. In most woodland Indian societies, war chiefs traditionally had temporary and limited authority, deferring in normal circumstances to the wise counsel of older civil or village chiefs. But in the new world of warfare that engulfed North America, war chiefs rose in prominence. European allies bolstered their prestige with medals and supplies of firearms, expecting them in return to rally their warriors for the king's campaigns. Generations of Indian people grew up in a world where warfare was endemic and in communities that existed on a war footing.

Warfare also became endemic in areas distant from face-to-face contact with European soldiers, as Indian peoples felt the impact of European influences in how and why they went to war. On the Great Plains, balances of power shifted around the possession of guns and the acquisition of horses. After the Spaniards introduced them into the Southwest in the sixteenth century, horses spread rapidly north and eastward, along routes of trading and raiding, passing through the Rocky Mountains, over the plains, and into Canada by the early eighteenth century. Guns entered the region via French and British traders from the north and east. Both transformed the warfare of Plains Indians and helped turn the Plains into a cauldron of conflict. Some Indians adopted the Spanish practice of covering their mounts with armor, using layers of hide, but armor restricted mobility and was soon abandoned.

The Spanish arrival in the Southwest disrupted intertribal relationships, thus fueling competition and intensifying patterns of conflict. The new goods, livestock, and horses they brought to the Pueblos made those communities inviting targets for Apache and Navajo raiders, who, now mounted on horseback, could carry off more plunder than ever before. In Elizabeth A. H. John's words, the Apaches in the seventeenth century "were catching a rising tide—revolutionizing their lives with horses and metal, expanding their range and powers, scoring against old enemies and new rivals on every side." Escalating Apache raids helped precipitate the great Pueblo Revolt of 1680, when, in an unprecedented display of united and synchronized action, the Pueblos drove the Spaniards out of their homeland for a dozen years.

The various Apache tribes held undisputed sway on the southern plains in the early part of the eighteenth century. Mounted on horses and using Spanish-style lances, Apaches pushed Pueblos westward and Indian farmers on the western tributaries of the Mississippi eastward. But Comanche Indians, migrating south and out of the Colorado mountains, swept the Apaches from the plains. Spanish authorities tried to keep guns out of Apache hands, but Comanches obtained weapons from French traders via Osage and Wichita intermediaries. By the time of the American Revolution, Comanche bands dominated an area from Texas to the Nebraska border, and from the Rocky Mountains in the west to the lands of the Pawnees and Osages in the east. The Apaches found themselves shoved farther south into desert and mountain regions of Arizona and New Mexico, and into increasing conflict with the northern frontier of New Spain.

On the northern plains, the Shoshones' experience in the eighteenth century illustrates the fluctuating and precarious balance of power as horses and guns arrived. The eastern Shoshones or Snakes, who lived in southern Idaho and western Wyoming, had horses by about 1700, having obtained them in trade from Ute and Comanche relatives farther south. The Shoshones enjoyed a distinct edge over unmounted neighbors, and they pushed out on to a huge area of the northwestern plains. An old Cree Indian named Saukamappee, who lived with the Blackfeet, told fur trader David Thompson how Shoshone cavalry had changed warfare on the northern plains in his lifetime. Recalling a battle that took place when he was a boy, some time before 1730, Saukamappee described how unmounted Shoshone and Blackfeet warriors lined up in ranks behind large rawhide shields and shot arrows until nightfall put an end to the skirmish. Horses and guns finished this kind of warfare for good. The Blackfeet soon encountered a new weapon, when Shoshone cavalry swinging heavy war clubs rode down on them "as swift as the deer," killing many of their best men. But the Shoshones could not preserve their equestrian advantage, and the Blackfeet had horses by the second quarter of the century. Soon after, the Blackfeet began to obtain guns, first from Cree and Assiniboine Indians to their east and then directly from French and British traders who built posts on the Saskatchewan River. The tables were turned. The Blackfeet gunned down the Shoshones in their next encounter and then proceeded to keep the trade in firearms out of Shoshone country. When the American explorers Lewis and Clark headed west in 1804–5, they found the Shoshones huddled in the foothills of the Rockies, fearful of Blackfeet enemies. They welcomed the Americans as a new source of trade and firearms, and a new cycle of war began on the northern plains.

Meanwhile, Sioux Indians, edged out of their Minnesota homelands by gun-toting Ojibwas or Chippewas, and attracted by the horse and buffalo culture that was developing on the plains, began to move west. Eventually, they would establish themselves as the dominant power on the northern and central plains, pushing aside less powerful tribes. By the time the United States began to make its presence felt on the plains, the world there was very different from what it had been in 1600. Horses and guns had created new reasons for going to war and generated new ways of waging war. Plains Indians traded captives, furs, and horses for guns, powder, lead, and steel-edged weapons. The mounted and armed Indian warrior of popular stereotype was a product of the new world created on the plains by European invasion of America. The jostling for position that occurred in the eighteenth century also brought to the plains new peoples who would then defend the region from American latecomers.

In a world of competition, Plains Indian societies placed tremendous importance on warfare. Success in war became the path to status for young men, and a warrior culture, in which young men prayed for visions and invoked sacred power as they rode to battle, became ingrained in many societies. American soldiers sent to the plains after 1850 confronted warrior societies that had emerged in response to the revolutionary impact of horses and guns there. The U.S. Army had no chance of defeating mobile warriors at their own game. Instead, like their colonial forebears, they resorted to total war, breaking the resistance and independence of the Plains Indians. They systematically slaughtered buffalo herds, burned Indian villages in wintertime, and killed pony herds whenever possible. Immobilized warriors with starving families drifted in from the frozen plains to life on the reservations.

The experience of the early Indian wars left its imprint on American society in many ways. Warfare in America was significantly different from that practiced in Europe at the time, and the new ways of fighting contributed in some measure at least to the winning of American independence. The Indian wars also left an enduring impression in the minds of Americans as to the character of Indian people. War became so common in Indian country, wars against Indians such a recurrent feature of early American history, that it was easy to assume that Indians were warlike by nature and therefore merited treatment as "savages." The Indian wars also, some would say, left a more sinister mark on American culture: a nation built on conquest could not escape the legacy of its violent past.

Six

✶

New World Diplomacy and New World Foreign Policies

CONTACTS BETWEEN INDIANS and Europeans often took the form of violent confrontations in which the only dialogue was the hum of arrows and the crash of gunfire. Yet, from their first meetings, Indians and Europeans also tried to cultivate diplomatic relations and reach understandings that avoided bloodbaths. Even as Hernando de Soto cut his bloody swath across the Southeast, he pursued his goals through diplomacy as well as butchery. The European invasion of North America, and subsequent rivalries between European powers for tribal allies and continental hegemony, changed forever the diplomatic landscape. Indian peoples had to develop a range of foreign-policy responses if they were to survive in increasingly perilous times. Indian leaders found it expedient to work with as well as against Europeans. Some tribes survived, and even prospered, in the new world of imperial rivalries by playing one European power off against another. Some Indians and some Europeans fashioned important new roles for themselves as intermediaries. The diplomacy of early America often involved Indian chiefs wearing uniform coats and medals given to them by European allies, negotiating with European emissaries who smoked the calumet and spoke on wampum belts while mixed-blood or other bicultural individuals translated their words.

Political and diplomatic decisions rested more and more in European hands—and in European and colonial capitals—but acting on such decisions in Indian country required skillful maneuvering and a knowledge of local politics and politicians. Europeans had to adjust their imperial ambitions to the realities of operating in Indian country and the fact that Indians controlled most of the continent. Europeans courted Indian chiefs and adopted the protocols of Native diplomacy even as they disturbed traditional political arrangements. Writing to his successor as governor of New Mexico in 1754, Don Tomás Vélez Capuchin outlined the kind of situation that required European powers to cultivate Indian alliances and pay attention to Indian diplomacy. "The condition of this government and its circumstances, due to its organization and the diversity of the nations which surround it, must be ruled more with the skillful measures and policies of peace than those which provoke incidents of war," he wrote. The nomadic Comanches, Utes, and Apaches were formidable foes, and "the small forces which this province has would be crushed by tribes of their size if they conspired against it." There was not an Indian nation in the region "in which a kind word does not have more effect than the execution of the sword," maintained Vélez, who had tried both approaches.

On the matter of the best way to receive visiting Comanche chiefs, he advised: "Sit down with them and command tobacco for them so that they may smoke as is their custom. . . . Show them every mark of friendship, without employing threats," he advocated. "I have done so and have been able to win the love they profess for me." Lest his successor underestimate the need to master Indian diplomacy, Vélez reminded him that Spain lacked the armed forces to resist Comanche attacks and that the French were competing for Comanche allegiance: "If this tribe should change its idea and declare war, your grace may fear the complete ruin of this government." Vélez followed his own advice. When he became governor a second time in 1762, he found the Comanches on the brink of war with New Mexico. He quickly dispatched six Comanche women captives as emissaries, inviting the Comanches to come to Santa Fe for peace talks. When the Comanche delegation arrived a month later, they were armed with guns, powder, and shot obtained from the French. Vélez reestablished peace and "sent them away well-fed and loaded with presents, some clothing they esteemed, adornments, and bundles of tobacco, so that, in the councils of their chiefs, principal men, and elders, they might smoke and consider well their resolution in regard to my purposes."

The conquest of America is often portrayed as a simple story of racial conflict, in which white invaders fought and defeated the Indians. That conveys the broad outlines of what happened but obscures and distorts historical reality. European invaders entered a world in which various Indian groups pursued different foreign policies with regard to other Indian friends and enemies. Europeans therefore found a ready supply of Indian allies as well as Indian enemies; had they not done so, the story of conflict, from Cortez to Custer, would have been very different. By the same token, arranging alliances with one Indian nation often earned the suspicion or even the open hostility of others, who had their own reasons for enmity toward that nation. International and intercolonial rivalries added to and complicated intertribal rivalries, turning North America into a kaleidoscope of competing, overlapping, and changing foreign policies.

Frontier diplomacy in early America involved negotiations between tribes and colonies rather than simply between Indians and whites. Each Indian tribe pursued its own set of relations with other Indian tribes, with one or more European powers, and with one or more of the individual colonies, which were themselves divided as often as united. Just as Europeans played various Indian tribes against one another, so Iroquois, Creeks, Choctaws, and others manipulated rival European powers and even rival colonies of the same nation. Capable Indian leaders, like Powhatan and Massasoit of the Wampanoags, cultivated relations with early English settlers on the East Coast in part as potential allies against Indian enemies to the west. Indian leaders traveled to European capitals, accepted European agents, traders, and missionaries, held out the promise of military support, and shifted ground as necessary, all in an effort to secure constant supplies of trade goods and occasional military aid while at the same time preserving their independence.

In a world of increasing warfare, the on-again, off-again neutrality of certain tribes frustrated European allies and enemies, but the Indians were marching to their own drummer not to a distant monarch's. In 1684, an Iroquois chief assured the English that "Wee have putt our selves under the great Sachim Charles [II] that lives over the great lake," but in almost the same breath he declared, "We are a free people uniting ourselves to what sachem we please." An Abenaki chief, speaking before both the French and the English in 1752, declared, "We are allies of the king of France. . . . We love that monarch, and we are strongly attached to his interests." However, he asserted, the Abenakis were "entirely free," and he made it clear they intended to remain so.

Success and survival in this dangerous new world required innovative and skillful diplomacy by all participants. When the French made alliances with the Montagnais, Algonkin, and other tribes of the St. Lawrence Valley in the early seventeenth century, they laid the basis for trading connections with Indian peoples as far away as the Ottawas and the Hurons. In time, the French constructed their New World empire based on a network of alliances with Indian tribes from the mouth of the St. Lawrence to the mouth of the Mississippi. As Richard White has shown in his prize-winning book, *The Middle Ground,* keeping such alliances intact, amid the centrifugal pressures of cultural misunderstandings, conflicting interests, and shifting bases of power, meant not only constant attention but willingness to compromise and endless negotiation. In their efforts to build workable relationships, Indians and Frenchmen together created a complex and dynamic world that was new to everyone. Bestowing gifts, mediating disputes, and counseling modera-tion, the French tied multiple Indian groups to them in a precarious alliance. Indians employed traditional rituals and reciprocal relations to turn French strangers into real or metaphorical kinspeople, referring to the French as their "fathers" and "brothers." The French channeled trade goods into Indian villages via selected chiefs, recognizing their traditional role of re-distributing goods among their people. The French also reinforced the influence of their client chiefs. Some chiefs developed new roles as "alliance chiefs," working to maintain the alliance that was also the source of their power.

Keeping the peace was not an easy task. What, for instance, were French officials and Indian chiefs to do about murder? For Indians, identifying the individual murderer was often less important than knowing the group to which he belonged. If the murderer's people were allies, then the victim could be "covered" or "raised" by the ritual of giving and receiving gifts and smoothing over the incident. If the murderer belonged to non-allies, how-ever, his deed demanded vengeance against them. Violence between individ-uals could lead to blood feud and clan vengeance. The French made a different distinction, between murder and "legitimate" killings in wartime. Finding a way of reconciling such cultural incongruities taxed the resilience of Indians and Europeans alike, but both persisted, since the alternative might well be a bloodbath. "The result," concludes White, "was an odd imperialism where mediation succeeded and force failed, where colonizers gave gifts to the colonized and patriarchal metaphors were the heart of politics."

The very success of the French in establishing and maintaining alliances with the Indian peoples of Canada and the Great Lakes region undermined their ability to achieve such relationships with the Iroquois tribes of New York. The Iroquois had long-standing rivalries with neighbors to the east, north, and west, which French presence and competition for the fur trade aggravated. For much of the seventeenth century, French and Iroquois engaged in a kind of cold war punctuated by open hostilities, and most Iroquois supported the English colonies in the early round of Anglo-French conflicts.

Other Europeans confronted the same dilemma in different times and places. Juan Bautista de Anza, governor of New Mexico from 1778 to 1787, scored a major diplomatic coup when he made peace with the Comanches. In 1779, supported by Pueblo allies, Anza attacked a Comanche camp in southeastern Colorado and killed the war chief Cuerno Verde. This victory laid the basis for the peace he negotiated with the Comanche chief Ecueracapa in 1786, which held for a generation. However, Anza had to practice some fast diplomatic footwork to avoid antagonizing the Utes and the Jicarilla Apaches, enemies of the Comanches, who looked with suspicion on what had happened.

The diplomatic map of North America was continually changing. Yesterday's enemies were tomorrow's friends, and vice versa. Only those leaders and peoples who charted careful and far sighted courses could hope to survive. The Five Nations of the Iroquois—the Mohawks, Oneidas, Onondagas, Cayugas, and Senecas—were united in a great league of peace, but by 1700 they were feeling the effects of recurrent warfare. They had lost half of their warriors and badly needed a period of recuperation. Iroquois statesmen decided on a new course of action and initiated a new era in Iroquois diplomacy. Though the French wanted them to remain at odds with the western tribes, and the English wanted them to remain at odds with the French, the Iroquois succeeded in making peace with everyone, thus securing through diplomacy what they had been unable to win in war. They first made peace with the western tribes, which gained them access to western hunting territories: "Let this peace be firm and lasting," Iroquois spokesmen said to their former enemies, "then we shall grow old and gray-headed together; else ye warr will devour us both." Then they negotiated treaties with the French and the English, informing them that henceforth the Iroquois would remain neutral in other peoples' wars, but trade would stay open. Any infringement of Iroquois neutrality would risk alienating the confederacy, something neither the French nor the English could afford to do. The formal neutrality was not totally effective: Mohawks sometimes supported the British in the east, and Senecas occasionally joined non-Iroquois neighbors in the west in supporting the French. Nevertheless, the new policy allowed the Iroquois to play the French and the English against each other, rather than being caught in their crossfire. "To preserve the Ballance between us and the French is the great ruling Principle of the Modern Indian Politics," wrote one colonial observer in 1750. Colonial delegates recognized the importance of retaining Iroquois friendship, and Onondaga featured as significantly as Williamsburg, Boston, and Quebec in the diplomacy of early America. Iroquois fortunes and Iroquois population rebounded, until the American Revolution split the confederacy and pitted tribe against tribe.

The Iroquois were not the only people to exploit European imperial rivalries. The Creek confederacy—a loose coalition of towns in Georgia and Alabama—for a long time held the balance of power in the Southeast and pursued adroit diplomacy to maintain that role. Brims, the Creek chief, played Spaniards and English against each other in the early eighteenth century, making sure that Europeans knew the Creeks were independent allies, not subjects. Creek emissaries traveled as far as Mexico City to negotiate with Spanish officials. In 1742, a Creek headman declared that Creek land "belonged" to both the British and the French and to neither of them, meaning that "both had liberty to Come there to Trade." In the international rivalry that dominated the Southeast after the American Revolution, the Creek chief Alexander McGillivray continued his predecessors' policies, allowing himself to be courted by Spain, Britain, and the new United States, but persistently pursuing Creek interests.

The Choctaws of the lower Mississippi Valley numbered about twenty thousand and occupied a region of crucial strategic significance in the eighteenth-century contests for empire. French, Spanish, English, and finally Americans all cast covetous eyes on their lands and courted their support as the major Native power in the region. Choctaws fought alongside the French in their wars against the Natchez and Chickasaws in the 1730s and 1740s, but the Choctaw nation comprised approximately fifty towns in several districts; different villages and even different village and clan chiefs sometimes pursued separate goals. Various Choctaw groups cultivated relationships with different European powers, for trade and support. Europeans thought the Choctaws hopelessly divided into factions, but in a sense it was the Europeans who were being exploited, since no nation dared cut the Choctaws off, and all nations felt they had some friends in Choctaw country. One Choctaw, a warrior named Red Shoe, so successfully exploited the diplomatic turmoil created by the competing interests of the British, the French, and the established Choctaw chiefs, that he rose rapidly, and sometimes ruthlessly, in prestige, until an assassin's dagger ended his career in 1747.

Few Indian peoples could operate from a position of power the way the Iroquois and Choctaws did, but all had to learn to survive in a new world where dealing with white men and the impact of their presence was unavoidable. By the mid-eighteenth century, the Catawbas in Carolina had declined to less than fifteen hundred people, and the future looked bleak as Indian enemies and colonial planters pressed into Catawba country. Governor James Glen of South Carolina feared "the Total destruction of that poor Nation." But the Catawbas survived, thanks largely to the ability of Hagler, chief from 1750 to 1763, to satisfy the needs of his own people while meeting the demands of their colonial neighbors. Hagler traveled to colonial capitals, became skillful in dealing with colonial and Crown officials, and managed to maintain amicable relations with Virginia and North and South Carolina. Colonial officials showered him with gifts and medals. However, he remained firmly wedded to Native traditions and Catawba interests. He spoke some English, but refused to do so in meetings with white officials, forcing them to negotiate in his language. He walked a fine line that required innovation and delicate handling of potentially explosive situations. In 1754, for instance, a drunken young Catawba killed a colonist's child. If Hagler were to retain his good standing with his colonial neighbors, he would have to execute the murderer. How could he avoid alienating the murderer's relatives and possibly sparking a cycle of clan vengeance? Hagler made sure he had the support of the Catawba council, and then he appointed a kinsman of the murderer to carry out the execution. By such deft maneuvering, Hagler avoided conflict with the English (justice was done) and within Catawba society (the whole tribe approved the execution). As James Merrell notes, Hagler balanced "a firm attachment to traditional native custom with a shrewd understanding of the Anglo-American colonial world."

Indian leaders and Indian tribes often found that they had to deal with several English colonies, which were not united in their Indian policies or in much else. So the Iroquois pursued separate relations with New York,

Pennsylvania, Maryland, and Virginia; Cherokees, with South Carolina, Georgia, and Virginia. In that very complexity lay opportunities for Indian leaders to court colonial officials yet keep them at arm's length, to secure their good will and their trade while avoiding commitments to any one power. But therein also lay the seeds of confusion and misunderstanding.

Colonists who were not always united themselves demanded unity from the Indian tribes with whom they dealt. They adopted a "take me to your leader" approach; and where they found no clear leaders, they endeavored to create them. They constantly expected spokesmen to represent and act for all their people, and they held the whole tribe responsible for the actions of a particular group or village. Such pressures had significant repercussions among Indian peoples. Cherokee society, for example, traditionally comprised many separate and autonomous towns, each pursuing its own policies. However, English colonists' treaties, which they expected to be binding on the whole Cherokee Nation, caused Cherokee political structure itself to change. By the 1750s, political authority was centralized at the capital town of Chota. Moreover, colonists generally were most interested in matters relating to war and trade and sought out the men as those responsible; as a result, the influence of women in Cherokee politics and diplomacy seems to have declined.

Indian peoples found increasingly that their dealings with Europeans revolved around questions of land. Christian nations claimed the "empty lands" they found in North America as theirs by "right of discovery." Indians came to realize that, in international diplomacy, Europeans transferred lands from one power to another without consulting the Native occupants of those lands. Peace treaties negotiated by diplomats in the halls of European capitals, rather than around Indian council fires, shifted territory back and forth like chips at a gaming table. Abenakis reacted in fury to news that their French allies had ceded Abenaki land to the English by the Treaty of Utrecht in 1713; Britain's Indian allies were "thunderstruck" to learn the king had granted their lands to the United States by the Peace of Paris in 1783. But Indians were quick studies. When Sir William Johnson and the British Crown sought to extend the line of settlement westward in 1768, the Iroquois sold them Shawnee and Cherokee hunting territories at the Treaty of Fort Stanwix, satisfying the British while diverting settlement from Iroquois country.

Indians came to understand that granting lands to Europeans would be interpreted as ceding all rights to those lands: Indian people could no longer expect to be able to hunt or plant there. Recognizing that the European demand for land seemed insatiable, Indian leaders sought ways to divert the tide of settlement if they could not halt it, selling off lands to gain time and space for their people. Such policies by older chiefs often angered younger warriors, who accused them of betraying the tribe to the whites. The result was generational struggles within Indian societies.

Indian leaders also had to step gingerly in the new world where alliance with Europeans was an economic necessity but could prove to be a political liability. Chiefs increasingly found themselves having to function for two constituencies, representing their people's interests to outsiders and their allies' interests to their people. The coats, commissions, and medals an Indian chief obtained from his European allies bolstered his position and signaled his ability to acquire trade goods and perhaps military support for his people, but they might equally well raise questions about the chief's ability to remain "his own man." The interference of outsiders in creating and sustaining a chief rendered a leader's power base all the more unstable. Indian delegates at treaty meetings were often hard-pressed to meet the demands of European allies in distant capitals and retain the support of their own people.

✳

In 1633, a group of Wicomesse Indians killed three colonists and some cattle. The governor of Maryland demanded that the killers be handed over to the English for punishment, but the Indians offered to give wampum in atonement for the deed, pointing out that "since that you are heere strangers, and come into our Countrey, you should rather conforme yourselves to the Customes of our Countrey, then [*sic*] impose yours upon us." Many Europeans, convinced that their ways were superior, found adopting the customs of the country difficult if not impossible, but if their imperial aspirations were to succeed, they had little choice.

First and foremost, Europeans had to learn the languages of this new world, which numbered in the hundreds. Effective conduct of business in such an environment required a constant source of interpreters, of Indian, European, or mixed heritage. John Heckewelder, a Moravian missionary among the Delaware and other Indians of the Ohio Valley in the eighteenth century, wrote that "even if an Indian understand English he prefers communicating to a white man through an interpreter."

Early English and French explorers on the coasts of New England and Canada kidnaped Natives, took them to Europe, and later returned with them as translators in dealings with the Indians. One of Samuel de Champlain's guides in 1604 was a Micmac chief named Messamouet, who spoke French because he had already been to France, where he had stayed with the governor of Bayonne. In 1621, the Pilgrims at New Plymouth were astonished when an Abenaki named Samoset "came bouldly amongst them, and spoke to them in broken English." Samoset had been captured by Englishmen and taken from Maine to Cape Cod, where he lived among the local Wampanoags. He introduced the Pilgrims to Squanto. Squanto, a Patuxet Indian who came to serve as the Pilgrims' interpreter and their guide to the new land, had been kidnaped by Englishman Thomas Hunt in 1614. Hunt had shipped about twenty Indians to Spain to be sold as slaves. Squanto somehow managed to escape and made his way to England, where he lived for a time in London. Returning to New England with another English expedition, he found his people had been all but wiped out by disease. The arrival of the Pilgrims gave him a role and a purpose in a world that must have seemed quite empty.

Well-traveled and bilingual Indians were not unusual. But most early interpreters were colonists who mastered a Native language, not Indians speaking English, French, or Spanish. Successful interpreters needed to be able to do more than offer word-for-word translations. Indian speakers at formal treaty councils were generally seasoned orators, and their use of metaphor and imagery taxed the abilities of all but the most skillful interpreters. "Metaphor is largely in use among these Peoples," said Jesuit Paul Le Jeune in 1636. "Unless you accustom yourself to it, you will understand nothing." To convey accurately the full sense and nuances of an Indian speaker's sentiments, interpreters had to have an intimate understanding of Indian concepts, customs, and concerns. They had to understand Indian and European worldviews as well as words. They had to explain rituals and actions and speeches; they had to show Indians and Europeans how to do business in the other's terms; and they sometimes had to show them with whom to do it. Successful interpreters usually lived among Indians for a time and thought like them to some extent.

The new world created by the interaction of Europeans and Indians produced many individuals capable of fulfilling such roles. Many captives, former captives, and children of mixed marriages found a valuable niche in Indian-white relations, since they, and sometimes they alone, had the experience, expertise, and contacts in both worlds to act as intermediaries and communicators.

Jacques Cartier took two sons of the Iroquoian chief Donnacona with him to France in 1534. They learned French and returned with Cartier on his second voyage the next year, and Cartier's conversations with them produced a small French-Iroquoian dictionary. In 1713, when Louis Jucheron de Saint Denis was sent by Sieur Antoine de la Mothe Cadillac to explore what is now northwestern Louisiana, up the Mississippi and Red Rivers into the heart of Caddo country, he took along as his interpreters two brothers, Pierre and Robert Talon. As children, the Talons had accompanied La Salle's expedition (Robert was born during La Salle's voyage across the Atlantic) and had been adopted by Indians. Pierre had lived with the Hasinais; Robert, with the Karankawas. They had made their way back to France in 1690, but had been sent to the Gulf of Mexico with Iberville. Now, Saint Denis took them to Texas, hoping that their tattooed faces and their knowledge of Native languages would guarantee his party safe passage.

Andrew Montour, an interpreter and a culture broker on the Ohio frontier in the mid-eighteenth century, was proficient in Delaware, Miami, Shawnee, and several Iroquois languages. He had ties to the Oneidas and the Delawares and on occasion spoke for the Indians in council, rather than just interpreting for them. Sometimes known by his English name, sometimes by his Indian name Sattelihu or Eghisara, Montour wore European clothing and Indian face paint and ornaments. Simon Girty shaped a similar role for himself in the era of the American Revolution. Taken captive in 1755 at age fourteen and adopted by the Senecas, Girty was liberated after Pontiac's Revolt (1763). He spent the rest of his life working as an intermediary and an interpreter. His dual identity, his command of several languages, and his knowledge of both Indian and white worlds put him in a unique position in the Ohio Valley during the crucial years of the Revolution and its aftermath. At one multitribal council, the Indians would allow no white men to be present "but Simon Girty, whom they considered one of themselves." Casting his lot with the Indians and the British, Girty devoted his skills and the best years of his life to preserving the kind of multicultural world that had created him and in which he felt at home. For that, he earned the hatred of his American contemporaries—who put a price on his head—and a lasting reputation as a "white savage." James Dean, who was raised by Indians and served the Americans as interpreter during the Revolution, was said to speak Oneida better than any other white man, without a trace of an accent.

The presence of an interpreter did not necessarily mean that negotiations between Indians and Europeans went smoothly. Interpreters wielded great influence in formal treaty councils, since they could embellish, distort, or suppress the words they heard, subtly shaping the direction negotiations took. An incompetent, dishonest, or intemperate interpreter could produce layers of misunderstanding and derail peace talks.

Some interpreters commanded several Indian languages, but none spoke them all. So it was not uncommon for Europeans and Indians to have teams of interpreters in attendance at treaty councils to ensure communication despite multiple language barriers. That could mean a series of translations before a speaker's words reached the intended audience. In 1598, when Juan de Oñate led a Spanish expedition into New Mexico, he found two Mexican Indians, members of an earlier expedition, who had been living among the Pueblos for fifteen years. They served as Oñate's primary interpreters, translating Pueblo speeches into Mexican Indian languages, so that other, more fluent Spanish-speaking Mexican Indians could translate them into Spanish. In 1748, the Oneida Shickellamy, an intermediary on the Indian-white frontier in the Ohio Valley, went to considerable lengths to converse with a German visitor. A colonist translated the German's words into Mahican, then a Mahican woman translated them into Shawnee for her husband, who in turn translated them into Oneida. Shickellamy's reply went through the several translators in reverse order: Oneida to Shawnee to Mahican to German. More than two thousand miles to the west, the American explorers Lewis and Clark encountered similar problems in opening diplomatic relations with the Flathead Indians in 1805. No one in the American party spoke Salish, the Flatheads' language. To communicate, the Americans delivered their speech in English, which François Labiche, one of the party, translated into French. Toussaint Charbonneau translated the French version into Hidatsa; his Shoshone wife, Sacagawea, who had lived among the Hidatsas, translated the speech into Shoshone. Finally, a Shoshone boy living with the Flatheads translated it into Salish. One wonders how much of the original speech remained intact after traveling the length of this elaborate linguistic chain. But it was by such means that Europeans and Indians often attempted to communicate across barriers of language and culture.

Europeans had to learn new symbolic languages as well. From de Soto to Lewis and Clark, expeditions into Indian country took along stores of glass beads and other trade goods to give as gifts, to curry favor with local chiefs, and to lubricate the wheels of diplomacy. In Indian cultures the giving and receiving of gifts had symbolic meanings that outweighed utilitarian values. Gifts denoted sincerity and good will. They symbolized the giver's position and intentions. The acceptance of gifts often implied certain understandings and appropriate obligations. Hatchets and pipes, wampum and beads of different colors and in particular arrangements, tobacco and feathers, all carried clear messages in the symbolic language of Indian country. As James Merrell observes, "Colonists had to read a foreign text."

Colonists soon learned the symbolism and the implications of giving and receiving gifts. In the winter of 1621–22, the Narragansett sachem Canonicus sent Governor William Bradford of Plymouth Colony a gift of several arrows wrapped in a snakeskin, thereby proclaiming Narragansett dominance in southern New England. Bradford viewed it as a blatant challenge to the power of the English and turned to Squanto for advice. The governor then sent the snakeskin back to Canonicus filled with bullets. Canonicus refused to accept it and returned it to Plymouth. By the act of mutual rejection, each party announced its refusal to submit to the other.

Colonists not only endeavored to master Native symbol systems; they also added symbols of their own, presenting chosen chiefs with medals, silver gorgets, swords, brightly colored military uniforms, and other European insignia of leadership. Such adornments proclaimed the allegiance of the chief and identified him to his people as a man of influence with powerful European backers. The same symbols and actions often had different meanings for Indians and Europeans, who frequently resorted to diplomatic maneuvering to get the other to accept the implications of their own protocol. When Powhatans and Englishmen met on the Chesapeake early in the seventeenth century, each group regarded itself as dominant and tried to demonstrate its superiority. Powhatan captured and adopted John Smith and seems to have appointed him as a werowance for the newcomers, the equivalent of a village chief in his confederacy. The English therefore constituted another subordinate tribe, and Smith was a kind of subchief to Powhatan. The English tried to crown Powhatan as a vassal of King James I. Powhatan refused to come to Jamestown, and he would not kneel when the English came to him. He did accept the crown they offered him, however: such gifts were appropriate from vassals.

European diplomats had to learn new codes of behavior. Agents of imperial powers eager for allies or of colonial governments anxious to acquire Indian lands had to curb their desire to "get down to business." Indian councils sometimes went on for weeks, with speakers performing elaborate ceremonies of condolence to prepare the minds of the participants, giving lengthy recitals of past meetings, and even recapitulating what the previous speaker had said. There was much activity away from the council and lengthy deliberation to achieve consensus. Europeans and Americans often tried to hurry things along, but not always with success. Quaker William Savery noted of the negotiations between U.S. commissioners and Iroquois delegates at the Treaty of Canandaigua in 1794: "It is to no purpose to say you are tired of waiting, they will only tell you calmly, 'Brother, you have your way of doing business and we have ours; we desire you would sit easily on your seats.'" Like many colonial diplomats before him, Savery resigned himself to doing things the Indian way: "Patience, then, becomes our only remedy," he said.

Wampum belts and calumets or peace pipes were indispensable in the successful conduct of intertribal and interethnic diplomacy. The calumet is popularly assumed to have been a thoroughly Indian artifact, but French and Métis traders spread the calumet and its associated ceremonies throughout much of North America. Red-stone pipes, their stems decorated with feathers, served as passports through Indian country, and the ceremony of smoking a pipe as a sign of peace was observed from the St. Lawrence River to the mouth of the Mississippi. The calumet ceremony was not just a formality but a prerequisite for negotiation and an essential foundation for good relations. When La Salle entered the villages of the Quapaws in 1682, the Indians greeted the French with a calumet dance, a feast, and an exchange of gifts; in this way they established ritual ties with the newcomers and gave them status within their social system.

Wampum, from the Algonkian word *wampumpeag,* was originally fashioned from quahog shells drilled and strung into belts. Mass-produced cylindrical beads, obtained from European traders, soon replaced traditional shells. Woodland Indian people used wampum for a variety of purposes, as gifts, jewelry, and trade items, but its most widespread use was as an essential lubricant of council-fire diplomacy. Intricate designs, usually of purple against a white background, conveyed messages and ideas; sometimes the symbolism was more graphic and more simple: belts painted red signified war; white belts, peace.

European emissaries and Indian agents found they had to learn the language of wampum diplomacy and familiarize themselves with its protocol. Indian speakers often opened council proceedings with lengthy speeches of welcome, urging the participants to have good thoughts and open minds, and offering belts of wampum to symbolically remove any impediments to the talks. Speakers punctuated their words by handing wampum belts across the council fire. The wampum signified that what they said was true and came from the heart; taking the wampum belts meant that the recipients had heard, understood, and accepted. Words not accompanied by wampum might not be binding; rejecting or, as sometimes happened, casting the wampum dramatically aside indicated a refusal to accept what the speaker said and perhaps even a complete breakdown of negotiations. The wampum belts given and received served as a mnemonic record of what took place at councils and treaty meetings and constituted a tribe's record of its foreign relations. The Iroquois deposited their wampum belts at Onondaga, the physical and political center of their league of five (later six) nations. The wampum keepers were responsible for safe storage of the belts and for interpreting their meaning. Indian speakers, meeting in council with Europeans or delegates from other tribes, were able to produce wampum records from previous meetings and cite chapter and verse of what had happened, reminding the parties of their commitments and pointing out where transgressions had occurred.

The French and the British devoted considerable attention to calumet and wampum diplomacy. Recognizing the extent to which their imperial ambitions in North America hinged upon Native American support, these Old World rivals dispatched agents to live in Indian country where they were to cultivate key chiefs and learn the language of Indian diplomacy. The British Indian department, contrary to popular stereotypes, was not composed of haughty redcoated officers in powdered wigs who thought it beneath their dignity to sit around a council fire talking with "savages." It employed English, Scots, Irish, French Canadian, Indian, and Métis people, who spent much of their lives in Indian country, often wore Indian clothing, and generally sympathized with Indian people. On occasion, members of the

An Indian orator holding a wampum belt addresses Colonel Henry Bouquet. (From William Smith, *An Historical Account of the Expedition against the Ohio Indians in the year 1764* [Philadelphia, 1766]. Dartmouth College Library)

British Indian department identified more strongly with the interests of their Indian friends and relatives than they did with the interests of the British Crown. Men such as Sir William Johnson among the Mohawks, Alexander Cameron among the Cherokees, and Matthew Elliott among the Shawnees married into the tribe and served as the key link between the Indians and their British "father." Mohawks at the Albany Congress in 1755 referred to Johnson as "our lips and our tongue and our mouth." His home at Johnson Hall in New York became a meeting ground for British and Indian diplomats: "All the Six Nations and other Indians to the Westward stop at his house," said Cadwallader Colden.

Indian agents were ambassadors among their own relatives, and in the swirling waters of international, interethnic, intertribal, and intratribal politics, they needed to be skilled practitioners of the art and the protocol of forest diplomacy. They had to be able to follow what was going on in Indian council meetings and in private. They needed to know whom to court, whom to avoid offending, and how different individuals could be expected to react in different circumstances. Conrad Weiser had more experience in Indian diplomacy than almost any other white man. An adopted Mohawk, he served as an interpreter and as Pennsylvania's "ambassador to the Indian nations"—he was virtually ubiquitous in colonial Indian affairs. In the summer of 1743, entrusted with a delicate mission to Onondaga to smooth over matters between Pennsylvania and the Iroquois, Weiser sought out the Onondaga spokesman, Canasatego, for a private meeting in the bushes: "I would tell him all my Business, and beg his Advice how to speak to everything when the Council should be met." Knowing when to remain silent was sometimes as important as knowing what to say.

For their part, Indians had to learn how Europeans conducted treaty negotiations. Just as Europeans learned to adopt Indian ceremonies, wampum diplomacy, and metaphors in their meetings with tribal delegations, so Indians had to become accustomed to European symbolism and new ways of doing business. Comanche Indians visiting the governor of New Mexico in 1762 carried crucifixes as a sign of peace. Indians dealt with Europeans who insisted on referring to themselves as "father" and to Indians as "children," yet who rarely understood that in many Indian societies the role of father carried more obligation than authority. Indian delegates became accustomed to, and sometimes came to expect, rum and frequent toasts as both an "ice breaker" and an incentive to reaching agreement. They had to put up with scribes writing down their words and live with the knowledge that, once interpreted and put on paper, those words could take on a life of their own and a very different meaning from what the speaker intended. Indians, as members of an oral culture, normally attached far greater importance to the words and wampum exchanged at a treaty conference than to the written record made of the talks. Europeans, as members of a culture that valued the written word, attached primary importance to the final treaty document rather than to the discussions that preceded and produced it. Their written documents sometimes bore little resemblance to what Indian delegates remembered they had agreed to, something the Onondaga orator Canasatego attributed to the "Pen-and-Ink Work" of the colonists. Indians also had to accept that, in European eyes, granting land meant more than simply allowing colonists to share its resources; the property was permanently conveyed from Indian to white hands.

European ambitions, innovations, understandings, and misunderstandings, imposed on a Native American background, gave diplomacy in North America a new and unique character and appearance. Indian treaty councils, by which so much of America passed from Indians to whites, grew out of the meeting of Indian and Europeans in colonial times and continued through much of the nineteenth century, until Congress in 1871 declared an end to treaty making, preferring to regard Indian people as wards of the government rather than as separate nations. But the United States put a new slant on Indian diplomacy long before 1871.

In colonial America, where Indian power remained formidable and many sought Indian favor, Europeans paid careful attention to protocol and made a point of following Native American procedures. When the American colonies became the United States and European rivals withdrew from the picture, however, diplomacy in North America entered a new era. The "middle ground" arrangements that first the French and then the British had maintained with Indian tribes dissolved as American invaders discarded old ways of conducting Indian diplomacy and attempted to dictate from a position of strength. The new nation was interested less in having Indian allies and more in having Indian land. The need to cultivate Indian peoples and to play the diplomatic game according to Indian rules declined. In their dealings with Indian tribes after the Revolution, United States treaty commissioners dispensed with much of the old protocol and council-fire rhetoric. They took the position that the Indians had forfeited their lands by siding with the

British in the war and that Indian lands now belonged to the United States "by right of conquest." Sometimes with troops at their backs, they dictated terms to Indian delegates, demanding hostages and territory as the price of peace, and rejected wampum belts with contempt. Such posturing was not new in Indian diplomacy, and, for a time, Indian power demonstrated the flimsy nature of American pretensions to having obtained their land by right of conquest. But American power was new, growing, and here to stay. Future negotiations would be conducted on American, not on Native American, terms. The diplomacy of North America was never the same again.

Seven

:✦:

New Nomads and True Nomads

POPULAR STEREOTYPES AND many history books tell us that European colonists were settlers and Indians were nomads. In reality, most Indian peoples in the eastern woodlands and many in other areas of the country were horticulturalists; they moved with the seasons and harvested a variety of resources. When European immigrants arrived in America, many of them moved frequently, even frantically, it must have seemed to Indian eyes, their migrations motivated by the desire for more land or for distance from neighbors, rather than by the seasonal exploitation of what land they already occupied. Confronted with the influx of thousands of Europeans, Indian people must have felt much like the citizens of imperial Rome as hordes of Huns, Goths, and Vandals invaded their world. In the wake of such invasions, many Indian peoples became migrants themselves. Their societies disrupted by wars and diseases, Indians moved to new locations and often built multi-ethnic communities out of refugee camps. The original American pioneers, Indians became pioneers again as they tried to rebuild their world and their lives, often in unfamiliar environments and surrounded by strangers.

Many tribal legends fix the origins of particular Indian peoples firmly in their historic homeland. Although most scholars accept the theory of migration across the Bering Strait (between Siberia and Alaska) during the ice age as the explanation of ancient human presence in America, many Native Americans reject this "first immigrants" interpretation in favor of their own stories of genesis in this continent. Some tribes recall their own ancient migrations in legend—the Choctaws and the Chickasaws came to their Mississippi homelands from the west, for example—but all seem to have developed their identity as a people in connection with a particular place. Legends explained how they came to be where they were; past lives rooted them to their homeland. Indians did not wander aimlessly across the land; they belonged to it.

Nevertheless, Indians did travel frequently and extensively long before Europeans arrived. Moccasin paths and canoe routes, networks of commerce and communication, crisscrossed the country and linked Indian communities as far apart as the Ohio Valley and the Gulf of Mexico, the Great Lakes and New England. Indian paddlers covered immense distances following the watercourses of North America. In the twentieth century, writer John McPhee heard the story of an Indian living in a remote community in Ontario who developed an urge to see New York City. "He put his canoe in the water and started out. From stream to lake to pond to portage, he made his way a hundred miles to Lake Timiskaming, and its outlet, the Ottawa River. He went down the Ottawa to the St. Lawrence, down the St. Lawrence to the Richelieu, up the Richelieu to Lake Champlain, and from Lake Champlain to the Hudson. At the Seventy-ninth Street Boat Basin, he left the canoe in the custody of attendants and walked on into town."

James Fenimore Cooper and other writers created and perpetuated the image of North America before European settlement as a "trackless wilderness." In reality, the continent was laced with well-traveled trails. At first glance, rock carvings on the Colorado River Reservation in Arizona appear to have been placed haphazardly, but they belong to an ancient system of markers that pointed Indian runners to trails spanning vast distances. In the eastern woodlands, Indian paths, created by moccasined feet and sometimes marked by blazed trees, formed an elaborate web of trails. The Great Warriors' Path, for example, was fed by Indian trails from all parts of Iroquois country and headed south to Shamokin (Sunbury, Pennsylvania), where several offshoots led south, east, and west, connecting with other trail systems. Although the path served Iroquois war parties heading south to raid the Cherokees or the Catawbas, it was also traveled by Iroquois ambassadors going to meet delegates from other tribes or commissioners from Pennsylvania, Maryland, and Virginia.

"When an Indian lost his way in the woods, as he sometimes did," remarks Paul Wallace, tracing the numerous Indian paths in Pennsylvania, "it was as likely as not because there were *too many* tracks and he had taken the wrong one." Indians possessed remarkable skill in woodcraft and could make their way through the forest with an ease that impressed Europeans, but they "had the same reason for keeping to the beaten path that motorists have for preferring paved highways to plowed fields." Diplomats and messengers covered enormous distances along such paths. People visited friends and relatives for social, economic, and ceremonial purposes. The traffic along woodland trails made the forest, in Wallace's words, "a busy place." Travelers frequently met others on the trail, smoked with them, and shared hospitality before continuing on their journeys.

Many Indian paths were so well planned and kept the level so well, even in mountainous country, there was little reason to change their routes before the coming of the automobile, and sometimes not even then. Indian trails became bridle paths, then wagon roads, and finally motor highways. As the British struggled to move troops and supplies through the forests during the Seven Years' War, General John Forbes acknowledged that the Indians "have foot paths . . . through these deserts, by the help of which we make our roads." An Indian path that for centuries had followed the great curve of the Appalachian Mountains became the Virginia Road by the mid-eighteenth century (present U.S. 11) and the major route for settlers migrating into the southern backcountry.

Indian peoples knew intimately the homelands they inhabited, but many knew their continent as well. Consequently, when Europeans arrived in North America, Indian people were able to show them the way, pointing out rivers and trails, interpreting the landscape, leading them inland to other tribes, and providing information on tribes they had yet to meet. As the French historian Fernand Braudel observed, "Europeans often rediscovered the world using other peoples' eyes, legs and brains." Indians participated in the European rediscovery of America, providing guides, maps, and a fund of knowledge derived from extensive travels. European explorers and fur traders followed Indian canoe routes into the heart of the continent. Indians traced maps in the sand with their toes and fingers, etched them on birch bark, and drew them on deerskins and buffalo hides. They showed Frenchmen the way from the St. Lawrence River to the Ohio, from the Great Lakes to the Mississippi, and out on to the Great Plains.

Beginning with Cartier and Champlain, the French made a practice of kidnaping Indians to serve as guides. Indians showed Spaniards the way across the American Southwest and from Florida to the Mississippi. Hernando de Soto's expedition benefited from having an Indian guide who had "such thorough knowledge of the country that the night before he could tell everything they would find on the road the following day." In 1540, an Indian whom Spaniards called "the Turk" guided the expedition of Don Francisco Vásquez de Coronado in its search for "Quivira," a fabled rich city rumored to be somewhere on the plains. Instead of finding cities of gold, the Turk led Coronado to the Caddo Indian villages near Wichita, Kansas. The Spaniards strangled him. A map drawn by a Yavapai Indian guided Juan de Oñate across the Arizona desert to the Colorado River in 1605; an Indian drew René Robert Cavelier de La Salle a map of the Mississippi River in 1681.

Englishman John Lawson, who traveled widely in the Carolina upcountry in 1700–1701, said that Indians were "expert Travellers" who could locate riverheads five hundred miles away and, given pen and ink, could draw accurate maps of the country. On the northern plains in the late eighteenth century, French Canadian trader Jean Baptiste Truteau saw Indians make accurate skin maps of the countries with which they were familiar. "Nothing is wanting but the degrees of latitude and longitude," he said. During their two and a half years in the West, Lewis and Clark solicited thirty maps, sketches, and cartographic devices from Indian informants. The Mandan villages on the upper Missouri, where the expedition spent the winter of 1804–5, were a thriving trade rendezvous and gave the American explorers access to knowledge and information about routes and peoples as far west as the Rocky Mountains. When the expedition reached those mountains, a Shoshone chief created a temporary cartographic masterpiece, building up piles of sand to depict the daunting topography they were about to cross. Like their European predecessors, Lewis and Clark depended on Indians to point the way across America.

Indians no doubt also led strangers *away* from places—sacred sites, friendly villages, treasured resources. Pueblo Indians almost certainly encouraged Coronado to explore the Great Plains as a way of getting rid of the Spaniards. But European penetration of America could not have been what it was without Indian participation in the process. Armed with knowledge gained from Indians, Europeans produced maps of their own, which often became instruments of conquest. Maps not only provided valuable information to colonizers, soldiers, and land speculators; they also helped dispossess Indians and render them invisible. European cartographers routinely designated areas where Indian people lived as "wilderness," empty land awaiting settlement by Europeans.

The routes Europeans found with Indian help became fissures in Indian America, down which European explorers, traders, missionaries, and land speculators ventured. In time, the trickle became a flood. These same routes became the arteries by which immigrants from Europe headed into Indian country, or along which colonists felt themselves pushed by growing population pressures in the East. Sometimes population moved in a series of chain reactions: in the decade before the Revolution, most immigrants to Kentucky came from North Carolina, which was itself being flooded by emigrants from Virginia and Pennsylvania, and from Germany and Scotland. The pioneers who confronted Indians in that "dark and bloody ground" were the product of a vast series of population pressures that reached through the eastern colonies, back across the Atlantic, and into the heart of Europe. Sometimes, though, individuals and groups ventured far afield rather than shunting on to the next "available" land.

The massive movement of peoples from Europe, across the Atlantic, and into the interior of North America was a momentous event in human history. At first, American migration was simply an additional outlet for people already in motion, a spillover of patterns in Europe, which sent people from the German states east as well as west, and which sent a constant flood of humanity from throughout Britain to London. In time, however, the American magnet began to shape European movements. American land speculators looked to Europe to recruit the settlers they needed to realize a lucrative return on their investments; agents, family ties, and rumor directed immigrants to areas of America where they could expect to find their own kind. In Bernard Bailyn's words, "We know only in the vaguest way who the hundreds of thousands of individuals who settled in British North America were, where precisely they came from, why they came, and how they lived out their lives." Their migrations involved "an untraceable multitude of local, small-scale exoduses and colonizations, the continuous creations of new frontiers and ever-widening circumferences, the complex intermingling of peoples in the expanding border areas, and in the end the massive transfer to the western hemisphere of people from Africa, from the European mainland, and above all from the Anglo-Celtic offshore islands of Europe." Bailyn found the immigrants' population shifts in America "strange, irrational"; "multitudinous and complex almost beyond description"; "mysterious and chaotic." They translated into "almost frantic expansion." If European movements in North America so bewildered a historian surveying them from the vantage point of twentieth-century Harvard, how must they have appeared to Indian people in the eighteenth century?

In the seventeenth century, European immigration to North America had been significant, even devastating, but it was small-scale compared to what was to follow. Europeans established a series of footholds: the French in Canada and the Great Lakes; the Dutch, on the Hudson; the Swedes and Finns, along the Delaware River; the Spaniards, in New Mexico and Florida; and the English, in the Chesapeake and New England, along with some Germans and Scots—and began the creation of their New World societies, sometimes with the help of imported African labor. Population grew steadily, even dramatically. In the eighteenth century, however, internal population growth was less by natural causes than by massive immigration. In 1650, perhaps fifty thousand Europeans lived on the eastern shores of North America: New France had a mere two thousand colonists; New Netherland, a little over three thousand; and New England already outstripped its rivals with more than twenty-two thousand. In 1680, European population edged toward one hundred fifty thousand. By 1750, that number had jumped past one million. Immigrants from Europe, often victims themselves of wrenching economic changes, community destruction, and population dislocation, were settling and resettling large areas of North America. They came from dozens of countries, hundreds of regions, and thousands of communities, leaving a continent where land was scarce, heavily populated, and beyond most people's reach, for a world where land was plentiful, supposedly unoccupied, and "free."

Most seventeenth-century immigrants were English, and many came from the nobility, the gentry, and the yeoman classes. In the eighteenth century, most of the immigrants were non-English and came from the poorer classes in Germany and Switzerland, Scotland and Ireland. Many came as indentured servants, bound to labor for four to seven years in return for passage, food, clothing, lodging, and eventual freedom. They endured appalling shipboard conditions and suffered a mortality rate not much different from that of African slaves who were also being transported to America, crowded aboard slave ships in chains. On reaching America, many of the new immigrants pushed west, building new communities on the frontiers where they rubbed shoulders and exchanged blows with the Indian inhabitants.

An estimated ninety thousand German-speaking settlers, fleeing famine, war, and disease in Europe, sailed to the American colonies in the eighteenth century. They came from many different regions—the Palatine, Alsace, Baden, Bavaria, Hesse, and Switzerland—and their migrations were part of larger population movements within German lands. But they tended to migrate together and settle together. William Penn invited German Quakers, Moravians, and Mennonites to settle in Pennsylvania, and several thousand did so in the late seventeenth century. In the early 1700s, there came thousands of German Lutherans and Reformed settlers, attracted by the promise of cheap land and religious toleration. Since they spoke Deutsch, they became known as Pennsylvania Dutch, although some Pennsylvania Dutch actually were Dutch, from the border regions of Holland and Germany. People of German descent also settled in Maine, New York, New Jersey, Maryland, Virginia, Georgia, and the Carolinas. The path of eighteenth-century German settlement can be seen in place names for Herkimer, Mannheim, and New Berlin in New York; through Germantown, Bethlehem, Hanover, and Gettysburg, Pennsylvania; to Fredericksburg, Virginia; and New Bern, South Carolina. German place names, languages, and customs became prevalent in the mid-Atlantic region. Benjamin Franklin, seeing German population growth in Pennsylvania by mid-century, feared that they would "swarm into our settlements, and by herding together, establish their language and manners, to the exclusion of ours."

David Hackett Fischer has identified four great migrations from the British Isles to North America before the American Revolution. From 1629, when the Great Migration began with the settlement of Boston, until 1640, the mainstream comprised English Puritans from the eastern counties, such as East Anglia, to Massachusetts. Puritans eventually dominated the colonies of Massachusetts, Rhode Island, Connecticut, and New Hampshire. The mid-seventeenth century witnessed substantial migration from Kent, Devon, Warwickshire, and Northamptonshire to Virginia. Between 1675 and 1715, Quakers from the North Midlands fueled a steady migration to the Delaware Valley. For most of the eighteenth century, however, immigrants from the northern British and Celtic borderlands—Ulster, Scotland, Northumberland, Yorkshire, and Lancashire—led the British invasion of America. In Fischer's words, those immigrants "gradually became the dominant English-speaking culture in a broad belt of territory that extended from the highlands of Appalachia through much of the Old Southwest." They brought with them Old World habits of border belligerence, which shaped their societies and their lives on the American frontier. Alexis de Tocqueville, in the early nineteenth century, remarked, "I consider the people of the United States as that portion of the English people who are commissioned to explore the forests of the new world." But British migration to America drew people from widely different regions, ranks, religions, and generations.

The Scotch-Irish had a long history of emigration. When James VI of Scotland assumed the throne as James I of England, he invited Lowland Scots to settle in Ulster, promising inexpensive rents and religious toleration, as a means of colonizing Ireland. More than forty thousand Lowland Scots took advantage of the offer between 1610 and 1640. Oliver Cromwell continued the policy, and according to one estimate, one hundred thousand Scots lived in Ireland by 1672. More people went to Ireland after the defeat of James II at the battle of the Boyne. Then in the eighteenth century, famines racked Ireland, landlords raised rents, and Presbyterian Scotch-Irish endured growing persecution. Almost three hundred thousand Scotch-Irish migrated to America in the 1700s, "one of the most remarkable folk movements in history." Mostly Protestant and poor farmers, they flooded into many of the same backcountry areas favored by the Germans, and many more trekked south into the Carolinas and Georgia or crossed the Appalachians into Indian country. Germans and Scotch-Irish alike were attracted to Pennsylvania, where they could expect to find fertile lands and religious toleration. Philadelphia became a major port of entry, and Pennsylvania became the gateway for Scotch-Irish invasion and settlement of large areas of Indian America to the south and west. By the 1760s, the Great Philadelphia Wagon Road, which followed old Indian trails from Pennsylvania to Georgia, was the most heavily traveled route in North America— Scots, Ulstermen, Germans, English, and Welsh streamed down it. Scotch-Irish migrants moved rapidly and squatted quickly. James Logan, provincial secretary of Pennsylvania, expressed the commonwealth's alarm over the influx, noting that the new immigrants "crowd in where they are not wanted" and boldly take "any spot of vacant land they find." When the authorities tried to expel them and burned down their cabins, the Scotch-Irish simply moved on and squatted again. Logan noted that "the Indians themselves are alarmed at the swarms of strangers," but colonial officials encouraged Scotch-Irish people to settle on the western frontiers, where they served as a first line of defense or as shock troops against the Indians. Pennsylvania's non-Indian population leaped from 30,000 in 1720 to 180,000 in 1760.

The fifteen-year period from the defeat of the French in 1760 to the outbreak of the Revolution in 1775 brought at least 221,500 immigrants to the British colonies in North America, including more than 55,000 Protestant Irish, more than 40,000 Scots, more than 30,000 English, and at least 12,000 people from the German states and Switzerland. Highland Scots fleeing hard times, high rents, and the suppression of the clan system in the aftermath of the Jacobite Rebellion in 1745 made up a substantial proportion of the prerevolutionary immigration. Emigration to America became epidemic in the Highlands, and British authorities feared that it would depopulate the area. The mobility of the immigrants and their expectations of access to Indian land rendered British policies of frontier regulation unworkable, contributing to escalating Indian-white conflicts and to the alienation of colonists from the mother country that culminated in the American Revolution.

Between 1700 and 1775, more than 250,000 African slaves were transported to the American colonies. They came in chains and had no expectation of freedom, but they added to the effects of population movements felt throughout Indian America.

✦

European peoples moving into and across America generated successive reactions that affected and dislocated Indian peoples throughout the continent. American history textbooks, and some books on Indian history, frequently contain maps that purport to show the location of Indian tribes in 1492, thus "setting the stage" for what was to follow. Such maps often underestimate or totally ignore the reshuffling of Indian populations that occurred in the wake of European contact. The mobility and movement that were integral parts of traditional Indian life gave way to forced migrations. Indian peoples fled new diseases, were scattered by warfare, pursued new economic opportunities and new ways of life, were attracted or repulsed by mission villages, were edged out by white settlers, retreated from white soldiers, or gravitated toward forts for trade or protection. They jostled for position with new neighbors, and sometimes they created new communities and even new tribal or individual identities in the crucible of change and movement that was early America.

When Europeans first encountered a group of Indian people, they usually tried to identify them as members of a particular "tribe," and the identity that the Europeans gave them generally stuck. Europeans often failed to realize that their concept of tribe had little meaning to many Indian societies, which were bound by family, clan, and village rather than by a larger tribal allegiance. Moreover, by the time Europeans reached Indian country, the communities they encountered were often in a state of flux: the ripple effects of European diseases, European trade goods, and European wars, felt long before Indian people ever laid eyes on a European person, took their toll on the structure of Indian societies. What European observers thought were tribes might be refugee camps or new communities in the making. As James Merrell has demonstrated, the English were bewildered by the congeries of independent peoples scattered throughout the river valleys of the Carolina interior and by the confusion and profusion of names. In an effort to bring order out of chaos, the English seized on the name Catawba to define all these peoples. The name obscured complex ethnic realities, but it stuck.

Spanish invasion of America generated demographic disruption across large areas of what is now the southern United States. As de Soto's conquistadors cut through the Southeast the human landscape of the region changed forever. War and disease sent populations plummeting. Survivors reeled out of the invaders' way: villages relocated downriver or into the uplands, and much of northwestern Georgia and eastern Tennessee became depopulated, allowing Cherokee-speaking peoples to move into the area. Florida suffered massive depopulation in the century after de Soto's men passed through. Those Timucuans, Guales, and Apalachees who survived resettled around Christian missions after Spaniards built St. Augustine in 1565. In 1703-4, South Carolina militiamen and their Indian allies destroyed Florida's mission communities, carrying thousands of Timucuans and Apalachees into slavery. The rest scattered, and one group fled west. With the exception of a few Native enclaves huddled around St. Augustine, Florida had become a virtual population vacuum.

By the time William Bartram traveled through the Southeast on the eve of the American Revolution, the loose alliance of towns stretching across Georgia and Alabama known as the Creek confederacy consisted of "many tribes, or remnants of conquered nations, united." But the fluid nature of the confederacy allowed groups to move away and establish new communities. During the eighteenth century, various groups of Creeks gradually separated from the parent confederacy and went to the depopulated areas of northern Florida. The Spaniards called these people *cimarrón*, meaning wild folk or runaways, and in time they developed their own identity as Seminoles. The Seminoles built new societies on the fertile Alachua prairies, herding wild cattle that had once belonged to the mission communities; they also built large canoes from cypress trees and traveled to Cuba, where they traded deerskins, dried fish, and honey for Spanish coffee, sugar, tobacco, and alcohol.

Many northeastern Indian peoples also experienced relocations as rival European powers penetrated their world. People competed and shifted position to gain access to European trading posts and trade routes. The Hudson's Bay Company, which began operations under charter from Charles II in 1670, depended on Indian middlemen to convey furs obtained from more distant hunting bands to its posts on the Bay. Crees, Assiniboines, and Ojibwas were successful as middlemen in the late seventeenth and early eighteenth centuries. After 1763, rival traders from Montreal came to Indian country to deal directly with the Indians who did the trapping. The Hudson's Bay Company had no choice but to follow suit, and the Crees and Assiniboines lost their lucrative middleman position. Some bands migrated west to try to maintain that role; others relocated to pursue new roles, to supply, for example, the new fur trading-posts with buffalo meat. Competition for trade, exhaustion of fur-bearing animal populations, exploiting new territories, and responding to changing market forces, all caused recurrent population movements in Indian America.

In some cases the demographic repercussions were dramatic. The Iroquois "Beaver Wars" of the mid-seventeenth century destroyed the Huron Confederacy. Surviving Hurons amalgamated into Iroquois communities or took refuge with other tribes. Hurons who resettled in northern Ohio, along with refugees from the Neutral, Erie, and Tobacco nations who had suffered similar dispersal, became known as Wyandots. Many Indian peoples whom Frenchmen met in the Great Lakes region in the seventeenth century were already refugees, trying to build new communities in a world of chaos and violence.

The Shawnee Indians, who lived along the Ohio River when the French encountered them in the seventeenth century, also migrated because of pressure from the Iroquois. One group went to Illinois in the 1680s, then accepted an invitation from the Delawares to return east and settle on the Susquehanna River in Pennsylvania. Other Shawnees moved south and east toward the Carolinas, where the English first met them. Many Shawnees remained in the Southeast and developed strong ties with the Creek Indians in Georgia and Alabama. As English pressure increased, however, the majority of the tribe retreated back toward their traditional homelands. By the mid-eighteenth century, most Shawnees had regrouped in south-central

Ohio. There, they found themselves on the front lines of the battle between Indians and whites for the Ohio River. That battle gradually swung against them, and the Shawnees retreated farther and farther into northwestern Ohio, joining other displaced Indians in new, multiethnic communities. Traditionally, the Shawnees comprised five separate divisions, each with its own responsibility—such as war, politics, healing, or ritual—and each with its own villages. By the end of the Revolution, those distinctions became blurred as Shawnees from different groups crowded into new communities. By 1792, an estimated two thousand people lived in seven main towns—three Shawnee, two Delaware, one Miami, and an Anglo-French trading post—all within ten miles of the confluence of the Auglaize and Maumee Rivers. After General Anthony Wayne defeated the northwestern tribes at the battle of Fallen Timbers in 1794 and Indian leaders ceded most of Ohio to the United States in 1795, some Shawnees moved west to continue their resistance in Indiana and Illinois. Finally pushed across the Mississippi early in the nineteenth century, they met other Shawnees. Some time during the American Revolution, the Shawnee nation split, with about half the tribe leaving Ohio and moving eventually to Spanish-claimed territory in Missouri, where they built new communities near Cape Girardeau. In time, most Shawnees made new homes in Kansas, Oklahoma, and Texas.

The experience of the Shawnees' Delaware neighbors and relatives was similar. The Delaware or Lenni Lenape people first met Europeans when the Dutch landed in the Hudson Valley. Edged out of their homelands in Delaware, New Jersey, and eastern Pennsylvania in the seventeenth century, Delawares moved west to Ohio and then on to new homes in Ontario, Kansas, and Oklahoma. The nineteenth-century American artist George Catlin said that "no other tribe on the Continent has been so much moved and jostled about by civilized invasions." As place names of European origin took over in what was once Indian country throughout the eastern woodlands, so, in time, those Indian place names appeared west of the Mississippi. Exiled Indian people rebuilt communities and named them Chicopee, Genesoe, Seneca, Oneida, Cherokee, Chillicothe, and Miami in Oklahoma, Kansas, and elsewhere.

Some New England "tribes" produced "satellite communities," which sometimes asserted their own independence. Indians in John Eliot's praying towns in Massachusetts lived apart from their relatives and assumed new identities as members of their towns. Although some northeastern Indian peoples migrated west in the wake of European contact, many New England natives went north. The defeat of Metacomet's resistance movement in King Philip's War (1675–76) produced an Algonkian diaspora as Indians from southern and central New England fled north into Abenaki country. Some joined Abenaki communities; others kept going until they reached French Canada. Old tribal ties were sometimes replaced, sometimes supplemented by ties that bound Indians into new Christian communities. Tribal group- ings broke down, and fluidity and connections between groups increased. Individuals who lived and moved in this world often assumed multiple identities in the historical records. An Indian might be described as a Nip- muc, a Sokoki, a Pennacook, a Penobscot, or a St. Francis Indian, or as all of these, depending upon whether Europeans saw him in Massachusetts, Ver- mont, New Hampshire, Maine, or Quebec.

The Abenakis in turn came under pressure to defend their lands and culture from English expansion, and they pulled back from the invaders. Many withdrew into remote regions of their homeland, beyond the reach of English soldiers and out of sight of English settlers. Others trekked north. On the banks of the St. Lawrence River, French missions beckoned, promising the Indians salvation from both the English and their own "heathen" ways. New communities of displaced Abenakis and other New England Indians grew up at places like St. Francis, Bécancour, and Three Rivers. As in Florida and California, Indian people in Canada who built new lives and new com- munities within the sound of mission bells sometimes were identified by the nearby mission rather than by their tribal affiliation. Nominally Catholic, "St. Francis Indians" returned south during the French and Indian wars and raided the English forts and farms in their former homelands. Other Abe- nakis ventured farther afield. An Abenaki accompanied La Salle on his expe- dition down the Mississippi; Abenakis were living in Indian communities in the Midwest in about 1750; and Spanish records reported Abenakis west of the Mississippi after the American Revolution, all testimony to the continuing displacement of New England's Native American population.

Indians from seven tribes in southern New England, badly reduced in numbers and land by the time of the Revolution, moved west and created a new community called Brothertown, in Oneida country in New York. They found only temporary refuge there and were soon forced west again, but the community was the genesis of the Brothertown tribe, located today in Wisconsin.

Although most Indian people left New England by land, some went by sea. In the aftermath of the Pequot War and King Philip's War, the English sold many New England Indians, mainly women and children, into slavery in the Caribbean. After destruction of their traditional economies in the eighteenth century, many Indian men, from places such as Mashpee, Martha's Vineyard, and Nantucket, took work as sailors and whalers. The employment allowed them to make a living, but the work was dangerous. Husbands and fathers were away from home for months and sometimes years on end, and occasionally they were buried at sea or in some distant land. Many Indian people who remained in New England endured poverty and became transients as local officials moved them from town to town rather than accept responsibility for paying them poor relief.

For much of the colonial era, the Iroquois Five Nations of upstate New York held their territory intact against Indian and European alike. The philosophy of the Iroquois League envisaged embracing many peoples under the shelter of the Great Tree of Peace, and displaced Indians from throughout the eastern woodlands took refuge there. Many individuals were adopted and incorporated into Iroquois communities. By the middle of the seventeenth century, Jesuit missionaries reported that Iroquois villages contained "more Foreigners than natives of the country": peoples from seven different tribes lived with the Onondagas; and from as many as eleven, with the Senecas. In 1722, the Five Nations became Six when the Tuscaroras, migrating north after a bloody war with the English in their Carolina homelands, joined the league as a junior member. Other refugees settled along the banks of the upper Susquehanna River, where they also served to protect the southern borders of Iroquoia.

There was also migration away from Iroquoia. Some Iroquois migrated west in the eighteenth century. Taking up residence in the Ohio Valley, they became known as Mingoes, mixed with Delawares, Shawnees, and others, and established new communities, independent of the French, British, or Iroquois. Others, mainly Mohawks, converted to Catholicism. Leaving their relatives in New York, they moved to French mission villages on the St. Lawrence. Two thirds of the Mohawks were living in Canada by 1700. "We are All Scattered from Our Castles and formerly We used to Live together," Mohawks said in 1741. Caughnawaga emerged as a new community or "tribe" of Catholic Mohawks; St. Regis was founded on the south bank of the St. Lawrence in 1747 by disaffected people from Caughnawaga. The groups who moved to Caughnawaga and St. Regis became the modern communities of

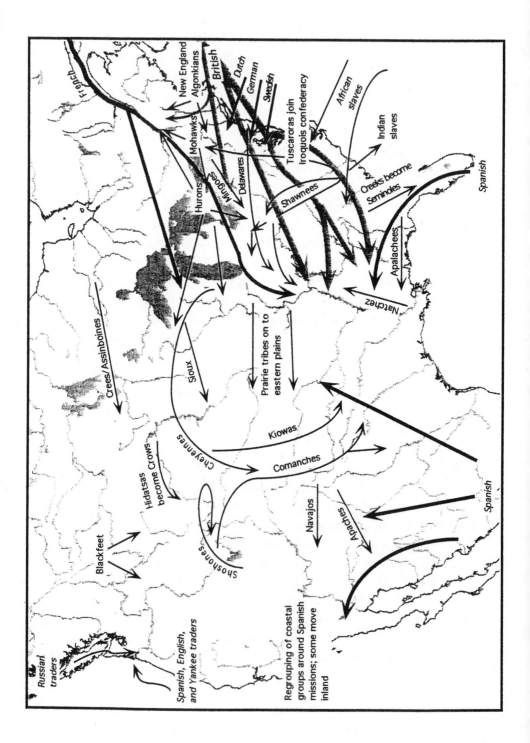

Kahnawake and Akwesasne. Pro-French Onondagas founded a new community at Oswegatchie, near present-day Ogdensburg.

Iroquois power and diplomacy kept the league essentially intact and in control of its homeland until the time of the Revolution. But the Revolution split the Iroquois. Most Mohawks, Onondagas, Cayugas, and Senecas fought for the British; most Oneidas and Tuscaroras supported the Americans. Driven from their Mohawk Valley homes, Joseph Brant and his Mohawks relocated to the British fort at Niagara, which rapidly emerged as the prime source for British attacks on the American frontier and as a refugee center for displaced Indian peoples. General John Sullivan's expedition into Iroquois country in 1779 drove the Senecas and many other refugees to Niagara. By November 1779, there were 3,329 Indians drawing rations at Fort Niagara: Mohawks, Senecas, Cayugas, Onondagas, and Tuscaroras; Delawares, Chugnuts, Shawnees, Nanticokes, and Mahicans; and other peoples caught up in the revolutionary diaspora in the eastern woodlands. After the war, most of the Senecas returned home and settled on reservations—the land was now claimed by the United States. Brant, the Mohawks, and many other peoples preferred exile in Canada to life in the United States, and they accepted a grant of land from the British on the Grand River in Ontario. The Iroquois League was permanently split, with one council fire at Onondaga, another on the new Six Nations Reserve in Ontario. The Oneidas, allies of the American revolutionaries, sought shelter in squalid refugee camps around Schenectady during the war. The Americans promised to protect their land, but speculators and agents swarmed into Oneida country once the Revolution was won. By the early nineteenth century, most Oneidas had migrated west, to new homes in Wisconsin and Ontario.

The Cherokees also experienced division and relocation during the Revolution. Cherokees who preferred to move farther west and continue the fight rather than accept the Americans' peace terms built new towns on the Chickamauga River in Tennessee and acted independently from the older towns. They became known as the Chickamaugas.

Similar demographic disruption occurred in the West. After de Soto's passage through Arkansas, human populations collapsed and animal popu-

---

Map 2. A New World of Movement: Simplified map showing major routes of European penetration of North America and selected migrations of Indian peoples, c. 1500–1800.

lations in the region flourished. Refugees from the Iroquois wars who had congregated in the Ohio Valley in the late seventeenth century now began crossing the Mississippi to hunt, as did Choctaw and Chickasaw hunters farther south. By the second half of the eighteenth century, the Caddoes and Quapaws in eastern Arkansas faced an influx of Miamis, Delawares, Shawnees, Piankeshaws, Peorias, Chickasaws, and Choctaws.

The introduction of horses by Spaniards in the Southwest produced chain reactions as Indian peoples transformed themselves from pedestrian to equestrian societies. Apache Indians so completely assimilated horses into their world and their myths that they regarded the animals as a gift from their gods, not a by-product of Spanish invasion.

Horses also attracted people on to the sparsely populated grasslands known as the Great Plains and produced population movements within the plains. Migrations there had been occurring since the Middle Ages in Europe, when Caddoan-speaking Pawnees and Wichitas from eastern Texas, Siouan-speaking Mandans and Hidatsas from the Ohio Valley, Athapaskan-speaking Apache peoples from northwestern Canada, and Algonkian-speaking Arapahoes and Gros Ventres moved on to the plains. The arrival of Europeans in America set in motion a second wave of migrations that began in the late seventeenth century. Eastern tribes, newly armed with European firearms, pushed Osages, Omahas, Poncas, Iowas, Otos, Quapaws, and Missouris out on to the prairies. Frenchmen first met Cheyenne Indians on the upper Mississippi in the 1660s, but in subsequent years the Cheyennes left their Minnesota homeland and migrated west to take up new lives as buffalo hunters. The Teton or Lakota Sioux, the western and largest division of the Sioux nation, pushed west by Cree and Ojibwa enemies armed with French guns, and attracted by the new way of life on the plains, began to move west in the eighteenth century. Groups who split from the Hidatsa Indians in North Dakota before 1700 and migrated west became a new tribe—the Crows—on the northern plains and in the Yellowstone Valley. Shoshones, who had previously inhabited the Great Basin and the Rocky Mountains, acquired horses and moved out across the plains in the early eighteenth century. They retreated to the Rockies later in the century as other tribes moving south and west pressed them out of the area. Comanche and Kiowa Indians, encountered by early European explorers on the northern plains, migrated south and pushed many Plains Apache groups into the deserts and mountains of Arizona and New Mexico. The Apaches and

Navajos had themselves produced significant population movement in the Southwest. Apache raids, combined with a severe drought, prompted many eastern Pueblos to migrate to the Rio Grande in the 1670s. The Pueblo Revolt of 1680 not only drove Spaniards south; it also displaced Indian communities as Christianized Indians fled with the Spaniards, and other peoples regrouped in the wake of the conflict.

Horses increased a people's mobility, range, and capacity to hunt and wage war. Indians traveled over vast distances, either on horseback or to acquire horses. On at least one occasion, Crow Indians from Montana raided into the desert Southwest; Indians from across the plains traveled to Santa Fe for horses; and Hidatsas raided as far west as the Rocky Mountains, which explains the presence of the Shoshone woman Sacagawea in their upper Missouri villages when the American explorers Meriwether Lewis and William Clark passed through in 1804. The world Lewis and Clark entered on their trek west from St. Louis to the Pacific was a huge arena of migration and movement by old and new Indian occupants.

Maps in history books that purport to depict Indian America at the time of Columbus often place Seminoles in Florida and Crows in Montana as if those tribes had lived there for all time. Such maps ignore the dislocations and migrations, and the consequent tribal fusions and formations, that were common throughout Indian country after European invasion.

✳

By the time the United States formed a new nation, thousands of people, born in the American colonies, had pushed farther into the country. Thousands more, born in Germany, Ireland, Scotland, or Africa, had migrated to America and then fanned out westward, settling and resettling new lands and building new societies. Thousands of Indian people also participated in the process of migration and resettlement. Pushed from their original homelands by war, disease, or the growing pressure of European population, Indians were attracted to new locations by better trade options and by access to horses or new hunting territories. Seeking security in increasingly perilous times, individuals, families, bands, and tribes migrated time and time again. European invasion of America created a world in perpetual motion. Natives and newcomers alike left their homelands, moved to new locales, met new neighbors, and moved on. Indian and European migrants built new lives and communities far from the places of their birth and far from their ancestors' graves.

Eight

✦

Crossing and Merging Frontiers

*T*HE BOUNDARIES THAT divided Indians and Europeans in early America were porous: the frontier operated as a sponge as often as a palisade, soaking up rather than separating people and influences. Some Indians and some Europeans crossed over to live in the other's world, and some became members of the other's society. Interactions in frontier zones served to connect and unite people as well as divide and alienate them, providing new economic, social, spiritual, and sexual opportunities and creating new networks of kinship, affection, commerce, and common interest. Some people ventured across cultural boundaries and made new lives for themselves; others found themselves living in another culture as a result of coercion and rebelled against it or adjusted to it only after time; still others returned with changed outlooks, new skills, and human contacts that enabled them to play valuable roles as intermediaries between Indian and European societies. Europeans and Indians collided in competition and open conflict, but they also forged paths of cooperation and uneasy coexistence that cut across ethnic boundaries.

When Hernando de Soto's conquistadors landed in Florida in 1539, they came upon a group of ten or eleven Indians, "among whom was a Christian, naked and sun-burnt, his arms tattooed after their manner, and he in no respect differing from them." The Spaniards might easily have killed him, but he remembered enough Spanish to call out, "Do not kill me, cavalier; I am a Christian! Do not slay these people; they have given me life." The "Christian Indian" turned out to be Juan Ortiz, "a native of Seville and of noble parentage." He had been a member of Pánfilo de Narváez's disastrous expedition in 1528 and had lived with the Indians for twelve years. He served de Soto as interpreter until his death in 1542.

More than eighty years later and more than a thousand miles north, the Pilgrims at Cape Cod came across an Indian burial mound that contained a "powerful, if enigmatic, sign of a mingled Indian-European destiny." Digging open the grave, the settlers discovered the skeleton of an adult male, with fine yellow hair still on the skull, and various objects of European manufacture. Buried alongside was the body of a small child. Juan Ortiz and the unknown European were early examples of a phenomenon that occurred regularly over the centuries and across the continent: Europeans, for a variety of reasons, lived with Indians, and their lives and sometimes their identities became mingled.

Europeans, and Anglo-American society in particular, were anxious to keep Indian and white distinct. Europeans who lived with and like Indians called into question assumptions of racial and cultural superiority and demonstrated the ease with which "civilized" persons could "degenerate" to the level of "savages" in this new world. "We are all savages," announced an enigmatic message one of La Salle's men etched on a board. According to Gabriel Sagard, Frenchmen in the seventeenth century "become Savages themselves if they live for even a short while with the Savages, and almost lose Christian form." Colonial legislatures in Virginia, Massachusetts, and Connecticut passed laws to try to prevent such "Indianization," imposing penalties on people who ran off and lived with or like Indians.

Nevertheless, from the first, Europeans lived with Indians, and some observers thought that happened with alarming regularity. For traders, living in Indian communities was a way of doing business in Indian country. Spanish traders participated in the trade fairs at Pecos, where Pueblo and Plains peoples crossed their own frontiers to exchange the products of hunting and horticulture; French Canadian and British traders lived and operated in the villages of Mandans and Hidatsas, which functioned as similar rendezvous for Plains hunters and Missouri Valley farmers. Traders in Indian country enjoyed casual sexual encounters with Indian women, but they also cultivated relationships that tied them into Indian kinship networks and gave them a place in the community. Marriage often proved a prerequisite to successful business dealings. It also obligated traders to follow the customs of the society in which they lived and did business. Some traders left Indian wives and mixed-blood children behind when they departed from

Indian country, but others made new lives for themselves: "Many of them settle among the Indians far from Canada, marry Indian women, and never come back again," Swedish traveler Peter Kalm said of Canadian fur traders in the eighteenth century. He also noted that many of the French trappers and traders painted and tattooed themselves like the Indians. Italian botanist Luigi Castiglioni, visiting North America just after the Revolution, remarked that they took up Indian habits, such as smoking, sang Indian songs, lived with Indian wives, and imitated Indian "superstitions." "They are accustomed," he said, "when they are traveling on a river in a contrary wind, to throwing a bit of lighted tobacco into the air, saying that this way they give the wind a smoke so that it will be favorable to them." One observer described Lewis Lorimer, a trader among the Shawnees, as "from long habit a savage."

European governments frequently utilized the expertise, experience, and connections of such men as members of their Indian departments, and these Indian agents often displayed or developed a real affinity for Indian ways and Indian people. Sir William Johnson, British superintendent of Indian affairs in the North prior to the Revolution, traded, hunted, and lived with the Mohawks. He dressed like a Mohawk and participated in their councils and war dances. "Something in his natural temper responds to Indian ways," observed a contemporary. He lived for fifteen years with a Mohawk woman, Molly Brant, fathered Mohawk children (who inherited clan membership through their mother and were therefore Mohawks, not "half-breeds"), and headed a dynasty that dominated the British Indian department for half a century. Irish and Iroquois culture mingled at Johnson Hall, where, said Johnson, every corner of the house was "Constantly full of Indians." Johnson may have learned more than Mohawk ways from his Mohawk friends and guests: several of them visited England; he himself never did. Alexander Cameron married a Cherokee woman and lived with the Cherokees so long that he had "almost become one of themselves."

Missionaries who went into Indian country did so for specific purposes and had no intention of becoming Indians themselves. They nonetheless exposed themselves to Indian influences, and some came to appreciate the attractions of an Indian way of life. Indians did not try to convert their missionaries to their religion, but what was going on when Sebastian Rasles confessed to thinking like an Indian?

In the view of Hector St. John de Crèvecoeur, Indian society held an "imperceptible charm" for Europeans and offered qualities lacking in European society. Benjamin Franklin said that "no European who has tasted Savage Life can afterwards bear to live in our societies." Franklin exaggerated, but he identified a phenomenon common in early America: many Europeans found life in Indian communities preferable to life in colonial towns and villages.

Many of these cultural converts entered Indian country as captives, against their will, but they were subjected to powerful acculturative pressures by their captors, and some came to prefer their new life to their old. Still others chose to live with Indians, whether in preference for the Natives' way of life or to escape from their own society. Some of these "white Indians" even fought alongside their Indian friends and relatives in their wars against the whites.

Pioneers on the American frontier viewed the prospect of being taken captive by Indians as a fate worse than death. The narratives of people who had endured and survived Indian captivity fueled this notion, often portraying Indians as bloodthirsty savages who tomahawked and tortured men, butchered children, and subjected women to "unspeakable horrors." Subsequent generations of writers and filmmakers more often perpetuated than challenged such notions. More recently, however, scholars have reconsidered the captivity narratives, which contain valuable information on Indian societies, on intercultural interaction, and on gender relations in early America. Captives in Indian societies sometimes provided ethnographic data and a view of events from Indian country. Their words and experiences also sometimes posed disturbing challenges to Euro-American assumptions about "civilized" and "savage" life.

Taking captives had traditionally appeased sorrowing relatives and assuaged the spirits of deceased kinfolk; after European invasion, it became a way of maintaining population levels as well as patching the social fabric torn by war and disease. Indian peoples who adopted members of other tribes into their communities afforded white captives the same courtesy. War parties often embarked on raids specifically for captives, taking thongs and extra moccasins for the prisoners. The imperial wars of England and France from 1689 to 1763 offered an additional incentive, since the French often bought prisoners to ransom to the English. During the French and Indian wars, more than sixteen hundred people were abducted from New England alone. Some died in captivity; many were sold to the French and ransomed to the

English or made new lives for themselves in Canada; others were adopted into Indian communities.

James Axtell has explored the reasons for "the extraordinary drawing power of Indian culture." Although the captives' fate and experience depended on the character of individual captors, chance happenings, and the decision of bereaved relatives back in the villages, Indian warriors seem to have displayed remarkable kindness to those who were likely candidates for adoption. Older people, adult males, and crying infants might be tomahawked and left for dead, but women and children were often treated with consideration once Indians escaped pursuit. Contrary to popular fears then and Hollywood stereotypes since, Indian warriors in the eastern woodlands did not rape female captives: preserving the purity of their war medicine demanded sexual abstinence, and intercourse with someone whom one's clan might adopt was incest. Hard travel in moccasins across rough terrain, irregular meals and an unfamiliar diet, sheltering in a hastily constructed wigwam, and being wrenched from family and home, all taxed the captives' resilience, but these experiences also initiated them into their new way of life.

Once the trek into Indian country was over, captives faced new ordeals. Arriving at an Indian village, they might have to run a gauntlet between ranks of Indians brandishing sticks and clubs (though sometimes that was a symbolic event marking passage from one society to another: Susanna Johnson and her family entered St. Francis and walked between lines of Abenakis, who touched them lightly on the shoulder as they passed). They might be dressed and painted Indian-style, and then ritually adopted into an Indian family. In addition, they doubtless endured psychological trauma not unlike that experienced by people taken hostage by terrorists in the twentieth century. But time and the wealth of kinship relations they found in Indian society healed many wounds. Some captives preferred not to return home even when the opportunity arose.

Children proved especially susceptible to such "Indianization." The daughter of Anne Hutchinson was captured by Indians when she was about eight years old. According to Puritan John Winthrop, she stayed with them for four years, by which time "she had forgot her own language, and all her friends, and was loath to have come from the Indians." Titus King, taken captive during the French and Indian wars, saw many English children held by Indians in Canada and reckoned that it took only six months for them to forsake their parents, forget their homes, refuse to speak their own language

"& Seemingly be Holley Swollowed up with the Indians." When Peter Kalm visited Canada in the mid-eighteenth century, his party hired an Indian guide from the Huron mission village at Lorette. "This Indian," observed Kalm, "was an Englishman by birth, taken by the Indians thirty years ago when he was a boy and adopted by them according to their custom in the place of a relation of theirs killed by the enemy." He became a Roman Catholic and married an Indian woman. He dressed like an Indian, and he spoke English, French, "and many Indian dialects." Captive taking had been so common during the French and Indian wars that many Indians whom Kalm saw in Canada were mixed-bloods, "and a large number of the Indians now living owe their origin to Europe." Joseph Louis Gill, a prominent Abenaki chief at Odanak at the time of the American Revolution, was the son of two English people who had been captured, adopted, converted to Catholicism, and married each other. Gill—"the white chief of the St. Francis Abenakis"—was English by blood but Abenaki by upbringing and allegiance.

Perhaps the most famous story of cultural conversion—and the most troubling to English Puritans at the time—is that of Eunice Williams. In February 1704, a French and Indian war party sacked the town of Deerfield, Massachusetts, and took captive more than one hundred residents. Among them were the town's minister, the Reverend John Williams, and his family. As the Indians fled north along the frozen Connecticut River, they tomahawked and killed Williams's wife, who had recently given birth and could not keep up. But the warriors carried, or pulled on toboggans, the captive children, including Williams's seven-year-old daughter, Eunice. When John Williams was liberated after two and a half years, he wrote an account of his experiences, which became a best-seller. *The Redeemed Captive Returning to Zion* expounded the Puritan view that captivity tested good Protestants, an ordeal in which, with God's help, they resisted the torments of Indian savages and their evil Jesuit backers.

But Eunice Williams's experience shed a different light on captives in Indian society. She stayed with the Indians, converted to Catholicism, and married an Indian from Caughnawaga. Despite repeated entreaties from her father and brother, she refused to return home. One emissary reported that Eunice was "thoroughly naturalized" to the Indian way of life and "obstinately resolved to live and dye here, and will not so much as give me one pleasant look." Another reported that the Indians "would as soon part with

A Little Captive. Captured children intended for adoption frequently experienced kind treatment from Indian warriors. Nineteenth-century engraving. (© All Rights Reserved The Rhode Island Historical Society, RHi X3 4914)

their hearts" as let her return home. To her father's dismay and her country-men's consternation, Eunice Williams lived with the Indians for more than eighty years and died among the people with whom she had made her life, her home, and her family.

Other captives at other times and places followed Eunice's example. Mary Jemison, captured about age fifteen in 1758, married an Indian, raised children, and to all intents and purposes lived the life of a Seneca Indian woman in the late eighteenth century. Like Eunice Williams, Mary Jemison turned down the chance to return to white society. By the time she died, "the white woman of the Genesee" had had two Indian husbands, borne eight children, and left thirty-nine grandchildren and fourteen great-grandchildren. Jemison became, and remains, a prominent name among the Senecas. Isaac Zane was captured as a boy and adopted by the Wyandots in northwestern Ohio. He married an Indian, raised a family, and refused to return to white society, but he acted as U.S. interpreter at the Treaty of Greenville in 1795.

François Marbois, on a journey to the Oneida Indians of upstate New York in 1784, had a remarkable guide. The man wore earrings, "bones hung at his nose, and his face was painted with bands of different colors," but he spoke excellent French. Captured during the French and Indian wars, he was adopted into the tribe and married an Indian woman. He recalled that the Indians had treated him "with extreme severity" at first, but after his adoption, they "taught me all that my new situation made necessary"—how to hunt, how to build a canoe, and how to live on little food for months at a time. He missed France, and he had tried to escape once, but was recaptured. Since then, he had written letters home and received no reply. Now, he said, "I have insensibly got used to the way of living of these people. I have several children. I have brothers and other adopted relatives. . . . I no longer think of leaving them; my age, my children, fix me here forever, and I shall regret my country less than in the past, since I can hope from time to time to see Frenchmen again."

Captives who did return to colonial society did not always come home rejoicing. After Colonel Henry Bouquet defeated the Indians of the Ohio Valley at Bushy Run in 1763, he marched into Delaware country the next year and dictated peace terms that required the Indians to hand over all captives taken during the French and Indian wars. The Shawnees and the Delawares complied, but with reluctance and misgivings. They reminded Bouquet that the captives "have been all tied to us by Adoption. . . . We have taken as

"The Indians delivering up the English Captives to Colonel Bouquet" in 1764. The "liberation" of these captives was a heartbreaking experience for the captives and for their adoptive Shawnee and Delaware families. (From William Smith, *An Historical Account of the Expedition against the Ohio Indians in the year 1764* [Philadelphia, 1766]. Dartmouth College Library)

much care of these Prisoners, as if they were [our] own Flesh, and blood." They would always regard them as their relatives and asked Bouquet to take special care of their well-being: "They are become unacquainted with your Customs and manners, and therefore, Father, we request you will use them tender, and kindly, which will be a means of inducing them to live contentedly with you." The Shawnees knew what they were talking about, having employed precisely that treatment to win over the white captives to the Indian way of life.

Many of the Shawnees' captives protested their "liberation." William Smith, who was present when the Indians delivered their captives to Bouquet, said that the children had become "accustomed to look upon the Indians as the only connexions they had, having been tenderly treated by them, and speaking their language," and "they considered their new state in the light of a captivity, and parted from the savages with tears." Some of the adult captives were equally reluctant to return, and the Shawnees "were obliged to bind several of their prisoners and force them along to the camp; and some women, who had been delivered up, afterwards found means to escape and run back to the Indian towns. Some, who could not make their escape, clung to their savage acquaintances at parting, and continued many days in bitter lamentations, even refusing sustenance."

Many captives who returned home were permanently changed by the experience. For some, it was a nightmare they never forgot. But others retained lasting connections in Indian communities and real affection for the Indian families who had adopted them. Having been captured and adopted by the Shawnee chief Blackfish, Daniel Boone had a "second family" among the Shawnees. He also had enemies among the Shawnees, with whom he contested for the rich hunting grounds of Kentucky. When he moved to Missouri, he met old Shawnee acquaintances who had also trekked west ahead of the advancing line of settlement. It was not unusual for former captors to visit former captives back in the settlements, bringing news of Indian friends and relatives.

Some redeemed captives applied the knowledge, contacts, and experience they had acquired to construct new roles for themselves as culture brokers and helped build a middle ground where they exercised significant influence. Phineas Stevens, a former captive of the Abenakis and a militia captain during the French and Indian wars, ran a trading post at Fort Number Four (now Charlestown, New Hampshire) on the upper Connecticut

River and apparently enjoyed the trust and the business of English settlers and Abenaki Indians alike. Simon Girty retained an allegiance to the Senecas, among whom he had lived as a captive, and occupied a pivotal role as an interpreter in the Ohio country during and after the American Revolution.

The choices these people made and the lives they lived were rarely easy, however. William Wells, captured as a boy, grew to manhood among the Miamis and married a daughter of the Miami chief Little Turtle. He not only accompanied the Indians on raids against frontier settlements, but he helped lure travelers on the Ohio River into ambush. Wells fought against Josiah Harmar's army in 1790, and he figured prominently in the rout of Arthur St. Clair's army the following year. Despite a lifelong attachment to the Miamis, Wells of his own free will left the tribe prior to the battle of Fallen Timbers in 1794 and enlisted as a scout in General Anthony Wayne's army, which was marching against his adopted people. He was invaluable as a mediator between the Indians and the Americans, and he met his death fighting to protect white people against Indians. His death symbolized his life: dressed as an Indian, with his face painted black as was the Miami custom when confronting certain death, Wells escorted the garrison and their families from Fort Dearborn (later Chicago) in 1812, only to see them attacked and killed by Potawatomi Indians. Potawatomi warriors killed Wells, chopped off his head, and tore out his heart, an act of respect for his courage.

Some people became "white Indians" voluntarily, either to escape their own society or to embrace the Indians' way of life. When Samuel de Champlain began a policy of sending French boys to live with the Indians for a winter so they could learn the language, one youth, Etienne Brulé, "went Indian." He lived and traveled extensively with Indians in the Great Lakes region, until the Hurons killed him in 1633. Deserters from the British army hid among the Senecas and other western tribes at the end of the Seven Years' War. After the Revolution, François Marbois met "a rather fine looking squaw, whose color and bearing," he said, "did not seem quite savage." He asked her in English who she was. At first she pretended not to understand, but when pressed she told him she had been a servant in a wealthy planter's home in New York State. Tired of harsh treatment and working while others rested, she ran away to the Indians, who welcomed her, and she had lived happily ever since. "Here," she told Marbois, "I have no master, I am the equal of all the women in the tribe, I do what I please without anyone's saying anything about it, I work only for myself,—I shall marry if I wish and be unmarried again when I wish. Is there a single woman as independent as I in your cities?"

Others, it appears, had less to escape from in European society, but found something enriching in Indian society. Jean Vincent d'Abbadie, baron de Saint Castin, was the son of a noble family from the district of Béarn in the lower Pyrenees. He arrived in Quebec in 1665 as a young ensign in the Carignan-Salières Regiment and probably served in campaigns against the Iroquois. In 1670, he was given responsibility for restoring the fort at Pentagouet on Penobscot Bay in Maine and assumed command of its small garrison. He acted as a liaison with the local Abenakis and helped secure their allegiance to the Crown. When his brother died in 1674, Jean Vincent at twenty-two became the third baron de Saint Castin. Instead of returning to France to claim his inheritance, however, he remained with the Indians and married the daughter of a local chief. Though he continued to serve as a vital agent for the French, he became increasingly Abenaki in his loyalties and sentiments. The English, fearing his influence, tried to have him assassinated. His activities during King William's War (1689–97) earned the conflict the local title "Castin's War." A contemporary traveler, the baron de Lahontan, said Castin had lived among the Abenakis for twenty years "after the savage way." In 1701, Castin finally returned to France to sort out his affairs. He died six years later without ever seeing Maine again.

Etienne de Véniard, sieur de Bourgmont, was another Frenchman of social standing who lived for years at a time with the Indians. Arriving in the lower Missouri country around 1712, Bourgmont was an explorer and an ambassador to the tribes there, becoming "a power and a legend" among them. Although he had a French wife, he married a Missouri Indian woman, who bore him a son. He lived with the Missouris for five years, traveling on diplomatic missions as far as the Padouca Apaches, and he arranged for Indian delegations to visit Paris. "For me," Bourgmont boasted, "with the Indians nothing is impossible. I make them do what they have never done." Bourgmont died back home at Cerisy in Normandy in 1734. Four years earlier, the village priest had recorded the baptism of "Marie Angelique, Padouca slave of E. Veniard de Bourgmont." Two years later, the woman married. Presumably she lived the rest of her life in Normandy, the Apache wife of a French husband.

Men like Castin, who cast their lot with the Indians, ran the risk of being condemned as "renegades" by the society they had chosen to leave. Men who could abandon their own kind to live with the Indians were deemed capable of the most heinous acts. It was believed that they fought alongside Indians against their own people. Some did. Joshua Tefft married a Wampanoag Indian woman and lived with or near her people. When King Philip's War broke out in 1675, the Wampanoag women, children, and noncombatants took refuge with the Narragansetts of Rhode Island, and Tefft accompanied them. The English interpreted the Narragansett offer of sanctuary as an act of hostility, or a pretext for war, and launched a winter attack on the tribal stronghold. Tefft's role in the Great Swamp Fight is unclear, but shortly after the battle he was wounded and captured by the English in a clash with a Narragansett raiding party that was stealing cattle. He was dressed like an Indian, and his captors had no doubt of his guilt. Tefft protested that he was the Narragansetts' prisoner and had not borne arms, but the English accused him of masterminding the construction of the Narragansett fortress (after all, how could Indians have performed such a feat alone?). Condemned for having forsaken his people and his God, Tefft was hanged, drawn, and quartered. The English stuck his head on a gatepost as a warning of a traitor's sure punishment.

In the wars of early America, some individuals literally turned against their own kind after they had gone to live with Indians. According to Sir William Johnson, such people often proved to be "the most Inveterate enemies" of the whites. John Ward was captured in 1758 at three years of age by the Shawnees, who adopted him. He married an Indian woman, and they had three children. He fought against the Virginians at the battle of Point Pleasant in Lord Dunmore's War, where his natural father was killed. In 1792, he participated in a skirmish against a Kentucky militia that included his brother; a year later he was killed in a clash in which another brother fought on the opposing side. Another "renegade," George Collett also fought at Point Pleasant, exhorting his Shawnee friends to fight on against "the white Damnd. Sons of bitches." After the battle, Collett was found among the Indian dead. His brother, who was in the Virginian army, identified the body.

Those who had grown up among or lived close to Indians frequently demonstrated their cultural allegiance in less violent ways, or operated as intermediaries between two worlds, in the borderland areas where those worlds overlapped and merged. Here, whites who had lived with Indians and now served as their emissaries to colonial society passed Indians who had lived with whites and were traveling as emissaries into Indian country.

From very first contacts, Indian people traveled to Europe. Recent research suggests that as many as two thousand Indians, from Labrador to Brazil, may have crossed the Atlantic before the Pilgrims set foot on Cape Cod. Spanish, French, and English explorers kidnaped Indians and took them home as slaves, as curiosities, in the hope that they could be guides and interpreters on later expeditions, and as envoys to the capitals of Europe. The two sons of Donnacona, whom Cartier took to France, returned to France in 1536 after Cartier's second voyage. This time Donnacona himself and several other Iroquoians accompanied them. None of them ever saw Canada again: five years later they were all dead, including Donnacona, "who died in France as a good Christian, speaking French." Champlain's Micmac guide, Messamouet, had lived in France, and Champlain took another Indian named Savignon back to France with him.

An Indian from the Chesapeake Bay region was captured by the Spanish in 1559. They gave him the name Don Luis and took him to Spain, where missionaries baptized and educated him. He remained in Spain for two years and met King Philip II. Don Luis managed to find his way home via Cuba, promising to find gold and converts for Spain. Once back in Virginia, he escaped to his people and rallied the local Indians in a revolt against the Spanish colonists there.

Pocahontas, the daughter of Powhatan, married Englishman John Rolfe in 1613. Three years later, she and several other Indians sailed to England with Rolfe. There she was received as a princess, met King James I and Queen Anne, and had her portrait painted. Waiting to board ship for home in 1617, Pocahontas contracted a disease and died. John Rolfe was killed in 1622 when the Powhatans went to war with the English colonists. Pocahontas's son, Thomas Rolfe, returned to America in 1641. He became a successful businessman and was an ancestor of some of the great families of Virginia.

Two Indians from North Carolina were taken to England in 1584; both returned later as guides for the English. In 1605, an English expedition seized five Abenakis on the coast of Maine. Two of them, Maniddo and Assacomoit, were going back to Maine when the English ship on which they were traveling was attacked by a Spanish fleet. The English crew and their Abenaki passengers were taken to Spain and thrown into jail. Maniddo's fate is unknown, but the English ransomed Assacomoit, and nine years after his original kidnaping, he made it home to Maine. Another of the kidnaped Abenakis, Dehanda, "lived long in England" and then came back as a guide for the English. Squanto, the Patuxet Indian famous in American history for helping the New England Pilgrims survive their first hard years, also had been abducted. Taken to Spain, he then made his way to London and found passage to New England with another expedition.

These individuals were just some of the many Indian people who visited Europe, willingly or not, during the first century or so of contact. Others followed in later years: a delegation of "four Mohawk kings" (actually three Mohawks and one Mahican, none of them kings) visited Queen Anne in 1710; Cherokee delegations arrived in London in 1730, 1762, and 1764; Governor James Oglethorpe took a Creek chief from Georgia to England in 1735; Hendrick, one of the four "kings" who visited London in 1710, returned in 1740; Mohegan missionary Samson Occom visited England and Scotland on a fund-raising tour in 1766–68; representatives from the Six Nations went to London in 1766; and several Indian delegates from New England went to Old England to protest to the king about illegal encroachments on their lands. Mohawk Joseph Brant went to London in 1775, where he visited George III. The celebrated artist George Romney painted his portrait. Brant also joined the prince of Wales in enjoying the London nightlife. He returned after the Revolution. Peter Otsiquette, an Oneida Indian, accompanied the marquis de Lafayette to France in 1784 and spent several years there. One account described him as "probably the most polished Savage in Existence. He speaks French and English perfectly, is Master of Music and many Branches of Polite Literature, and in his Manners is a well-bred Frenchman." Otsiquette returned home and died while representing his people in treaty negotiations with the United States in Philadelphia in 1792.

A delegation of Creek and Cherokee Indians made the trip to England in 1790–91, led by an adventurer named William Augustus Bowles. Bowles, at various times, was a soldier, artist, actor, musician, baker, diplomat, interpreter, hunter, chemist, and lawyer. He wore Indian clothes, had an Indian family, and masqueraded as an Indian chief in the hope of creating an independent Indian state with British support. In London he moved freely in British social and political circles. His travels did not end there: he circumnavigated the globe as a Spanish prisoner and died in a dungeon in Havana.

Other European capitals received their share of visiting Indians who came as emissaries to secure political, economic, and military alliances. European governments were eager to impress the visitors with their wealth and power, and the Indians usually received considerable attention. However, they were not always impressed with what they saw: poverty in the midst of opulence, corporal punishment of children, begging in the streets, and imprisonment of criminals and public hangings had no parallels in Indian society.

As Europeans built new societies in North America, Indians became regular visitors to those communities too, and sometimes they participated in the life of the community. Indians and Spaniards mingled in mining towns, ranches, and haciendas in the Southwest and in California. An Apache Indian, Manuel Gonzalez, became alcalde of San Jose, California, and the Cherokee chief Oconostota joined the Scottish Society of St. Andrews in Charleston, South Carolina, before the Revolution. New England Indians supplied the early Pilgrims with food and assistance, but, according to Robert Cushman in 1622, the English returned the favor: "When any of them are in want, as often they are in the winter, when their corn is done, we supply them to our power, and have them in our houses eating and drinking." In some areas of colonial New England, Indians not only worked alongside English neighbors; they also lived with them. Frontiersman Daniel Boone won renown as an Indian fighter but, in the words of his most recent biographer, Indians "knew they could find food, drink, and a place to sleep at the Boone homestead." When war brought an abrupt halt to such peaceful interactions, Indians and colonists often recognized individuals they knew among their adversaries. During the Shawnees' siege of Boonesborough in 1778, both parties exchanged profanities and personal insults.

As Indian nations pursued diplomatic relations with various colonial governments, it was not unusual to see Indian statesmen walking the streets of Quebec, Montreal, Albany, Philadelphia, Williamsburg, Charleston, St. Augustine, New Orleans, San Antonio, or Santa Fe. Thomas Jefferson recalled that in Virginia before the Revolution, Indians "were in the habit of coming often, and in great numbers, to the seat of our government." On the edges of Indian country, delegates visited frontier posts and garrison commanders for similar purposes.

Indians also came to colonial settlements and cities to trade and participate in the communities' economic life. Indians in the fur and deerskin trades were key components in the labor force of early America: Indian men hunted and trapped; Indian women prepared the skins; Indian canoes transported the skins to market. Some Indians lived and worked as indentured servants, signing an agreement to work for colonists for a term of years in exchange for food and lodging. Indian people continued to follow traditional ways of life as long as they could, but European invasion disrupted their traditional economies, and many earned a living by taking advantage of new economic opportunities.

Women, whose household, farming, and foraging activities did not require huge areas of land or bring them into sustained contact with Europeans, usually found this easier to do than did men. Women took on housework or light farm work in the colonial economy, tasks that resembled their traditional ones. They sold baskets, pottery, and food in the marketplaces of colonial towns, or peddled them door-to-door. A Delaware woman named Hannah Freeman, who related a brief story of her life to the overseer for the poor of Chester County, Pennsylvania, in 1797, lived and worked as an independent day laborer in rural Pennsylvania, moving among colonial society rather than maintaining ties with traditional Delaware bands who had migrated west. Hannah worked for several farming families for wages (3 shillings 6 pence a week, which was about what white women in the rural labor force earned), sometimes as a live-in employee. Later, she "moved about from place to place making baskets & staying longest where best used." By the 1790s, she was described as "having forgot to talk Indian and not liking their manner of living so well as white people's." In her declining years, she worked for room and board at local farmsteads. In the 1750s, after the British built Fort Loudoun in Cherokee country, Cherokee women brought corn to the garrison, sometimes giving it to the soldiers but more often selling it at inflated prices. Indian women were servants, wives, or mistresses to the Spanish more often than in the English colonies, and Spaniards adopted from them corn tortillas, Native pottery, and many techniques and implements of food preparation. Pueblo and other Indian women wove textiles in the weaving shops of Santa Fe.

Men's activities were more severely curtailed. Raised to be warriors and hunters, they often found they could be neither. In order to earn a living in the colonial economy, they had to become laborers, learn new skills, or take up the plow. Christian Indians in seventeenth-century Florida cleared and maintained roads, cut lumber, operated ferries, and worked on Spanish farms and cattle ranches. Some high-ranking Apalachees owned their own ranches. In Virginia, colonists hired Powhatan men to kill wolves, build fishing weirs, and work as guides and hunters. Traveling past a small Pamunkey town in Virginia in the mid-eighteenth century, the Reverend Andrew

Burnaby found that the main employment of the community was "hunting and fishing for the neighboring gentry." Indian men from Nantucket, Mashpee, and other Indian towns in New England signed on as sailors and whalers; others learned new trades as carpenters, coopers, and blacksmiths, and they became wage earners in the colonial economy.

Indians also learned new skills from those who conquered and colonized them. The English in Rhode Island taught Narragansett Indians stone masonry, so they would have a skilled labor force. In time, however, Narragansetts earned a living by it and incorporated it into their lives and traditions, even turning it into a badge of Narragansett identity. Franciscan friars introduced the Indians of Pecos Pueblo to carpentry; the Pecos mastered the craft and plied their skills from mission to mission.

Other Indians entered the colonial labor force under more direct coercion. It was not uncommon to find Indian slaves working alongside African slaves in southern English colonies: Indians were one quarter of the slave labor force in South Carolina in the first decade of the eighteenth century. Spaniards devised the *encomienda* and *repartimiento* systems to extract and control a steady labor supply from the Indian populations they subjugated. *Génizaros*—captive Apaches, Navajos, Comanches, Utes, Pawnees, and Wichitas—in colonial New Mexico worked as muleteers, household servants, day laborers, and shepherds, although some learned trades and became silversmiths, blacksmiths, masons, and weavers. According to Father Juan Agustin de Morfi in 1778: "Since they are the offspring of enemy tribes, the natives of this province, who bear long grudges, never admit them to their pueblos. Thus [the *génizaros*] are forced to live among the Spaniards, without lands, or other means to subsist except by the bow and arrow. . . . They bewail their neglect and they live like animals." *Génizaros* were baptized and given Spanish names, and they were auxiliaries and scouts in campaigns against enemy tribes. Nevertheless, they remained very much members of a servant class.

Where colonial and Native economies overlapped, the patterns of employment, exploitation, and entrepreneurship were not always simple. At the end of the eighteenth century, Seneca Indians sold baskets and beadwork to non-Indians and worked for them as laborers, yet the Seneca chief Cornplanter hired non-Indians to operate smithies and mills on his grant of land in Pennsylvania. While Cherokee warriors angrily protested the loss of tribal lands to white settlers in the 1770s, Cherokee chief Little Carpenter collected rent from white tenants. Joseph Brant also leased land to non-Indian tenants on the Grand River Reserve in Ontario after the Revolution. In the West, from the time of the earliest Spanish ranches, some of the first cowboys were Indians. For centuries, Indians worked as cowboys, so that "cowboying," ironically, became part of the heritage of some Indian tribes.

Europeans also brought Indians into their societies for purposes of cultural and spiritual conversion. Whereas French Jesuits traveled into Indian country in search of converts, Puritan English missionaries preferred to establish "praying towns" near English settlements and try to convert Indians to an English way of life as well as an English religion. English colonial authorities and mission groups sought to educate Indian children in English ways. John Eliot hoped that his Indian converts would become "all one with *English* men." In 1619, Governor George Yeardley of Virginia was instructed to "procure their children in good multitude to be brought upp and to work amongst us." The Indians proved reluctant to part with their children, and Yeardley decided his best plan was to relocate Indian families among English settlers. The 1650 charter of Harvard College provided for the "education of the English and Indian youth of this country," and charitable contributions supported construction of an Indian college building. No more than six Indian students attended Harvard before the Indian college was demolished in 1698. Governor Spotswood of Virginia opened a school for Indian children on the frontier early in the next century, and at one time the school had almost eighty pupils. But Indian chiefs objected: "They thought it hard, that we should desire them to change their manners and customs, since they did not desire us to turn Indians." In 1724, the College of William and Mary built the Brafferton school hall for Indian students, but, says James Axtell, "the few who attended came too late, left too early, and died or took sick in an urban setting."

At the Treaty of Lancaster in 1744, the commissioners from Virginia invited the Iroquois to send their young men to William and Mary to receive an English education. The Onondaga orator Canasatego thanked them for the offer, but pointed out that Indian alumni of English colleges had generally proved to be useless when they returned home, getting lost in the woods and not knowing how to fire a bow and arrow. With tongue in cheek, Canasatego suggested instead that the English send some of their young men to the Iroquois, and the Indians would teach them useful things like how to hunt and follow a trail. Almost thirty years later, the Onondagas were still resisting English efforts to teach their children. In 1772, the Onondaga council rejected Eleazar Wheelock's request to educate their youth. The Indians were appalled by how the English treated Indian students, trying to beat discipline and knowledge into them. "Brother," they said, "you must learn of the French ministers if you would understand, and know how to treat Indians. They don't speak roughly; nor do they for every little mistake take up a club & flog them."

A number of colonial colleges began with the intent of providing education for Indian students. Harvard, Yale, Dartmouth, and William and Mary all received funding on that basis. Eleazar Wheelock aimed to bring Indian children to his Charity School in Lebanon, Connecticut, where they could be educated far from the "pernicious Influence of their Parents' Example." Wheelock continued his educational mission with the founding of Dartmouth College in 1769, but some Indian students and graduates complained that they worked more than they studied. Dartmouth produced only three Indian graduates in the eighteenth century.

For Indian students and their parents, the time they spent in English colleges must have seemed a captivity, during which the captors sought to convert them to a new way of life. The Seneca orator Red Jacket anticipated the sentiments of later generations of Indian parents on seeing their children come home from U.S. government boarding schools. "You have taken a number of our young men to your schools," he said. "They have returned to their kindred and color neither white men nor Indians." However, English captors had much less success than their Indian counterparts. Benjamin Franklin and other contemporaries acknowledged in dismay that Indian students took every opportunity to go back to their own way of life. Crèvecoeur went further, saying that "thousands of Europeans are Indians and we have no examples of even one of those Aborigines having from choice become European."

Nevertheless, Indian alumni and college dropouts often gained valuable knowledge and skills they used to serve their people in their increasing contacts with Europeans. Samson Occom, a graduate of Wheelock's school, became a missionary to Indian peoples; Joseph Brant graduated and translated the Gospels into Mohawk. He also built himself a pivotal role in the international and interethnic diplomacy that was so crucial to Iroquois fortunes in the revolutionary and postrevolutionary eras. Others played less visible roles, but their experiences in colonial schools and colonial society shaped their lives. They in turn helped shape the direction of Indian and European interactions in the emerging new world.

✦

As Europeans and Indians moved in and out of each other's societies, sat and smoked at trading posts and treaty councils, and participated in the daily exchanges that characterized life in early America, they generated a new world of words. European immigrants brought many languages and dialects to a land already marked by linguistic diversity; during the conquest of North America, dozens of new languages mingled with hundreds of old ones, producing changes in them all. At the same time, Indian languages influenced one another more than before as escalating warfare, increased trade, migration, and multitribal responses to European expansion caused more contacts between Indian peoples. Linguistic changes and interchanges also serve as a microcosm of broader cultural interaction between Europeans and Indians: there was "linguistic hybridization" and change in both directions, but it was not fifty-fifty.

Travelers frequently commented that all the languages they heard were symptomatic of the intermingling of cultures that occurred in North America. William Penn described the people of the Delaware Valley as "a Collection of divers Nations in Europe," including French, Dutch, Germans, Swedes, Danes, Finns, Scots, Irish, and English; they mingled with Delaware and other Algonkian-speaking people. A traveler in New York at the beginning of the Revolution heard spoken on a daily basis English (often with heavy Irish and Scottish accents), High Dutch, Low Dutch, French, and half a dozen Iroquoian languages. Andrew Montour's sister, a Moravian convert at New Salem, Ohio, was described in 1791 as "a living polyglot of the tongues of the West, Speaking English, French and six Indian languages."

Early Europeans often denied that Indians had any "real language"; Indian speech struck them as strange and guttural and "savage," not as a system of oral communication as rational and complex as their own. Nevertheless, as Europeans entered Indian country and came into contact with Indian people, they had, of necessity, to try to master some of the languages they encountered there. In 1760, the bishop of Durango, on a tour of inspection through New Mexico, found Indians reciting the catechism in Spanish but not understanding what they were saying: "I ordered the missionaries to learn the languages of the Indians," he wrote. In 1779, Father Francisco Atansio Domínguez, having visited all the Franciscan missions of New Mexico, said that all the Pueblo Indians spoke "a kind of Spanish," but often not very well. Consequently, he argued, "if we and they manage some mutual explanation and understanding, it is in such a disfigured fashion that it is easier for our people to adjust to their manner of speaking than for them to attempt ours, for if one speaks to them rapidly, even without artifice, they no longer understand." Missionaries in Sonora reported that Pima Indians "do not all like to speak the Spanish language even though they have learned it quite well by constant association with the Spaniards living among them. When they are questioned in Spanish, they reply in their own language." Such linguistic fumblings, adjustments, and sparring occurred across North America as Indians and Europeans tried to communicate with each other.

Europeans picked up Indian words where no European equivalent existed for what they saw around them. The settlers needed a new vocabulary: "New circumstances," said Thomas Jefferson, "call for new words, new phrases, and the transfer of old words to new objects." So Europeans borrowed, modified, or mispronounced Indian words to describe Indian or uniquely American things. Their vocabularies increased to include moose, caribou, skunk, opossum, chipmunk, hickory, mahogany, mesquite, yucca, maize, hominy, squash, succotash, pemmican, wigwam, tepee, moccasin, wampum, tomahawk, sachem, sagamore, powwow, caucus, toboggan, smoke the peace pipe, bury the hatchet, and so on. Some words and phrases grew out of the interactions of Indians and whites. A "buck"—the standard item of the deerskin trade—became the term for its monetary equivalent, a dollar. The result was what Jack Weatherford calls the "Americanization of the English language." Modern American English contains more than a thousand words adopted from Algonkian, Iroquoian, Muskogean, Siouan, Eskimo, Aleutian, and other tribal languages. As Weatherford notes, English itself was a tribal language, in constant evolution as northern European peoples mixed on English soil. "When the language came to America, the Choctaw, Ojibwa, Cherokee, Muskogee, Seminole, and dozens of others added to the European tribal language of the Angles, Jutes, Saxons, Celts, Vikings, and Normans."

Some Europeans became fluent speakers of Indian languages. In 1601, Ginés de Herrera Horta reported meeting a Spanish boy who had had Pueblo Indian children as playmates and knew their language "better than the Indians themselves, and they were astonished to hear him talk." Sexual encounters with Indian women provided colonial traders access to excellent "sleeping dictionaries." From his observations of English traders who took "bedfellows" among southern Indian women as a means of learning "the customs of the country," traveler John Lawson reported that "this Correspondence makes them learn the *Indian* Tongue much the sooner, they being of the *French*-man's Opinion, how that an *English* Wife teaches her Husband more *English* in one Night, than a School-master can in a Week." Peter Fidler, whom the Hudson's Bay Company sent to winter with the Chipewyan Indians in northwestern Canada in 1791, found himself dreaming in Chipewyan after six months.

However, the changes in the Europeans' languages were superficial. English settlers incorporated Indian loanwords into their vocabulary, but they did not allow a few new words to alter their fundamental patterns of thought and speech. "As with so many other aspects of native culture," writes James Axtell, "Indian words were tools used to subdue the continent, no more and no less."

Indeed, European languages often showed a remarkable tendency to remain the same in their new environment. Although English continued to develop, change, and homogenize in the British Isles, English-speaking immigrants often preserved with minimal alteration the language they brought with them. English regional dialects, transplanted to various parts of America, survived, sometimes into the twentieth century. The "Yankee twang" of New England evidently evolved from the speech on East Anglia, whence most Puritans migrated. The American "midland dialect" of the Delaware Valley derived largely from the language of England's northern Midlands. Scottish Highlanders who settled North Carolina's Cape Fear Valley in the eighteenth century spoke Gaelic and so did their slaves; people still spoke Gaelic there into this century. Many English words survived in America long after they died out in England: eighteenth-century Virginians called a frying pan a "skillet," referred to schooling as "book-learning," and said "yonder" for distant, long after such phrases were regarded as archaic in England. By the time of the Seven Years' War, American colonists' speech struck British regular officers as foreign. The reason was that it had not kept pace with changes in the parent language, not that it had changed in America. Loyalists who fled to England after the American Revolution stood out because of their old-fashioned ways of speaking.

Indian languages also displayed evidence of change. Indian people came into contact with speakers of various dialects of French, Dutch, Spanish, English, Portuguese, German, Gaelic, and African languages, and they met more speakers of other Indian languages. It was useful and sometimes necessary for them to learn the languages of the people they dealt with. Refugee communities sometimes produced a babel of different dialects: when Mohegan missionary Samson Occom went to New Stockbridge, New York, in 1787, he found there "a vast concourse of People of many Nations," speaking as many as ten different languages.

Trade jargons developed as certain tribes—Choctaws, Chinooks, and Comanches, for instance—played pivotal roles in extensive trade networks and other Indians learned their tongues. When European traders tapped into these networks, they learned the functioning language of trade, adding their own words to create "trade pidgins." In some cases, the new language became the lingua franca. At Quebec in the early seventeenth century, the French traded with Montagnais Indians using a half-French, half-Montagnais pidgin. Micmac Indians in Nova Scotia and northern Maine learned Basque, Spanish, or French trade jargon in their dealings with European sailors. The Delaware jargon was the language of commerce and communication between Indians and colonists in New Sweden and New Netherland. Spanish emerged as the trade language of the Pueblos in colonial New Mexico. Mobilian—based on Choctaw but borrowing from neighboring dialects—became the lingua franca of Indians and French traders on the lower Mississippi and the Gulf Coast. In some areas, broken and modified English, French, or Spanish was the means by which Indians communicated with Indians of other language groups as well as with Europeans. The new patterns of speech produced some lasting impressions: for example, *bayou* entered the English language via the French, who picked it up from the Choctaw word *bayuk*.

Like the Europeans, Indians had to borrow or create words for what was new in their lives: God, Christ, Christmas, Easter, king, governor, horse, cat, cow, pig, book, clock, plow, gun, rum, and so on. Delaware Indians called chickens *tipas*, after the word Swedish settlers used to call poultry, and they adopted Dutch words *melk*, *suiker* (sugar), and *pannekoek* (pancake).

American Indian languages generally contained and contain no profanities, but Indians quickly acquired loanwords to fill the void. A Quaker shipwrecked on the coast of Florida in 1696 heard the local Indians say,

"English son of a bitch." John Lawson said that those Indians who spoke English "learn to swear the first thing they talk of." Captive James Smith heard an Indian say, "God Damn it." When Smith told him what it meant, the Indian "stood for some time amazed and then said if this be the meaning of these words, what sort of people are the whites?" Traders said it all the time, he noted, even when they were in good humor. When Lewis and Clark descended the Columbia River in 1805, they met Indian people who swore as colorfully as the European and Yankee sailors with whom they traded on the Pacific coast.

Indian people had little choice but to learn the language of the people who established themselves as the dominant power in their country. English was the primary language of Indians in Massachusetts by the mid-eighteenth century. Calusa Indians in southern Florida were speaking Spanish in 1743; most of the Seminoles whom William Bartram visited in northern Florida on the eve of the Revolution also spoke and understood Spanish. Sometimes, as happened in the transfer of Indian words into European languages, the Indians misheard or mispronounced European words, adding a totally new word to their language. Yaqui Indians in Sonora borrowed hundreds of Spanish words, creating a hybrid language. They misheard the Castilian word *cruz* (cross) as *kus,* and the word "became permanently embedded in Yaqui speech in that form."

Indian languages changed, and some died out, even before the U.S. government's programs of linguicide in the nineteenth century. Nevertheless, Indians often adapted words and phrases creatively. Even where English, French, or Spanish became the Indians' first language, those languages differed from the originals. Indians modified their new languages with words, phrases, idioms, and influences from their own. Consequently, "Indian English"—the English spoken by Indian people in their daily lives today—often differs from "standard" English in grammar, speech patterns, and pronunciations. There are also many varieties of "Indian English," and some people may speak "standard English" or "American English" in formal public settings and their own dialect of "Indian English" in their home communities.

Many Indian people learned the conquerors' language fully aware that knowledge of the "dominant" language often conveyed power and status. They approached the new written languages in a similar way. Indian students at colonial colleges might resent their lessons in reading and writing

English, but Indian leaders often recognized the power of the written word, either to communicate ideas and information at a distance or to deprive Indian people of their lands. "When I look upon Writing I am as if I were blind and in the Dark," said the Cherokee chief Skiagunsta in 1751. Iroquois leaders complained in 1769 that white people had been able to obtain Iroquois lands "by the help of their paper (which we dont understand)." The pen often proved mightier than the sword in acquiring Indian lands, and Indians knew it. Some parents who sent their children to colonial colleges no doubt recognized that literacy was important to their survival. Literacy also gave one status in colonial society.

When Indians and Europeans met, they each adopted some of the other's languages to help them survive in the new world created by their meeting. Some Europeans learned Indian languages; colonists employed the language of wampum in their treaty councils; and Indian words made their way, often in distorted form, into European languages, giving the newcomers an expanded vocabulary with which to describe and understand their new world. Many Indians learned European languages; some became adept at reading and writing; and European words made their way, often in distorted form, into Indian languages. But the exchange remained in balance for only a moment. Conquest and dominance allowed the Europeans to dispense with Indian languages as little more than a pool of new words for new things; conquest and dominance also placed Indian peoples in a perpetual struggle simply to keep their languages alive.

Nine

⁘

New Peoples and New Societies

EUROPEANS CAME TO America to create new societies. Their invasions added new peoples to the human landscape. However, the conquest of North America was not a simple process in which Indian peoples were removed and their places taken by European and African immigrants. Europeans might aspire to displace Indians and create societies that were pristine duplicates of Old World societies, but they could not. They occasionally uncovered disturbing evidence that the societies they were trying to destroy were in some respects superior to their own. The mingling and mixing of peoples produced new kinds of people and societies, different from what had existed in North America and in Europe. Many of the new societies were embryonic and did not necessarily survive as permanent communities, but they were part of the landscape of early America. European colonists encountered and constructed new social and physical environments.

Although English colonists often went to great lengths to avoid "miscegenation" and protect their supposed racial purity, they could not prevent the mixing of peoples that occurred throughout North America as Indians, Europeans, and Africans met and intermarried. Surveying the Carolina backcountry in the eighteenth century, for example, historical geographer D. W. Meinig found that it was "a loose pattern of ethnic districts," comprising English and Scottish traders, mixed-blood packers and hunters, "remnants and renegades" from half a dozen Indian tribes, various religious sects from northern Europe, and so forth. Slave-holding Carolina brought Indians, Europeans, and Africans into close working relationships that demanded development of new ways of living. "Nor was this vital process simply an encounter among three peoples," writes Meinig. "There were Europeans from several sources, especially England, Ireland, and France, as well as Whites with years of experience in the West Indies, local Indians, Indian slaves from various inland tribes, and Blacks from many parts of Africa, some of whom had spent some seasons or years in the American tropics." Colonial society differentiated these peoples into categories by race, status, occupation, wealth, and privilege, but in daily life they worked closely together in an emerging regional economy. In such conditions, a considerable amount of racial mixing inevitably occurred. On the other edge of the continent, the northwestern Pacific coast sea otter trade attracted English, Yankee, Spanish, and Russian traders and sailors, on ships that sometimes included Africans, Asians, and Sandwich Islanders among their crews. These men met, and often mated with, Chinooks, Nootkas, Bella Coolas, Aleuts, and others, leaving a mixed progeny.

Some people advocated racial intermarriage as a way of alleviating ethnic and cultural conflicts and accelerating a union of Indian and European societies. The French experimented with racial intermixing as an instrument of empire building "in order that . . . they may form only one people and one blood." Puritan minister Cotton Mather referred disparagingly to the war parties that raided New England from Canada in the seventeenth century as composed of "half Frenchified Indians and half Indianized French." Even in Anglo-America, there were proponents of "miscegenation." English traveler John Lawson recommended coexistence and intermarriage as the best way to avoid conflict, "civilize" Indians, and gain knowledge of the Indians' skill in medicine and surgery. They would "become as one People with us," he said. One hundred years later, Thomas Jefferson echoed Lawson's sentiments. At a reception for visiting Delaware, Mahican, and Munsee Indians in 1802, the president held out the promise of a new union of new people if the Indians would agree to live under American law and institutions: "You will unite yourselves with us, join in our great councils and form one people with us, and we shall all be Americans; you will mix with us by marriage, your blood will mix with ours, and will spread, with ours, over this great island." Jeffersonian philanthropists urged racial blending, to incorporate Indians into the new society, but the realities of Indian-white dealings and American Indian policy in the early republic tended to exclude rather than include

Indians. Racial intermarriages did occur, but they gave rise to epithets like "squaw man" and "half-breed," and families with Indian ancestry often denied that component of their heritage.

Sometimes the offspring of Indian and European parents developed their own communities and their own ethnic identity. In the southern Appalachians, the Melungeons developed from a frontier population of Indian, African, and European people. The Lumbees of North Carolina, who survive today as the largest Indian group east of the Mississippi and the largest tribe not formally recognized by the federal government, intermarried with outsiders from first contacts. One theory traces their origins to English colonists from Roanoke and Croatan Indians near Cape Hatteras; other theories suggest Cherokee, Tuscarora, or Siouan origins.

Throughout New France, trappers and traders lived with Indian women, producing whole communities of people of mixed ancestry. Originally applied to the offspring of French fathers and Cree Indian mothers, the term "Métis" came to refer to all children of Franco-Indian unions. Métis peoples developed their own distinct cultures and ways of life, and they were important in the history of the Canadian West. According to Canadian historian Denys Delâge, the Métis demonstrated that a symbiosis of Indian and European cultures was not impossible; whites and Indians lived together, "teaching each other to hunt and farm and peopling the world of their imagination with Indo-European and Amerindian tales." Although the Canadian government—for whom, says Delâge, Métis society represented the very antithesis—destroyed that society in the nineteenth century, the government today recognizes Métis as a distinct group of Native peoples.

Intercourse and intermarriage between Indians and Europeans occurred most often in areas of Spanish colonization. The author of one chronicle of the de Soto expedition of 1539–43 was a Peruvian mestizo, Garcilaso de la Vega, known as "the Inca." The son of a Spanish conquistador and an Incan noblewoman, he was "the first of a new race of people born of unions between the Spanish conquerors and the Native American peoples they conquered." Spanish conquistadors in the Southeast abducted Indian women, and intercourse was common and intermarriage not unusual at Spanish frontier posts, where there were few Hispanic women, but Indian women went regularly to trade. After English and Indian raids from the north destroyed the Spanish missions in Florida in 1704, refugee Indians flooded into St. Augustine, joining the Spanish and Indian communities there. In 1736, as

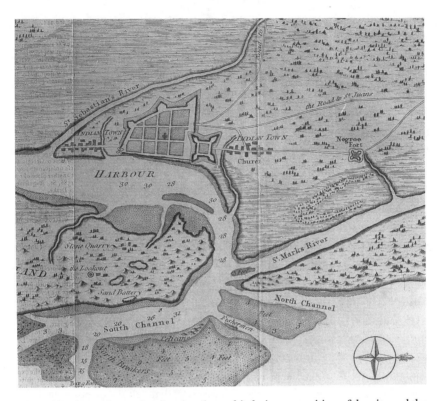

Plan of St. Augustine, 1762, showing the multiethnic composition of the city and the location of the Indian Town and church. (Courtesy St. Augustine Historical Society)

many as 1,350 Indian people lived in half a dozen towns around St. Augustine. The city had an Indian church. Spaniards and Indians traded, worked out labor arrangements, lived together, and intermarried. "Spanish-Indian intermarriage began immediately," writes Kathleen Deagan, "and continued consistently through two centuries of Spanish occupation." St. Augustine parish records show that marriages took place with some regularity between both free and slave blacks and Indian men and women from the mid-seventeenth century onward.

Tucson, Arizona, which was an important Northern Piman settlement in the mid-eighteenth century, grew into a Spanish military and colonial outpost where the garrison mixed with refugees from a variety of Indian groups. Northern Piman and other neighboring Indians from rancherias wracked by disease congregated at Tucson, and even some western Apache bands settled near the post. Nevertheless, the Indian population in and around the post continued to decline while the Spanish and mestizo population grew rapidly. When the presidio was established in 1776, about 240 Pimas lived around Tucson. In little more than twenty years, the town's demographic profile changed dramatically to include some 784 people of diverse origins. By 1797, the Indian population of Tucson had risen to 289, but only 78 of these were Pimas; 211 were migrant Papagos. A hundred or so western Apaches also settled in the area. The rest of the area's population—about 395 people—was Spanish or mestizo. Native American depopulation and Spanish fecundity ensured Hispanic settlement in southern Arizona.

When Juan de Oñate established the first permanent European colony in New Mexico, he hoped to keep Indian and Spanish peoples and societies separate, and for a long time people were officially either Indians or Spanish. However, Santa Fe was 1,500 miles and six months' travel from Mexico City, and Hispanic settlers in New Spain's isolated northern province, in historian Andrew Knaut's words, "could not escape almost total immersion in the ways and beliefs of the land's overwhelming Pueblo majority." Interaction and intercourse produced new ways of living and new kinds of people that strained to breaking point Spanish attempts to preserve ethnic and cultural separation. As intermarriage increased, people of mixed ancestry proliferated—as early as 1671, a Franciscan complained that "all the pueblos are full of friars' children." Spaniards created new categories to identify and define the "new" people. The child of a Spanish father and an Indian mother was a mestizo; the child of a Spanish father and a black mother was a mulatto; the offspring of a mestizo father and a Spanish woman were castizos, and so on. Obsessed with maintaining their status in the New World, Spaniards in eighteenth-century New Mexico distinguished between Spaniards born in Old Spain and those born in New Spain, between Indians who spoke Spanish and those who did not. In Ramon Gutíerrez's words, "There were defined categories for every possible combination between Spaniard, Amerindian, and Black." In Spanish colonial Tucson, people were categorized as Spaniard, coyote, morisco, and mulatto. A Spaniard who mated with an African produced a mulatto; a Spaniard who mated with a mulatto produced a morisco. Coyote probably denoted someone who was three quarters Indian and one quarter European. As demographer Henry Dobyns notes, however, "by a complicated series of matings, a Coyote could also be 7/64 Indian, 257/512 Negro and 271/512 European." The very proliferation of categories indicates the breakdown of efforts to keep Indians and Europeans separate and distinct.

In a society where status and prejudice predominated, people of mixed ancestry tended, where possible, to hide their Indian heritage and emphasize their Spanish blood. Consequently, Indians who could speak Spanish and wore Hispanic clothing might be regarded as mestizos, and many mestizos tried to pass as white. Spanish colonial authorities apparently sold "certificates of whiteness" to Indians who had mastered enough Spanish language and culture so they could earn the money to buy the certificate. There were even different categories of Indians: *génizaros* occupied the lowest ranks of society in New Mexico.

English colonial authorities also passed legislation to regulate the status of mixed and nonmixed groups of people. In Virginia, Indian people declined in number and African slaves increased, causing the English more concern with maintaining their position. They placed Indians in the inferior category of nonwhites, curtailing their ability to bear arms, to testify in court, to marry freely, and not to be enslaved. In 1691, Virginia passed a law prohibiting whites from intermarrying with "Negroes, Mulattoes and Indians." Indians were expected to occupy society's lowest ranks, along with slaves and "Free Negroes." In 1705, Virginia included Indians among the people subject to its "black code." As elsewhere in the South, white society moved to create a biracial system, and Indian people found themselves consigned to the wrong side of the dividing line: in white eyes and according to white laws, they were "black."

Whatever the status race-conscious whites accorded them, Indian people of mixed ancestry became a permanent and growing part of the mosaic of American society. Indeed, as their numbers plummeted, intermarriage was one way of bolstering population in those Indian societies that were matrilineal: children of an Indian mother were considered members of her clan and tribe, no matter who the father was. However, intermarriage is a two-way street: Indian populations displayed growing evidence of European ancestry, and many Europeans who were becoming Americans had Indian ancestors, whether or not they admitted it.

✴

The new societies that Indian people inhabited after European invasion often were falling apart. Economic dependency, alcoholism, demographic disaster, political realignment according to European rather than Indian interests, and steady cultural assault, all served to destabilize Native communities. Indians' traditions, political structures, social arrangements, and values, which had provided guidance and unity in the past, faced unprecedented challenges. Some communities disappeared from history as tribes, and their members resurfaced in colonial society and colonial records as "people of color," or poor people of Indian descent, petitioning the authorities for relief or trying to eke out a living. Theirs was a new world of poverty, dependence, and debt, and they lived subject to colonial laws rather than by tribal custom.

Indian-European interactions produced new peoples, and they produced new communities. Europeans created the concept of "Indian"; European pressures also created new Indian "tribes." As seen in chapter 7, the repercussions of European invasion, warfare, disease, and Christianity, which dislocated Indian peoples throughout North America, generated new communities and shattered old ones. Many tribes were postcontact creations: either they emerged out of the demographic chaos produced by European invasion or they existed first in the minds of Europeans who needed some organizing label for the bewildering array of family bands, clans, temporary and permanent alliances, coalitions of villages, and loose confederacies they encountered in Indian America. Unaccustomed to dealing with fluid band societies, Europeans pressed Indians to centralize and function as political units, and some Indian groups came to operate like the "tribes" Europeans assumed they were.

The Spanish invasion of the Southeast in the sixteenth century produced massive transformations in Indian societies. "When first encountered by Europeans," writes Jerald T. Milanich, "the native peoples of interior La Florida must have been incredible to behold." Powerful Mississippian chiefs demanded tribute and redistributed resources among their followers. Costumed in magnificent feather cloaks and beautifully crafted accoutrements reflecting their high status, they went in canopied litters carried on their subjects' shoulders and met the Europeans. Great chiefdoms, like Coosa in Georgia, held more than thirty thousand inhabitants. Populous towns contained plazas and temples built atop earthen mounds. By the late seventeenth century, the powerful chiefs and their densely settled chiefdoms had disappeared; only mounds and overgrown ruins remained in silent testimony to the civilizations that had once flourished there. The Indians who survived the Spanish onslaught "reorganized themselves to meet the challenges of the modern world." When the French and the English penetrated the southern interior, refugees from the chiefdoms and new immigrants had rebuilt, or were rebuilding, new societies from the ruins. Living in relatively small villages, Indian people banded together in loose confederacies, becoming the Catawbas, Creeks, Cherokees, Choctaws, Chickasaws, and other tribes and confederacies of the South. The Indian peoples encountered when English traders first penetrated the Southeast after the founding of Charleston (1670) were already "postcontact" societies.

The new societies of North America were ethnically as well as tribally mixed. Indian communities that adopted captives added a European strand to their social fabric. And many new communities, especially on the frontier, were almost from their beginnings multiethnic societies. Arriving at Charlestown, New Hampshire, then the northern frontier of New England, as a girl in 1744, Susanna Johnson found nine or ten families living in cabins, and numerous Indians "associated in a friendly manner with the whites." Looking back in her old age to that time, she recalled: "In these days there was such a mixture on the frontiers of savages and settlers, without established laws to govern them, that the state of society cannot easily be described." In 1774, Governor Patrick Tonyn of Florida said the Indians in his colony were "settled amongst our Plantations, they have daily intercourse with them, and are as it were a People interwoven with us."

Many new communities that emerged from the meeting of Indians and Europeans were short-lived social experiments. In New England in the early seventeenth century, Thomas Morton established a notorious settlement at Merry-Mount, where English men lived with Indian women. Puritan authorities were alarmed at its implications for English claims to superiority and its threat to their creating a new England, and they suppressed it. Governor William Bradford complained that Morton and his followers "set up a maypole, inviting the Indian women for their consorts, drinking and dancing about it like so many fairies." Accused of fornicating with Native women and supplying guns to the Indians, Morton was arrested and exiled. In western Massachusetts, English missionaries in the 1730s established a model mission community at Stockbridge, where Christian Indians lived alongside English families and shared town government with them. But the English population increased; the Indian did not. Indian lands became English, and Indians were gradually excluded from town government. By the end of the

Revolution, Stockbridge was a white town; it still is. What happened at Stockbridge occurred time and again across the country.

In other areas, the kind of society that so alarmed Governor Bradford and that proved so short-lived at Stockbridge was more common and more enduring. Many towns and settlements that grew into America's cities began life as trading posts, which by their nature encouraged close interaction of Indians and Europeans. Schenectady, New York, for example, was on the overland route between Iroquois villages and Dutch settlements on the Hudson River. The community of Dutch origins and Dutch people was frequented by Iroquois Indians, French trappers, African slaves, and, from the 1690s, English soldiers and settlers. Like neighboring Albany, it was a community "where whites and Indians lived together, traded with each other, slept in the same rooms, and ate at the same table." Countless cities, towns, and villages across America began in similar fashion, springing up or emerging from existing Indian settlements at the junction of trade routes that brought together disparate peoples. Quebec, Montreal, Albany, Philadelphia, Pittsburgh, Charleston, Detroit, St. Louis, and many others all, at one time or another, depended on the fur trade and the Indians who provided most of its pelts and its man- and woman-power. French outposts in the Midwest were often cosmopolitan communities where Frenchmen met Indians from far and near, as well as people from different parts of Europe and Africa. Detroit, a multiethnic metropolis in the twentieth century, was a multiethnic community in the eighteenth century. When Sieur de la Mothe Cadillac founded Detroit in 1701, he planned to settle Indians and Europeans together, so that they would intermarry and form one people. A visitor to Fort Pitt in 1772 described the future city of Pittsburgh as a village of about forty log houses, the headquarters of the Indian traders, and "the resort of Indians of different & distant tribes." Auguste Chouteau and his younger brother, Pierre, the "Founding Family of St. Louis," established a family fortune and a city's future on the basis of trade with the Indians of the Mississippi and Missouri Valleys. The pattern was repeated farther west. Reviewing the nineteenth-century origins of Pueblo, Colorado, fur trade historian Paul C. Philips wrote: "The crude adobe fort known as Pueblo was 'home' to a bizarre melange of American adventurers, French coureurs de bois, Canadian Iroquois, Mexican trappers and traders, Negroes, and European immigrants." American cities today face challenges that frighten many as they try to accommodate—or exclude—peoples of different ethnic back-

Pencil sketch of a tavern scene near Montreal around 1775, by John André. The landlady holds a candle over a group composed of Indians, soldiers, trappers, women, and a small child, who dance to the music of an Indian drum (*at right*) and a piano (*not visible*). (Courtesy the William L. Clements Library)

grounds. This is not strictly a twentieth-century phenomenon: the scale of the challenge, not the challenge itself, is unprecedented.

✦

Not only did Indians and Europeans create new societies in the new world that emerged after contact, but existing societies experienced significant changes and responded to new influences. Those were greatest for Indian societies, of course, but Indian ways left subtle imprints in the societies of the Europeans who sought to displace them.

In 1987, two centuries after the adoption of the Constitution of the United States, the U.S. Senate passed a resolution that acknowledged "the historical debt which this Republic of the United States of America owes to the Iroquois Confederacy and other Indian Nations for their demonstration of enlightened, democratic principles of government and their example of a free association of independent Indian nations." Shortly after, several Iroquoian scholars signed an open letter to the *New York Times,* criticizing the Senate resolution for its misuse of history, but the notion that the Iroquois provided the model for the U.S. Constitution has remained popular—it is an article of faith in some circles. Those who believe that the founders used the Iroquois system point to evidence such as the speech of the Onondaga orator Canasatego to the commissioners of Virginia, Maryland, and Pennsylvania at the Treaty of Lancaster in 1744. On the final day of the conference (ironically, July 4), Canasatego urged the colonists to seek strength in unity: "Our wise Forefathers established Union and Amity between the *Five Nations;* this has made us formidable; this has given us great Weight and Authority with our neighboring Nations," he said. "We are a powerful Confederacy; and, by your observing the same Methods our wise Forefathers have taken, you will acquire fresh Strength and Power; therefore whatever befalls you, never fall out one with another." The message was not lost on Benjamin Franklin, who later wrote that "it would be a very strange Thing, if six Nations of ignorant Savages should be capable of forming a Scheme for such a Union, and be able to execute it in such a Manner, as that it has subsisted [for] Ages, and appears indissoluble; and yet a like Union should be impracticable for ten or a Dozen Colonies, to whom it is more necessary, and must be more advantageous." Some writers insist that the Iroquois system and Indian ideas of liberty provided Franklin and other leaders the rationale for the American Revolution.

As had the Iroquois, the founding fathers created a system of government where power was distributed not concentrated, where new tribes or states could join, where authority was derived from the people, where individual freedoms, group autonomy, and freedom of speech were protected, but where member groups united on matters of common concern. Like the Iroquois League of Peace, the United States became a haven for refugee people. Evidence that the founders copied the Iroquois model in drawing up the Constitution, however, is largely circumstantial and inferential. The fact that they knew about the league and the remarkable Iroquois system does not mean that they sought to emulate it. There was much in the Iroquois matrilineal, clan-based system that the founders chose not to use: they rejected the idea of government by consensus, excluded women from participation, separated church and state, and protected individual rather than communal property rights. If the founders looked to the Indians to help build the new nation, it was the Indians' lands, not their systems of government, they were interested in.

The debate over the Iroquois and the Constitution is part of a larger question concerning Indian influences on American liberty. Even as Europeans sought to displace and destroy Indian societies, some found much to admire. Indian ways seemed to infiltrate their own societies, and, at the very least, they were exposed to Indian ideas and social values. To say that American democracy emerged as a synthesis of European and Indian political traditions may be an overstatement, but to deny it may be placing too much weight on the written record: ideas and customs tend to seep subtly from one group to another rather than being formally acknowledged. Such indirect influences are difficult to establish with certainty, but they would be in keeping with the flow of Indian ways into Euro-American societies.

Many have attributed to American Indians an impact on European social thought. From Roger Williams and the baron de Lahontan in the seventeenth century, to Thomas Jefferson and Benjamin Franklin in the eighteenth, and on to the present, numerous writers have found much to admire in Indian societies. French missionary Marc Lescarbot compared the social ills of European society with the merits he found in Micmac communities: "If only through considerations of humanity, and because these people of whom we shall treat are men like ourselves, we have reason to be roused with the desire of understanding their modes of life." Montaigne, Rousseau, and others used Indian society—that is, their understanding of it—as a yardstick by which to judge European civilization. Canadian historian Alfred Bailey suggested that by alerting Frenchmen to the inequities in their own society, contact with the Indians was "a remote precursor of the French Revolution." Historian William Brandon argues that Indian notions of liberty filtered into European social thought via reports from the New World. Seneca John Mohawk and Onondaga Oren Lyons claim democracy as an "export item, perhaps Native America's greatest contribution to the world," which toppled European monarchies and resulted in the formation of the United States. Wendat (Huron) scholar Georges Sioui sees a degenerate Europe finding the sources of its own regeneration in Native America. "A dehumanized European civilization," he writes, "began to rediscover the reality of human nature and, with the help of its Amerindian teachers, lead the rest of the world along the path of world socialization."

Certainly, some American colonists and European philosophers were impressed by the freedom, egalitarianism, and communal ethics they saw in Indian society. Indians lived in functioning democracies, enjoyed "natural" rights and freedom, and were not burdened by "unnatural" monarchy and government oppression. Roger Williams noted that Indian chiefs in New England led by "gentle persuasion" and would do nothing "unto which the people are averse." Daniel Gookin agreed that Indian sachems won and retained support by "acting obligingly and lovingly unto their people, lest they should desert them." William Penn said that Indian chiefs "move by the Breath of their People." Trader James Adair, who lived among the Indians of the Southeast before the Revolution, said the Indians' "whole constitution breathes nothing but liberty." Trader John Long said the Iroquois "laugh when you talk to them of Kings; for they cannot reconcile the idea of submission with the dignity of man." Cadwallader Colden said that each Iroquois nation was "an Absolute Republick by itself, governed in all Publick affairs of War and Peace by the Sachems or Old Men, whose Authority and Power is gained by and consists wholly in the opinions of the rest of the Nation in their Wisdom and Integrity. They never execute their Resolutions by Compulsion or Force Upon any of their People." A French officer, writing in the closing years of the French regime, commented that Frenchmen who lived among Indians found greater freedom than they had ever been accustomed to: " 'Liberty,' they say, 'is no where more perfectly enjoyed, than where no subordination is known, but what is recommended by natural reason, the veneration of old age, or the respect of personal merit.' " A Mohawk said more simply: "We have no forcing rules or laws amongst us."

Indian communities were living proof that human beings could construct and maintain societies based on liberty, examples of political systems where those who governed derived their authority from the people. Some colonists went to live in these societies, and some writers advocated injecting healthy doses of Indian-style freedom and equality into their own ailing societies. John Lawson maintained that Indians were "the freest People in the World," and he urged settlers to emulate their ways.

Some Europeans saw in Indian societies practices that put "civilization" to shame. Father Claude Chauchetière was impressed by the sharing, hospitality, and patience in dealing with children he witnessed in Indian communities. "In fine," he said, "all our fathers and the French who have lived with the savages consider that life flows on more gently among them than with us." Crèvecoeur maintained that Indians had "in their social bond something singularly captivating, and far superior to anything to be boasted of among us." In marked contrast to Europe, where wealth and poverty existed side by side, Recollect missionary Gabriel Sagard reported that the Hurons "make hospitality reciprocal and are so helpful to one another that they provide for the needs of all, so that there are no poor beggars in any of their towns and villages." William Wood, in *New England's Prospect,* reported that the Indians were "reddy to communicate the best of their wealth to the mutual good of one another." Roger Williams pointed out that, in contrast to European society, Indians had "no beggars amongst them, nor fatherlesse children unprovided for." Revolutionary writer Thomas Paine said that Indian societies lacked "any of those species of human misery which poverty and want present to our eyes in all the towns and streets of Europe."

Sharing in Indian societies was not an ideal; it was an obligation. People acquired honor and established reciprocal relations by giving things away, not by accumulating them. Observing how an item given to an Indian "may pas twenty hands before it sticks," William Penn said, "Wealth circulateth like the blood, all parts partake." Refusal to share was regarded as antisocial, even hostile behavior: in 1712, Cree Indians around Hudson Bay killed seven Frenchmen who would not share food and ammunition with a band of Indians who were on the verge of starvation. Indians thought Europeans were selfish and uncaring; many Europeans felt that Indians who gave things away and failed to "get ahead" were "shiftless" and "improvident."

Many Indian societies also accorded women and children a measure of respect unusual in Europe. In societies where women produced food as well as prepared it, their economic role seems to have translated into higher status than that of their European or colonial counterparts. Iroquoian women in particular exerted an influence undreamed of by Europeans. "All real authority is vested in them," wrote Joseph François Lafitau in the seventeenth century. "The land, the fields, and their harvest all belong to them. They are the souls of the Councils and the arbiters of peace and of war. . . . The children are their domain, and it is through their blood that the order of succession is transmitted." While women gave and sustained life, raising crops and rearing children in the villages, men took life, fighting and hunting away from the villages.

Gender relations often changed after contact with Europeans. Women's participation in public affairs sometimes declined, since Europeans insisted on dealing with men, and the new demands generated by the fur trade and the increased absences of men on hunting and war expeditions placed additional economic burdens on women. Europeans interpreted egalitarian gender relations as a lack of social and family hierarchy, and they sought to subordinate women in their program of restructuring Indian societies along European lines: men, not clan mothers, must dominate society.

European travelers frequently noted that Indian people were indulgent parents, eschewing corporal punishment in child-rearing. Cabeza de Vaca said, "These people love their offspring more than any in the world and treat them very mildly." What attracted de Vaca in the sixteenth century, however, alarmed Puritans in the seventeenth century. They feared the effects of the New World and its Indian inhabitants, and they worried that in building a new "civilization" in America, they might become like the Indians they sought to displace. The Puritan minister Cotton Mather lamented that "tho' the first English planters of this country had usually a government and a discipline in their families that had a sufficient severity in it, yet, as if the climate had taught us to Indianize, the relaxation of it is now such that it seems wholly laid aside, and a foolish indulgence to children is become an epidemical miscarriage of the country, and like to be attended with many evil consequences." Increase Mather also lamented the decline of family government and the indulgence of parents and masters toward children and servants: "Christians in this Land, have become too like unto the Indians," he said. Subordination of children, as of women, was part of the invaders' agenda for Indian society. Nevertheless, travelers noted, backcountry settlers often seemed to follow Indian examples in their indulgent treatment of children.

Colonists who borrowed from Indian societies and shook off the restraints of eastern elites created what scholars of French-Canadian history call "new social types." Denys Delâge notes that one can only imagine the impact of egalitarian and freedom-loving Indian societies on coureurs de bois, who generally were the sons of indentured servants and other members of the underclasses. Some Europeans found liberty and equality more threatening than attractive and endeavored to keep them out of the societies they were building. Delâge points to the colonists' dilemma: "It was the very existence of these relatively egalitarian societies, so different in their structure and social relationships from those of Europe, that exercised the greatest influence on the newcomers and, at the same time, repelled them most."

The egalitarian nature of Indian societies was antagonistic to the class societies of Europe. Individual freedom threatened to undermine patterns of hierarchy, discipline, and self-restraint. To contemporaries, the freedom of Indian society was largely inherent in what they saw as a wilderness environment, where land was plentiful and colonial authority was weak. In the seventeenth century, William Hubbard worried that the settlers scattered along New England's frontier "were contented to live without, yea, desirous to shake off all *yoake of Government,* both *sacred* and *Civil,* and so *Transforming* themselves as much as well they could into the manners of the Indians they lived amongst." In the 1750s, Louis Antoine de Bougainville complained that Montcalm's soldiers became "corrupted . . . by the example of the Indians and Canadians, breathing an air permeated with independence."

The patterns of communal sharing, leadership dependent upon the good will of one's followers, individual liberty, and egalitarian relations that typified many Indian societies contrasted starkly with the vision of society articulated by John Winthrop in a sermon to fellow Puritans aboard the *Arbella:* "God Almighty . . . hath so disposed of the Condition of mankind, as in all times some must be rich[,] some poor, some high and eminent in power and dignity; others mean and in subjection." The collision and occasional fusion of different concepts of society is part of the American historical experience, but how far European colonists, or American founding fathers, went in adopting Indian ways as they modified Winthrop's vision is difficult to say. Awareness and even admiration of Indian political systems and social ethics did not mean that Europeans would adopt them as permanent features of the new societies they were creating. Immigrants tended to cling to many of their own ways and to adopt new ways of life when and for as long as it suited them to do so. Gary Nash reviews the process by which admired values came to be suppressed:

> Idealistic Europeans saw the "wilderness" of North America as a place where tired, corrupt, materialistic, self-seeking Europeans might begin a new life centered around the frayed but vital values of reciprocity, spirituality and community. . . . Yet as time passed and Europeans became more numerous, it became evident that the people in North America who best upheld these values were the people who were being driven from the land. . . . Indians seemed to embody these Christian virtues almost without effort while colonizing Europeans, attempting to build a society with similar characteristics, were being pulled in the opposite direction by the natural abundance around them—toward individualism, disputatiousness, aggrandizement of wealth, and the exploitation of other humans.

In the end, European imperial ambitions, settlement patterns, laws, and institutions prevailed at the expense of idealistic notions that a truly new world could be created that incorporated the best of Indian and European societies. Ultimately, the invaders of North America succeeded in their goal of building new societies that were more like their old ones in Europe than the Native societies they encountered in America.

Nevertheless, those societies developed where Native American roots ran deep. How much of what was new in them derived from the human environment and how much from the physical is difficult to ascertain, but the early settlers themselves often regarded Indians and "wilderness" as inseparable. European colonists, like the Indians whose world they invaded, were compelled to combine old and new ways, to experiment and innovate as well as adhere to traditions for guidance. Although many social experiments did not endure, by the end of the colonial era, Europeans, Indians, and Africans had all created new societies. Each one, in James Merrell's words, was "similar to, yet very different from, its parent culture." The New England town meeting is a far cry from Winthrop's vision of an ordered and orderly society and displays more attributes of Algonkian government by consensus than of Puritan government by the divinely ordained.

Conclusion

.✴.

New Americans and First Americans

ACCORDING TO INDIAN trader John Long, Sir William Johnson was once sitting in council with a group of Mohawks when "the head chief told him, he had dreamed last night, that he had given him a fine laced coat, and he believed it was the same he then wore." Johnson smiled and asked the chief if he really dreamed it. The Mohawk assured him he had. "Well then," said Sir William, observing Indian custom, "you must have it." Immediately he pulled off his coat and gave it to the Indian, who left the council well pleased.

The next time they met, Johnson told the chief "that he was not accustomed to dream, but that since he met him at the council, he had dreamed a very surprising dream." The Indian asked what it was. "Sir William, with some hesitation, told him he had dreamed that he had given him a tract of land on the Mohawk River to build a house on, and make a settlement, extending about nine miles in length along the banks." The chief smiled and told Johnson that if he really had dreamed it he should have it, "but that he would never dream again with him, for he had only got a laced coat, whereas Sir William was now entitled to a large bed, on which his ancestors had frequently slept." Johnson took possession of the land, apparently some sixty-six thousand acres on the Mohawk River, by virtue of a deed the chiefs signed, "and gave them some rum to finish the business."

The story appears in several versions—the Mohawk is usually identified as Hendrick, but another rendition features Conrad Weiser and Shickellamy—and may be apocryphal, but it illustrates a process repeated time and again in early America: Europeans learned Indian ways to further their own goals and to help them take possession of what was once Indian country. As Richard Slotkin points out, a recurrent character and a potent symbol in America mythology is the "frontier hero," who has knowledge of both Indian and white ways, but who never quite becomes an Indian himself. Sometimes he works as a mediator, but more often he functions "as civilization's most effective instrument against savagery—a man who knows how to think and fight like an Indian, to turn their own methods against them." Slotkin had in mind fictional characters like Hawkeye in James Fenimore Cooper's *Last of the Mohicans,* but history furnishes numerous examples: Benjamin Church, Robert Rogers, Daniel Boone, and others. Ultimately, European power, European numbers, and European germs dictated that Europeans would prevail in the struggle for early America, though when and where the issue hung momentarily in the balance, European adaptation of Indian ways often helped tip the scales.

In 1492, there were no Indians in America, only Native people. By 1800, the descendants of those original inhabitants were called Indians. There were far fewer of them, and most lived in ways undreamed of by their ancestors and on a fraction of their ancient homelands. The people responsible for their decline had taken and applied Indian ways as they took over the Indians' lands. Despite their determination to remain who they were, they had also changed.

As James Axtell has shown, the Indian presence in America's past profoundly shaped the ways in which early American history unfolded. Europeans had to take account of Indians in their wars, diplomacy, and daily lives. They lived alongside Indians and had to know something about them. But they did not, most of them, become Indians. "To have become truly Indian, the colonists would have had to think like Indians, to value the same things that the Indians valued, and most important, to identify themselves as Indian and their future with native society." On the contrary, Puritans in New England, colonists in New France, and Spanish nobles in New Mexico used Indians as a foil, to help themselves identify what they were not. They worked at remaining English, French, and Spanish.

Nevertheless, their very efforts not to change indicated that they sensed the pressures to change. They did not become Indians, but they did become something other than what they, or their ancestors, had been. The New World brought new identities for all: there were no Indians until European invaders lumped them all together under a single name; there were no

Americans until discontented colonists looked to what distinguished them from their European counterparts. By the early nineteenth century, former colonists no longer thought of themselves as British. They were Americans. French-speaking inhabitants of the British colonies that remained in the north thought of themselves as Canadians. Descendants of Hispanic settlers and Native people were forming a new, Mexican, national identity.

To use James Axtell's metaphor, English colonists "forged their particular American identity . . . on an Indian anvil." In Axtell's view, "Without the steady impress of Indian culture, the colonists would probably not have been ready for revolution in 1776, because they would not have been or felt sufficiently Americanized to stand before the world as an independent nation. The Indian presence precipitated the formation of an American identity." Historians differ as to how far the colonists had gone in declaring a new collective identity by the time of the Revolution, but most agree that any distinctive identity they had developed stemmed from their encounter with the American environment and its Indian inhabitants.

Indians, too, were concerned about their identity in this new world: "We are Indians, and dont wish to be transformed into white men," a group of Iroquois told a missionary in 1745. Like the European invaders, Indians had to work at remaining who they were. As outward manifestations of culture and identity—clothing, housing, patterns of speech, economic activities, forms of public worship, and even physical appearance—changed at what must sometimes have been a dizzying rate, many Indian people clung all the more steadfastly to core values and inner strengths—reciprocal relations, clan memberships and kin networks, ancient stories, traditional beliefs and rituals—that enabled them to survive as Indians behind a veil of change. Even as they retained clan and tribal identities, however, some Native Americans began to embrace a "pan-Indian" identity in opposition to Europeans. The multitribal movements led by Pontiac in 1763 and by Tecumseh in the early nineteenth century united people who increasingly identified themselves as "Indians," members of an indigenous American ethnic group as well as of a particular clan or tribe. Puritans and other early colonists defined themselves in opposition to Indians, and Indians began to define who they were in opposition to Europeans.

In many ways, though, Indians were becoming more like Europeans and Europeans were becoming more like Indians. European colonists borrowed and adapted from Indians to help them survive in and subdue their new world. They appropriated Indian ways to their own uses and came to regard those ways, ultimately, as "American," not Indian. But when Indians borrowed and adapted from Europeans, Europeans interpreted *their* strategies of survival as acts of cultural suicide. They assumed that Indians who changed ceased being Indians, and those who survived by adopting European ways became "invisible." Most of the new Americans saw no Indians in their nation and saw nothing Indian in themselves. In becoming somewhat like what they had tried to destroy, they no longer saw anything distinctive in Indian people who had become somewhat like them and survived. In a society where systems of racial discrimination divided human beings into "whites" and "people of color," old and new Americans alike often had reason to conceal their shared Indian heritage.

Early America was a cloth woven from many threads, but the Indian strands that ran through it have often been ignored, forgotten, and allowed to fade from the nation's history. Indian people, gradually and inexorably, were squeezed out of their homelands and out of the picture as Europeans settled alongside them, then dispossessed them, and finally disregarded them. The new Americans strove to exclude the first Americans from the new nation they were building, into which many first Americans merged anonymously. American history became the story of Europeans and their descendants in America. But Indian people and Indian ways of life remained a part of the national experience. Denied center-stage in American history except in moments of open conflict, Indians continued, as they had for centuries, to make history and participate in American life.

Bibliographical Essay

The historical literature on colonial America is vast, and the ethnohistorical literature on the Indian peoples of early America is extensive and growing rapidly. The works cited here are limited to those that consider formative interactions between Indians and Europeans or provide examples given in the text.

General Works, Preface, and Introduction

Readers familiar with the work of James Axtell will recognize his influence on this book. Axtell's many works include *The Invasion Within: The Contest of Cultures in Colonial North America* (1985), the first book in a projected trilogy, and three collections of essays on the ethnohistory of colonial America: *The European and the Indian: Essays in the Ethnohistory of Colonial America* (1981, which provides the Moreau de Saint-Méry quotation as epigraph); *After Columbus: Essays in the Ethnohistory of Colonial North America* (1988); and *Beyond 1492: Encounters in Colonial North America* (1992). Jack Weatherford offers a rather more popularized discussion of similar themes in *Native Roots: How the Indians Enriched America* (1991) and *Indian Givers: How the Indians of the Americas Transformed the World* (1988). Christopher L. Miller discusses the Spokan prophecy in *Prophetic Worlds: Indians and Whites on the Columbia Plateau* (1985).

American appeals to Indians as brother Americans are printed in Colin G. Calloway, ed., *Revolution and Confederation*, in Alden T. Vaughan, gen. ed., *Early American Indian Documents: Treaties and Laws, 1607–1789*, vol. 18 (1994).

Frederick Jackson Turner's essay, "The Significance of the Frontier in American History," was published in *The Annual Report of the American Historical Association for the Year 1893* and has been reprinted many times. Felix Cohen's comments are from "Americanizing the White Man," in *American Scholar* 21 (1952):

177–91, and are quoted in Bruce E. Johansen, *Forgotten Founders: Benjamin Franklin, the Iroquois, and the Rationale for the American Revolution* (1982). Frank Shuffleton edits a collection of essays, *A Mixed Race: Ethnicity in Early America* (1993). Gary Nash explores the collision of cultures in colonial America in *Red, White and Black: The Peoples of Early North America*, 3d ed. (1992).

Richard White, *The Middle Ground: Indians, Empires, and Republics in the Great Lakes Region, 1650–1815* (1991), is essential for understanding French-Indian relations. Terry M. Jordan and Matti Kaups explore Finnish-Delaware interactions in *The American Backwoods Frontier: An Ethnic and Ecological Interpretation* (1989). Peter Kalm's observations are in Adolph B. Benson, ed., *Peter Kalm's Travels in North America* (1937). T. H. Breen's essay "Creative Adaptations: Peoples and Cultures" is in Jack P. Greene and J. R. Pole, eds., *Colonial British America: Essays in the New History of the Early Modern Era* (1984); James H. Merrell offers *The Indians' New World: Catawbas and Their Neighbors from European Contact through the Era of Removal* (1989) and " 'The Customes of Our Countrey': Indians and Colonists in Early America," in Bernard Bailyn and Philip D. Morgan, eds., *Strangers within the Realm: Cultural Margins of the First British Empire* (1991), reprinted in Philip D. Morgan, ed., *Diversity and Unity in Early North America* (1993). John Canup traces national roots in *Out of the Wilderness: The Emergence of an American Identity in Colonial New England* (1990). David J. Weber examines Spanish-Indian interactions in *The Spanish Frontier in North America* (1992). David Hackett Fischer explores cultural roots in *Albion's Seed: Four British Folkways in North America* (1989), which also includes the reminiscence of the Welsh immigrants in Pennsylvania.

Chapter 1
Imagining and Creating a New World

Some Indian statements on the changing nature of their world, including Miantonomi's speech, are reproduced in Colin G. Calloway, ed., *The World Turned Upside Down: Indian Voices from Early America* (1994).

The speech of the Natchez is in Seymour Feiler, trans. and ed., *Travels in the Interior of North America, 1751–1762,* by Jean-Bernard Bossu (1962). On pre-Columbian America, see, for example, Alvin M. Josephy Jr., ed., *America in 1492: The World of the Indian Peoples before the Arrival of Columbus* (1992), which contains an introduction by N. Scott Momaday and an epilogue by Vine Deloria Jr. The Taos Pueblo statement is quoted by Alfonso Ortiz in Frederick E. Hoxie, ed., *Indians in American History* (1988). Karen Ordahl Kupperman, ed., *America in European Consciousness, 1493–1750* (1995), considers the extent to which knowledge of America caused European thinkers to alter their conception of the world, as does Roger Schlesinger, *In the Wake of Columbus: The Impact of the New World on*

Europe, 1492–1650 (1996), which also provides a concise overview of the European repercussions of the "discovery" of America. William Brandon examines American influences on Europe in *New Worlds for Old: Reports from the New World and Their Effect on the Development of Social Thought in Europe* (1986). Emerson Baker et al., eds., *American Beginnings: Exploration, Culture, and Cartography in the Land of Norumbega* (1994), provide a cartographic-based discussion of early encounters in Maine; they include an essay by the late Brian Harley on maps as instruments of conquest.

Works examining the environmental consequences of European invasion and contact include William Cronon, *Changes in the Land: Indians, Colonists, and the Ecology of New England* (1983), from which much of the information in this chapter is derived; Carolyn Merchant, *Ecological Revolutions: Nature, Gender, and Science in New England* (1989), which carries the story of ecological change into more modern times; and Timothy Silver, *A New Face on the Countryside: Indians, Colonists, and Slaves in South Atlantic Forests, 1500–1800* (1990). William Bartram's observations are from his *Travels Through North & South Carolina, Georgia, East & West Florida* (1792), parts of which are reprinted, along with other relevant writings, in Gregory A. Waselkov and Kathryn E. Holland Braund, eds., *William Bartram on the Southeastern Indians* (1995). David J. Weber includes ecological repercussions in his overview, *The Spanish Frontier in North America* (1992). Broader perspectives are offered by Alfred Crosby in *The Columbian Exchange: Biological and Cultural Consequences of 1492* (1972), and *Ecological Imperialism: The Biological Expansion of Europe, 900–1900* (1986). Charles F. Carroll examines early English inroads in *The Timber Economy of Puritan New England* (1973). D. W. Meinig offers a different perspective in *The Shaping of America: A Geographical Perspective on 500 Years of History,* Vol. 1, *Atlantic America, 1492–1800* (1986).

Calvin Martin's insightful but controversial *Keepers of the Game: Indian-Animal Relations and the Fur Trade* (1978) discusses the spirits of wildlife, diseases, and Indians' retaliation. Critiques of Martin's thesis are offered in Shepard Krech III, ed., *Indians, Animals, and the Fur Trade* (1981). The effects of the maritime trade on the Northwest Coast are surveyed in Douglas Cole and David Darling, "History of the Early Period," in Wayne Suttles, ed., *Handbook of North American Indians,* Vol. 7, *Northwest Coast* (1990), 119–34.

On Indian uses of fire, see Stephen J. Pyne, *Fire in America* (1982). The discussion of Choctaw deer hunting is drawn from Richard White, *The Roots of Dependency: Subsistence, Environment, and Social Change among the Choctaws, Pawnees, and Navajos* (1983). Adoption of and reactions to domestic animals are discussed in Virginia DeJohn Anderson, "King Philip's Herds: Indians, Colonists, and the Problem of Livestock in Early New England," *William and Mary Quarterly,* 3d ser., 51 (1994): 601–24. Robert Beverley's comment on Powhatan improvidence is quoted in Helen C. Rountree, *Pocahontas's People: The Powhatan Indians of Virginia through Four Centuries* (1990).

Chapter 2
Healing and Disease

The standard work on Native American medicine is Virgil J. Vogel, *American Indian Medicine* (1970). Vogel provides an extensive appendix, "American Indian Contributions to Pharmacology." Jack Weatherford devotes considerable space to Indian medicine in *Native Roots* (1991). Dean Snow edits James W. Herrick, *Iroquois Medical Botany* (1995). Bobette Perrone, H. Henrietta Stockel, and Victoria Krueger examine the continuing role of native ways of healing in *Medicine Women, Curanderas, and Women Doctors* (1989). Gladys Tantaquidgeon, a Mohegan, provides lists of plants and remedies in *Folk Medicine of the Delaware and Related Algonkian Indians* (1972). Maureen Trudelle Schwarz explores how the Hanta virus was tracked down in "The Explanatory and Predictive Power of History: Coping with the 'Mystery Illness' of 1993," *Ethnohistory* 42 (1995): 375–401. Jonathan D. Sauer's essay "Changing Perception and Exploitation of New World Plants in Europe, 1492–1800" is in Fredi Chiapelli, ed., *First Images of America: The Impact of the New World on the Old,* 2 vols. (1976), 2:813–32. The distinguished Iroquois scholar William N. Fenton traces the exchange of knowledge in "Contacts between Iroquois Herbalism and Colonial Medicine," in *Annual Report of the Board of Regents of the Smithsonian Institution* (1941). Information on medical practices in Europe can be found in Lawrence I. Conrad et al., *The Western Medical Tradition, 800 B.C. to 1800 A.D.* (1995).

The account of the cure for scurvy by the Indians around Montreal is in Ramsay Cook, intro., *The Voyages of Jacques Cartier* (1993). Denys Delâge discusses Huron medicine in *Bitter Feast: Amerindians and Europeans in Northeastern North America, 1600–1664* (1993). Reuben G. Thwaites, ed., *The Jesuit Relations and Allied Documents,* 73 vols. (1896–1901), includes numerous observations of native practices and beliefs by French missionaries (the description of Huron diseases and their cures is from vol. 33: 199). Other works by early travelers who paid particular attention to Indian medicine and plant use include Hugh Talmage Lefler, ed., *A New Voyage to Carolina by John Lawson* (1967); Seymour Feiler, trans. and ed., *Travels in the Interior of North America, 1751–1762,* by Jean-Bernard Bossu (1962); Adolph B. Benson, ed., *Peter Kalm's Travels in North America* (1937); William Bartram, *Travels Through North & South Carolina, Georgia, East & West Florida* (1792); and Antonio Pace, trans. and ed., *Luigi Castiglioni's Viaggio: Travels in the United States of North America 1785–1787* (1983). John Heckewelder, *History, Manners, and Customs of the Indian Nations who once inhabited Pennsylvania and the Neighboring States* (1876), discusses Indian medicine and describes a sweat bath. Henry Tufts's account of his cure and his sojourn among the Abenakis is in *Narrative of the Life, Adventures, Travels, and Sufferings of Henry Tufts* (1807). On Molly Ockett, see Bunny McBride and Harald E. L. Prins, "Walking the Medicine Line: Molly Ockett, a Pigwacket Doctor," in Robert S. Grumet, ed., *Northeastern Indian Lives*

1632–1816 (1996), 321–47. Helen H. Tanner provides glimpses into a healer's life in "Coocoochee, Mohawk Medicine Woman," *American Indian Culture and Research Journal 3*: 3 (1979): 23–41. Andrew L. Knaut discusses Hispanic resort to Pueblo folk medicines and Pueblo losses to disease in *The Pueblo Revolt of 1680: Conquest and Resistance in Seventeenth-Century New Mexico* (1995). Richard I. Ford mentions trade in plants in his "Inter-Indian Exchange in the Southwest," in Alfonso Ortiz, ed., *Handbook of North American Indians*, Vol. 10, *Southwest* (1993), 711–22.

Scholarship in demography and epidemiology has grown dramatically in the past twenty years or so, and scholars apply increasingly sophisticated techniques to achieve their estimates of precontact Indian population and postcontact rates of decline. Nevertheless, considerable disagreement remains regarding the precontact estimates. William H. McNeill looks at the role of disease in human history in *Plagues and Peoples* (1976). Standard works for North America include Russell Thornton, *American Indian Holocaust and Survival: A Population History since 1492* (1987) and *The Cherokees: A Population History* (1990); William M. Denevan, ed., *The Native Population of the Americas in 1492* (1976); Alfred Crosby, *The Columbian Exchange: Biological and Cultural Consequences of 1492* (1972) and "Virgin Soil Epidemics as a Factor in the Aboriginal Depopulation in America," *William and Mary Quarterly*, 3d ser., 33 (1976): 289–99; Henry Dobyns, *Their Number Become Thinned: Native American Population Dynamics in Eastern North America* (1983); and John W. Veran and Douglas H. Ubelaker, eds., *Disease and Demography in the Americas* (1992). William Bradford's accounts of disease among the Indians of New England are in Harvey Wish, ed., *William Bradford, Of Plymouth Plantation* (1962). Dean Snow, *The Iroquois* (1994), provides statistics on Mohawk decline. Marvin T. Smith surveys southern tribes' disappearance in "Aboriginal Depopulation in the Postcontact Southeast," in Charles Hudson and Carmen Chaves Tesser, eds., *The Forgotten Centuries: Indians and Europeans in the American South, 1521–1704* (1994). The destruction of the indigenous population of Florida is the theme of Jerald T. Milanich, *Florida Indians and the Invasion from Europe* (1995). John H. Hann discusses Apalachee population collapse in *Apalachee: The Land between the Rivers* (1988). Willard H. Rollings surveys the devastating impact of disease in Arkansas in "Living in a Graveyard: Native Americans in Colonial Arkansas," in Jeannie Whayne, ed., *Cultural Encounters in the Early South: Indians and Europeans in Arkansas* (1995), 38–60. Robert Boyd examines diseases on the Northwest Coast in "Demographic History, 1774–1874," in Wayne Suttles, ed., *Handbook of North American Indians*, Vol. 7, *Northwest Coast* (1990), 135–48. Cole Harris looks at native accounts of smallpox in "Voices of Disaster: Smallpox around the Strait of Georgia in 1782," *Ethnohistory* 41 (1994): 591–626. Boyd and Harris disagree about the timing and extent of specific epidemics. Peter C. Mancall, *Deadly Medicine: Indians and Alcohol in Early America* (1995), surveys the impact of alcohol on Native American societies during the colonial era. James Cassedy surveys the state of medicine in the colonies in *Medicine in America: A Short History* (1991).

Chapter 3
The Stuff of Life

The analysis of Tapp's estate inventory is in Stephen Potter, *Commoners, Tribute, and Chiefs: The Development of an Algonquian Culture in the Potomac Valley* (1993). Extracts from William Wood's *New England's Prospect* (1634) and other early English colonization literature are reprinted in Peter C. Mancall, ed., *Envisioning America: English Plans for the Colonization of North America, 1580–1640* (1995). The trading at Hochelaga is reported in Ramsay Cook, ed., *The Voyages of Jacques Cartier* (1993). Denys Delâge analyzes Huron-French trading patterns in *Bitter Feast* (1993). James B. Langford Jr.'s essay "The Coosawattee Plate" is in David Hurst Thomas, ed., *Columbian Consequences*, vol. 2 (1990), 139–51. James Axtell considers the impact of European goods on seventeenth-century Indians in "The First Consumer Revolution," in his *Beyond 1492* (1992). James H. Merrell discusses some of the changes in everyday life in " 'The Customes of Our Countrey': Indians and Colonists in Early America," in Bernard Bailyn and Philip D. Morgan, eds., *Strangers within the Realm* (1991). Alexander Hamilton's observations are in Carl Bridenbaugh, ed., *Gentleman's Progress: The Itinerarium of Dr. Alexander Hamilton, 1744* (1948). Pierre Pouchot's comment is from Brian Leigh Dunnigan, ed., *Memoirs on the Late War in North America between France and England, by Pierre Pouchot* (1994). Convenient overviews of the northwestern maritime trade are provided in Wilcomb Washburn, ed., *Handbook of North American Indians*, Vol. 4, *Indian-White Relations* (1988), 375–90, and in Wayne Suttles, ed., *Handbook of North American Indians*, Vol. 7, *Northwest Coast* (1990), 119–34. Christopher L. Miller and George R. Hamell explore the spiritual associations of glass beads and other trade items in "New Perspectives on Indian-White Contact: Cultural Symbols and Colonial Trade," *Journal of American History* 73 (1988): 311–28.

Among the many works that discuss the impact of Native American foods on Europe is Jack Weatherford, *Indian Givers* (1988). Mortality and emigration figures resulting from the Irish potato famine are from Kerby A. Miller, *Emigrants and Exiles: Ireland and the Irish Exodus to North America* (1985). On Native American farming, see R. Douglas Hurt, *Indian Agriculture in America* (1987). Foods new to Europeans are discussed in Herman J. Viola and Carolyn Margolis, *Seeds of Change* (1991); and in Nelson Foster and Linda S. Cordell, eds., *Chilies to Chocolate: Food the Americas Gave the World* (1992). Peter Iverson lists Pawnee crops in his essay "Taking Care of Earth and Sky," in Alvin M. Josephy Jr., ed., *America in 1492* (1992). Lawson's comments on corn are in Hugh Talmage Lefler, ed., *A New Voyage to Carolina by John Lawson* (1967). David Freeman Hawke, *Everyday Life in Early America* (1988), and Timothy Silver, *A New Face on the Countryside* (1990), also discuss new foods. Nicholas P. Hardeman examines the adoption and influence of Indian corn in *Shucks, Shocks, and Hominy Blocks: Corn as a Way of Life in Pioneer*

America (1981). Carol O. Sauer, *Seventeenth Century North America* (1980), traces the northward spread of watermelons. Changes in Hopi subsistence are discussed in E. Charles Adams, "Passive Resistance: Hopi Responses to Spanish Contact and Conquest," in David Hurst Thomas, ed., *Columbian Consequences,* vol. 1 (1989), 77–91; California mission diets are examined in J. De Niro, "The Effects of European Contact on the Health of Alta California Indians," and Robert L. Hoover, "Spanish-Native Interaction and Acculturation in the Missions," both in Thomas, ed., *Columbian Consequences,* vol. 1. John Mack Faragher discusses the Indian origins of backwoods hunting culture in *Daniel Boone: The Life and Legend of an American Pioneer* (1992).

David Hackett Fischer discusses changing and continuing English material culture in *Albion's Seed* (1989). The population figures for London are from Roy Porter, *London: A Social History* (1995). Peter Nabokov and Robert Easton provide an excellent overview of Indian lodging in *Native American Architecture* (1989). Peter Kalm's observations on changing styles of Indian housing and clothing are in Adolph B. Benson, ed., *Peter Kalm's Travels in North America* (1937). Nicholas Denys discusses changing Indian ways in W. F. Ganong, ed., *The Description and Natural History of the Coasts of North America* (1908). The information on Oneida material culture at the time of the Revolution is drawn from Massachusetts Historical Society, Boston, Timothy Pickering Papers, reel 62, 157–74; that on the Cherokees from the archaeological reports of investigations at Chota and Tanasee prior to the flooding of those sites by the Tellico Dam in 1979, in Gerald F. Schroedl, ed., *Overhill Cherokee Archaeology at Chota-Tanasee* (1986). Patrick Campbell reports on his visit to Brant's home on the Grand River in H. H. Langton, ed., *Travels in the Interior Inhabited Parts of North America in the Years 1791 and 1792* (1937).

Material on changing culture in New Mexico, including Apache playing cards, is in Marc Simmons, *Coronado's Land: Essays on Daily Life in Colonial New Mexico* (1991). David J. Weber, *The Spanish Frontier in North America* (1992), is also useful for understanding changing material culture of Indians and Spaniards, in Florida, California, and New Mexico. John H. Hann reports the case of counterfeiting in "Apalachee Counterfeiters in St. Augustine," *Florida Historical Quarterly* 67 (1988): 53–88. John McPhee, *The Survival of the Bark Canoe* (1975), provides a lively chronicle of the construction of birchbark canoes and of a 150-mile canoe trip through the Maine woods.

Timothy J. Shannon suggests new ways of looking at the clothing of Indians and Europeans in "Dressed for Success on the Mohawk Frontier: Hendrick, William Johnson, and the Indian Fashion," *William and Mary Quarterly,* 3d ser., 53 (1996): 13–42.

The descriptions of Indian adoptions of European clothing in the Maine area are reproduced in Colin G. Calloway, ed., *Dawnland Encounters: Indians and Europeans in Northern New England* (1991), and in Harald E. L. Prins, "Turmoil on the Wabanaki Frontier, 1524–1678," in Richard W. Judd, Edwin A. Churchill, and Joel W. Eastman, eds., *Maine: The Pine Tree State from Prehistory to Present* (1995),

97–119. Examples of Indian clothing among backcountry settlers are taken from Colin G. Calloway, *The American Revolution in Indian Country: Crisis and Diversity in Native American Communities* (1995), chap. 1.

Chapter 4
A World of Dreams and Bibles

The fundamental source for any study of missionary activities in northeastern North America is Reuben G. Thwaites, ed., *The Jesuit Relations and Allied Documents,* 73 vols. (1896–1901). Henry Warner Bowden presents a convenient overview in *American Indians and Christian Missions* (1981). Other essential secondary sources include the works of James Axtell, especially his *The Invasion Within* (1985). John Webster Grant surveys Canadian developments in *Moon of Wintertime: Missionaries and the Indians of Canada in Encounter since 1534* (1984). Denys Delâge considers Huron and Iroquois responses in *Bitter Feast* (1993). George Tinker offers a Native American indictment in *Missionary Conquest: The Gospel and Native American Genocide* (1993).

Samuel Kirkland's experiences are recounted in W. Pilkington, ed., *The Journals of Samuel Kirkland* (1980). See Nancy Shoemaker, "Kateri Tekakwitha's Tortuous Path to Sainthood," in Shoemaker, ed., *Negotiators of Change: Historical Perspectives on Native American Women* (1995). Wanalancet's "conversion speech," recorded by Daniel Gookin, is in *Historical Collections of the Indians of New England* (1792). On Wanalancet, see Colin G. Calloway, "Wanalancet and Kancagamus: Indian Strategy and Leadership on the New Hampshire Frontier," *Historical New Hampshire* 43 (1988): 264–90; on the Mahican move to Stockbridge, see Patrick Frazier, *The Mohicans of Stockbridge* (1993), chap. 1. A French officer's observations on the limited success of missionaries among France's Indian allies are in Brian Leigh Dunnigan, ed., *Memoirs on the Late War in North America between France and England, by Pierre Pouchot* (1994).

Studies that consider how Indian peoples merged traditional and Christian beliefs include Kenneth M. Morrison, "Montagnais Missionization in Early New France: The Syncretic Imperative," *American Indian Culture and Research Journal* 10: 3 (1986): 1–23, and James P. Ronda, "Generations of Faith: The Christian Indians of Martha's Vineyard," *William and Mary Quarterly*, 3d ser., 38 (1980): 369–94. Neal Salisbury discusses Indian converts in "Red Puritans: The 'Praying Indians' of Massachusetts Bay and John Eliot," *William and Mary Quarterly,* 3d ser., 31 (1974): 27–54. Henry W. Bowden and James P. Ronda, eds., *John Eliot's Indian Dialogues* (1980), present a series of contrived conversations between converted and unconverted Indians, prepared by John Eliot as a guide to the kind of resistance Indian missionaries could expect to encounter when they returned to their people. Daniel Mandell examines the experiences of one praying town after the heyday of the mission towns in New England in " 'To Live more Like My Christian

Neighbors': Natick Indians in the Eighteenth Century," *William and Mary Quarterly*, 3d ser., 48 (1991): 552–79. Karen Anderson discusses missionary interference with gender relations in *Chain Her by One Foot: The Subjugation of Native Women in Seventeenth-Century New France* (1991).

David J. Weber describes Franciscan missionary efforts in *The Spanish Frontier in North America* (1992). Henry Dobyns discusses Francisco Garcés in *Spanish Colonial Tucson: A Demographic History* (1976), chap. 3. John H. Hann, *Apalachee* (1988), contains valuable information on Spanish missions in Florida, as does Jerald T. Milanich, *Florida Indians and the Invasion from Europe* (1995). David Hurst Thomas, ed., *Columbian Consequences*, vol. 2 (1990), includes a dozen articles on the same subject. John Kessel discusses the Spanish and the Pueblos in "From Crusading Intolerance to Pragmatic Accommodation," and E. Charles Adams describes the Hopis in "Passive Resistance," both in Thomas, ed., *Columbian Consequences*, vol. 1 (1989). The Domínguez-Escalante exchange with the Hopis is in Ted J. Warner, ed., *The Domínguez-Escalante Journal: Their Expedition through Colorado, Utah, Arizona and New Mexico in 1776* (1995). Ramon A. Gutiérrez, *When Jesus Came, the Corn Mothers Went Away: Marriage, Sexuality, and Power in New Mexico, 1500–1846* (1991), offers a controversial discussion of the Spanish missionaries' assault on the sexual practices and culture of the Pueblos. Andrew L. Knaut discusses Pueblo reactions to Franciscan missionaries in *The Pueblo Revolt of 1680* (1995). Robert H. Jackson and Edward Castillo take a critical look at Spanish missionary work in *Indians, Franciscans and Spanish Colonization: The Impact of the Mission System on California Indians* (1995). La Pérouse's observations are in Malcolm Margolin, intro., *Monterey in 1786: The Journals of Jean François de La Pérouse* (1989).

On David Brainerd's experiences, see Richard W. Pointer, " 'Poor Indians' and the 'Poor in Spirit': The Indian Impact on David Brainerd," *New England Quarterly* 68 (1994): 403–26. Alexander Hamilton's journey is in Carl Bridenbaugh, ed., *Gentleman's Progress* (1948). The community at Oquaga and Nicholas Cresswell's observations are discussed in Colin G. Calloway, *The American Revolution in Indian Country* (1995).

On Yaqui-Jesuit relations, see Edward H. Spicer, *The Yaquis: A Cultural History* (1980), chap. 1. For information on Father Rasles and the religious contest among the Abenakis, see Colin G. Calloway, ed., *Dawnland Encounters* (1991), chap. 2. Cornelius J. Jaenen, *The French Relationship with the Native Peoples of New France and Acadia* (1984), discusses the attempts by Father Nau and Rasles to conform to Indian ways.

Gregory Evans Dowd discusses the spiritual dimension of Indian wars of resistance in *A Spirited Resistance: The North American Indian Struggle for Unity, 1745–1815* (1992). Joel Martin considers a similar phenomenon in *Sacred Revolt: The Muskogees' Struggle for a New World* (1991). William Simmons and Cheryl Simmons, eds., *New Light on Separate Ways* (1982), provide background on Narragansett conversion. William Simmons documents the survival of native folk beliefs, often with European and African influences, in *Spirit of the New England Tribes: Indian History and Folklore, 1620–1984* (1986).

Chapter 5
New World Warfare and
a New World of War

General studies of warfare in early America include John E. Ferling, *A Wilderness of Miseries: War and Warriors in Early America* (1980), and Douglas Edward Leach, *Arms for Empire: A Military History of the British Colonies in North America, 1607–1763* (1973). Ian K. Steele provides a fine study of Indian and colonial conflicts in *Warpaths: Invasions of North America* (1994) and *Betrayals: Fort William Henry and the "Massacre"* (1990). Daniel J. Beattie discusses British adjustments in "The Adaptation of the British Army to Wilderness Warfare, 1755–1763," in Maarten Ultee, ed., *Adapting to Conditions: War and Society in the Eighteenth Century* (1986), 56–83. The essays in R. Brian Ferguson and Neil L. Whitehead, eds., *War in the Tribal Zone: Expanding States and Indigenous Societies* (1992), provide a broader perspective on the impact of Europeans on native warfare. Don Higginbotham gives a critique of the notion that a uniquely American way of war developed and a review of the literature in "The Early American Way of War: Reconnaissance and Appraisal," *William and Mary Quarterly*, 3d ser., 44 (1987): 230–73.

Champlain's account of the clash with the Iroquois is in H. P. Biggar, ed., *The Works of Samuel de Champlain*, 6 vols. (1922–36), 2: 90–101; the relevant extracts are reprinted in Colin G. Calloway, ed., *Dawnland Encounters* (1991). Daniel K. Richter considers the impact of the new warfare and the escalating "Beaver Wars" of the seventeenth century in *The Ordeal of the Longhouse: The Peoples of the Iroquois League in the Era of European Colonization* (1992), chap. 3. Scarouady's indictment of Braddock is in Paul A. Wallace, *Conrad Weiser* (1945).

A thought-provoking analysis of differing concepts of warfare as practiced and perceived by Spaniards and Aztecs is presented by Inga Clendinnen, " 'Fierce and Unnatural Cruelty': Cortes and the Conquest of Mexico," *Representations* 33 (1991): 65–100; David H. Dye's essay "Warfare in the Sixteenth-Century Southeast: The de Soto Expedition in the Interior" is in David Hurst Thomas, ed., *Columbian Consequences*, vol. 2 (1990), 211–22. Jerald T. Milanich surveys the impact of Spanish expeditions in *Florida Indians and the Invasion from Europe* (1995); Spanish accounts of the de Soto expedition are reprinted in Edward G. Bourne, ed., *Narratives of the Career of Hernando De Soto in the Conquest of Florida*, 2 vols. (1904), and more recently in Lawrence A. Clayton, Vernon James Knight Jr., and Edward C. Moore, eds., *The De Soto Chronicles: The Expedition of Hernando de Soto to North America in 1539–1543*, 2 vols. (1993). Patricia Galloway assesses the reliability of the various accounts of the de Soto expedition in *Choctaw Genesis 1500–1700* (1995), chap. 3. Cabeza de Vaca's comments on the prowess of Florida archers are in Cyclone Covey, trans. and ed., *Cabeza de Vaca's Adventures in the Unknown Interior of America* (1990). La Salle's views on the uselessness of swords are quoted in Anka Muhlstein, *La Salle, Explorer of the North American Frontier* (1994). J. Frederick Fausz discusses the impact of guns in "Fighting 'Fire' with Firearms: The Anglo-Powhatan Arms Race in Early Virginia," *American Indian Culture and Research Journal* 3: 4 (1979): 33–50, while Patrick M. Malone traces similar developments in seventeenth-century New England, with more attention to military technology, in *The Skulking Way of War: Technology and Tactics among the New England Indians* (1991). Alfred Cave gives the most complete account of *The Pequot War* (1996). John T. Juricek discusses the Westo war in "The Westo Indians," *Ethnohistory* 11 (1964): 134–38. French attempts to destroy the Fox are detailed in R. David Edmunds and Joseph L. Peyser, *The Fox Wars: The Mesquakie Challenge to New France* (1993). L. R. Bailey examines slavery in *Indian Slave Trade in the Southwest: A Study of Slave-taking and the Traffic in Indian Captives* (1966).

Francis Jennings offers a scathing comparison of warfare as waged by Indians and Europeans in the seventeenth century, in *The Invasion of America: Indians, Colonialism, and the Cant of Conquest* (1975), chap. 9, and discusses the Pequot War as total war (chap. 13). James Axtell and William C. Sturtevant discuss the evidence for scalping as a precontact phenomenon in "The Unkindest Cut, or Who Invented Scalping?" *William and Mary Quarterly*, 3d ser., 37 (1980): 451–72. On Indians in colonial armies, see Richard R. Johnson, "The Search for a Usable Indian: An Aspect of the Defense of Colonial New England," *Journal of American History* 64 (1977): 623–51. Daniel Mandell considers the impact of service in English armies in *Behind the Frontier: Indian Communities in Eighteenth-Century Massachusetts* (1996). Bougainville's views on France's Indian allies and the Seven Years' War are in Edward P. Hamilton, ed., *Adventure in the Wilderness: The American Journals of Louis Antoine de Bougainville, 1756–1760* (1964, 1990).

Henry Dobyns discusses Indian soldiers in the garrison at Tucson and the militarization of Northern Piman society in *Spanish Colonial Tucson* (1976). The Indian reference to being caught between the blades of a pair of scissors was reported by Moravian missionary John Heckewelder in the eighteenth century and is repeated in Ian K. Steele, *Warpaths*, and Colin G. Calloway, *Crown and Calumet: British-Indian Relations, 1783–1815* (1987). Calloway also surveys the involvement of Indian peoples in the American Revolution in *The American Revolution in Indian Country* (1995).

On the changing situations on the Great Plains, see Frank Raymond Secoy, *Changing Military Patterns on the Great Plains* (1953); Bernard Mishkin, *Rank and Warfare among the Plains Indians* (1940); John C. Ewers, "Intertribal Warfare as the Precursor of Indian-White Warfare on the Northern Great Plains," *Western Historical Quarterly* 6 (1975): 397–410, and *The Horse in Blackfoot Indian Culture* (1955); and Colin G. Calloway, "The Intertribal Balance of Power on the Great Plains, 1760–1850," *Journal of American Studies* 16 (1982): 25–48, and "Snake Frontiers:

The Eastern Shoshones in the Eighteenth Century," *Annals of Wyoming* 63 (1991): 82–92. Saukamappee's account is in Richard Glover, ed., *David Thompson's Narrative, 1784–1812* (1962). The Sioux move on to the plains is traced in Richard White, "The Winning of the West: The Expansion of the Western Sioux in the Eighteenth and Nineteenth Centuries," *Journal of American History* 65 (1978): 319–43. Peter Nabokov, *Two Leggings: The Making of a Crow Warrior* (1982), offers excellent insights into the warrior culture prevalent among Plains Indians by the nineteenth century. Elizabeth A. H. John discusses intensifying conflict between Pueblos and Apaches and shifting power struggles on the southern plains in *Storms Brewed in Other Men's Worlds: The Confrontation of Indians, Spanish and French in the Southwest, 1540–1795* (1975). The most recent study of the Pueblo Revolt is Andrew L. Knaut, *The Pueblo Revolt of 1680* (1995).

Chapter 6
New World Diplomacy and
New World Foreign Policies

Wilbur R. Jacobs examines the role of gift giving in Indian diplomacy in *Wilderness Politics and Indian Gifts: The Northern Colonial Frontier, 1748–1763* (1950). Richard White, *The Middle Ground* (1991) is the best recent study of the complexities of Indian-white diplomacy. Dorothy V. Jones examines treaties in British colonial America in *License for Empire: Colonialism by Treaty in Early America* (1982). The recommendations of Governor Tomás Vélez Capuchin are in Alfred Barnaby Thomas, *The Plains Indians and New Mexico, 1751–1778* (1940), 134–35, 151. White also traces the career of Red Shoe in David G. Sweet and Gary Nash, eds., *Struggle and Survival in Colonial America* (1981).

On the Iroquois, see Daniel K. Richter, *The Ordeal of the Longhouse* (1992); Francis Jennings and William N. Fenton, eds., *The History and Culture of Iroquois Diplomacy: An Interdisciplinary Guide to the Treaties of the Six Nations and Their League* (1985); and J. A. Brandão and William A. Starna, "The Treaties of 1701: A Triumph of Iroquois Diplomacy," *Ethnohistory* 43 (1996): 209–44. Gary Nash provides concise summaries of Iroquois and Creek diplomacy in *Red, White and Black,* 3d ed. (1992). For one Indian tribe's dealings with one colony, see Tom Hatley, *The Dividing Paths: Cherokees and South Carolinians through the Era of the Revolution* (1993). On Hagler and the Catawbas, see James H. Merrell, " 'Minding the Business of the Nation': Hagler as Catawba Leader," *Ethnohistory* 33 (1986): 55–70, and *The Indians' New World* (1989).

Dean Snow points out the French influence on the diffusion of the calumet in *The Iroquois* (1994). George Sabo III analyzes calumet ceremonies among the Quapaws and Caddoes at the time of La Salle's visit in "Rituals of Encounter: Interpreting Native American Views of European Explorers," in Jeannie Whayne, ed., *Cultural Encounters in the Early South* (1995), 76–87. Nancy L. Hagendorn examines the career of Andrew Montour as interpreter and culture broker in Margaret Connell Szasz, ed., *Between Indian and White Worlds: The Cultural Broker* (1994), and also discusses the role of interpreters in " 'A Friend to Go between Them': The Interpreter as Cultural Broker During Anglo-Iroquois Councils, 1740–1770," *Ethnohistory* 35 (1988): 60–80. Yasuhide Kawashima also discusses interpreters in "Forest Diplomats: The Role of Interpreters in Indian-White Relations on the Early American Frontier," *American Indian Quarterly* 13 (1989): 1–14. Colin G. Calloway sketches the life of Simon Girty in James A. Clifton, ed., *Being and Becoming Indian: Biographical Studies of North American Frontiers* (1989). Examples of interpretation by "linguistic chains" are from James H. Merrell's study of Shickellamy in Robert S. Grumet, ed., *Northeastern Indian Lives* (1996), 226–57, and James P. Ronda, *Lewis and Clark among the Indians* (1984). The nature of the British Indian department is discussed in Colin G. Calloway, *Crown and Calumet* (1987). Colden's comment on Johnson Hall is in *Documents Relating to the Colonial History of the State of New York* (1855–61), 6: 740–41. James Thomas Flexner provides a biography of Johnson in *Lord of the Mohawks* (1959); Lois M. Feister and Bonnie Pulis give information on Johnson's home and his Mohawk wife in "Molly Brant: Her Domestic and Political Roles in Eighteenth-Century New York," in Robert S. Grumet, ed., *Northeastern Indian Lives* (1996), 295–320. The volume contains several studies of individuals who learned to move between cultures. For a biography of Elliott, see Reginald Horsman, *Matthew Elliott, British Indian Agent* (1964).

Conrad Weiser's trip to Onondaga in 1743 is described in John Bartram, Lewis Evans, and Conrad Weiser, *A Journey from Pennsylvania to Onondaga in 1743* (1973). William Savery's observation at Canandaigua is quoted in Jack Campisi and William A. Starna, "On the Road to Canandaigua: The Treaty of 1794," *American Indian Quarterly* 19(1995), 467–90; quote at 488.

Chapter 7
New Nomads and True Nomads

John McPhee discusses Indian canoe routes in *The Survival of the Bark Canoe* (1975). Paul A. W. Wallace traces ancient trails in *Indian Paths of Pennsylvania* (1993). On Indian mapmakers, see Hugh Talmage Lefler, ed., *A New Voyage to Carolina by John Lawson* (1967); James P. Ronda, " 'A Chart in His Way': Indian Cartography and the Lewis and Clark Expedition," *Great Plains Quarterly* 4 (1984): 43–53; Malcolm Lewis, "Indian Maps: Their Place in the History of Plains Cartography," *Great Plains Quarterly* 4 (1984): 91–108; and Gregory Waselkov, "Indian Maps of the Colonial Southeast," in Peter H. Wood, Gregory A. Waselkov, and M. Thomas Hatley, eds., *Powhatan's Mantle: Indians in the Colonial Southeast*

(1989), 292–343. On the use of maps to dispossess Indians, see J. B. Harley, "Victims of a Map: New England Cartography and the Native Americans," in Emerson Baker et al., eds., *American Beginnings* (1994).

On the new sources of European, and especially British, migration in the eighteenth century, see David Hackett Fischer, *Albion's Seed* (1989); Angus Calder, *Revolutionary Empire: The Rise of the English-Speaking Empires from the Fifteenth Century to the 1780s* (1981); and D. W. Meinig, *The Shaping of America,* Vol. 1, *Atlantic America, 1492–1800* (1986). Bernard Bailyn examines prerevolutionary patterns of migration in *The Peopling of British North America: An Introduction* (1985) and *Voyagers to the West: A Passage in the Peopling of America on the Eve of the Revolution* (1986). Franklin's concern about German immigration is from James S. Olson, *The Ethnic Dimension in American History,* 2d ed. (1994); Logan's concerns about the Scotch-Irish are in Richard Hofstadter, *America at 1750: A Social Portrait* (1971).

On the Catawbas, see James H. Merrell, *The Indians' New World* (1989); on the chaos and refugee communities in the Great Lakes, see Richard White, *The Middle Ground* (1991), Helen H. Tanner, "The Glaize in 1792: A Composite Indian Community," *Ethnohistory* 25 (1978): 15–39, and Helen H. Tanner, ed., *Atlas of Great Lakes Indian History* (1987). Jesuit observations on the composition of Iroquois villages are in Reuben G. Thwaites, ed., *The Jesuit Relations and Allied Documents* (1896–1901), 43: 265. On the impact of Spanish invasion on Indian population movements, see Henry Dobyns, "Indians in the Colonial Spanish Borderlands" (and especially his excellent map, "Spanish and Native American Migrations, 1565–1800"), in Frederick E. Hoxie, ed., *Indians in American History* (1988). On Florida's population collapse, see Henry Dobyns, *Their Number Become Thinned* (1983), and Jerald T. Milanich, *Florida Indians and the Invasion from Europe* (1995).

Willard H. Rollings discusses population movements in "Living in a Graveyard," in Jeannie Whayne, ed., *Cultural Encounters in the Early South* (1995), 38–60. On the impact of the horse on Apache and Navajo folklore, see LaVerne Harrell Clark, *They Sang for Horses* (1966). Cree, Assiniboine, and Ojibwa migrations are discussed in Arthur J. Ray, *Indians in the Fur Trade: Their Role as Hunters, Trappers and Middlemen in the Lands Southwest of Hudson Bay, 1600–1870* (1974). Colin G. Calloway surveys Abenaki population movements in *The Western Abenakis of Vermont, 1600–1800: War, Migration, and the Survival of an Indian People* (1990). Evan Haefeli and Kevin Sweeney trace individual Indians through different locations and changing tribal identities in New England in "Wattanummon's World: Personal and Tribal Identity in the Algonquian Diaspora, C. 1660–1712," *Actes du Vingt-Cinquième Congrès des Algonquinistes* (1994): 212–24, and in "Revisiting the Redeemed Captive: New Perspectives on the 1704 Attack on Deerfield," *William and Mary Quarterly,* 3d ser., 52 (1995): 3–46. For the operation of New England systems of poor relief as applied to Indians, see Ruth Wallis Herndon and Ella Wilcox Sekatau, "The Right to a Name: The Narragansett People and Rhode Island

Officials in the Revolutionary Era," *Ethnohistory,* forthcoming. John Rydford provides information on the origins of Indian place names in Kansas in *Indian Place Names* (1968).

Chapter 8
Crossing and Merging Frontiers

Accounts of the Christian among the Florida Indians are related by Luys Hernandez de Biedna, the Gentleman of Elvas, and Garcilaso de la Vega in Lawrence A. Clayton, Vernon James Knight Jr., and Edward C. Moore, eds., *The De Soto Chronicles* (1993). John Canup discusses the burial mound at Cape Cod in *Out of the Wilderness* (1990).

John Lawson's comments on English traders are in Hugh Talmage Lefler, ed., *A New Voyage to Carolina by John Lawson* (1967). Peter Kalm's observations are in Adolph B. Benson, ed., *Peter Kalm's Travels in North America* (1937). Luigi Castiglioni's observations are recorded in Antonio Pace, trans. and ed., *Luigi Castiglioni's Viaggio* (1983); Crèvecoeur's views are expressed in *Letters from an American Farmer* (1782, and various modern editions).

James Axtell discusses the phenomenon of captives who refused to return home in "The White Indians of Colonial America" in *The European and the Indian* (1981). John Demos reconstructs the saga of Eunice Williams in *The Unredeemed Captive* (1994). In old age, Mary Jemison related her life story to New York physician James Seaver. The most recent edition is *A Narrative of the Life of Mary Jemison,* ed. June Namias (1992). Namias examines the experiences of several female captives in *White Captives: Gender and Ethnicity on American Frontiers* (1993). William Smith's account of the delivery of the Shawnee captives is given in his *Historical Account of the Expedition against the Ohio Indians in the year 1764* (1868). Examples of ties between redeemed captives and Indian "parents" are given in Evan Haefeli and Kevin Sweeney, "Revisiting the *Redeemed Captive*" (1995): 3–46. François Marbois' account is reprinted in Dean Snow, William Starna, and Charles Gehring, eds., *In Mohawk Country: Early Narratives of a Native People* (in press).

Colin G. Calloway's study, "Simon Girty: Interpreter and Intermediary," and other essays on bicultural individuals and shifting identities appear in James A. Clifton, ed., *Being and Becoming Indian* (1989). Paul A. Hutton gives Wells's biography in "William Wells: Frontier Scout and Indian Agent," *Indiana Magazine of History* 74 (1978): 183–222. Calloway considers the "renegade" phenomenon in "Neither Red Nor White: White Renegades on the American Indian Frontier," *Western Historical Quarterly* 17 (1986): 43–66, and in "Rhode Island Renegade: The Enigma of Joshua Tefft," in *Rhode Island History* 43 (1984): 136–45, and presents information on the baron de Saint Castin and other culture crossings in *Dawnland Encounters* (1991). The information on Bourgmont is drawn from Frank

Norall, *Bourgmont: Explorer of the Missouri, 1689–1725* (1988). On culture brokers in general, see Margaret Connell Szasz, ed., *Between Indian and White Worlds* (1994), and Frances Karttunen, *Between Worlds: Interpreters, Guides and Survivors* (1994), which provides sixteen case studies from the sixteenth to the twentieth century as well as an epilogue on the experiences of these people's children.

On Indians in Europe, see Carolyn Thomas Foreman, *Indians Abroad, 1493–1938* (1943), and Harald E. L. Prins, "To the Land of the Mistogoches: American Indians Traveling to Europe in the Age of Exploration," *American Indian Culture and Research Journal* 17:1 (1993): 175–95. The story of Peter Otsiquette is in Franklin B. Hough, ed., *Proceedings of the Commissioners of Indian Affairs Appointed by Law for the Extinguishment of Indian Titles in the State of New York* (1861), 179n. J. Leitch Wright Jr. relates the story of a remarkable life in *William Augustus Bowles, Director General of the Creek Nation* (1967).

John Mack Faragher provides instances of peaceful interaction typical on the frontier in *Daniel Boone* (1992). Marshall Becker recovers Freeman's life in "Hannah Freeman: An Eighteenth-Century Lenape Living and Working among Colonial Farmers," *Pennsylvania Magazine of History and Biography* 114 (1990): 249–69. Daniel H. Usner Jr., "American Indians in Colonial New Orleans," considers their involvement in the city's economy, in Peter H. Wood, Gregory A. Waselkov, and M. Thomas Hatley, eds., *Powhatan's Mantle* (1989), 104–27; Helen C. Rountree discusses the adjustments of Powhatan men and women to new economic conditions in *Pocahontas's People* (1990). The Reverend Andrew Burnaby's observations on the Pamunkeys are in his *Travels Through the Middle Settlements in the Years 1759 and 1760* (1904). D. W. Meinig includes examples of Indian interaction with Europeans and Africans in *The Shaping of America*, Vol. 1, *Atlantic America, 1492–1800* (1986). Tom Hatley mentions the activities of Cherokee women at Fort Loudoun in *The Dividing Paths* (1993). David J. Weber, *The Spanish Frontier in North America* (1992), includes examples of the mixing of Spanish and Indian cultures and peoples. Father de Morfi's "Account of Disorders in New Mexico, 1778," in which he discusses the position of *génizaros*, is in Marc Simmons, *Coronado's Land* (1991). John L. Kessell, *Kiva, Cross and Crown: The Pecos Indians and New Mexico, 1540–1840* (1979), provides the information on Pecos carpenters. Jerald T. Milanich surveys the activities of mission Indians in *Florida Indians and the Invasion from Europe* (1995), chap. 10.

Margaret Connell Szasz, *Indian Education in the American Colonies, 1607–1783* (1988), provides information on Indian students in colonial colleges. Versions of James Axtell's essay "The Little Red School" appear in his *The European and the Indian* (1981) and *The Invasion Within* (1985). Correspondence from Indian students and alumni is in James Dow McCallum, ed., *The Letters of Eleazar Wheelock's Indians* (1923), which also contains the Onondaga rejection of Wheelock's offer.

Jack Weatherford discusses the Americanization of the English language in his *Native Roots* (1991), chap. 14. Edward F. Tuttle considers how Europeans required a "new world of words," in "Borrowing Versus Semantic Shifts: New World Nomenclature in European Languages," in Fredi Chiappelli, ed., *First Images of America*, 2 vols. (1976), 2:595–611. Charles L. Cutler, *O Brave New Worlds: Native American Loanwords in Current English* (1994), provides historical context as well as lists. William L. Leap examines Indian adaptations and use of English in *American Indian English* (1993). James Axtell assesses the limited impact of Indian loanwords in *The European and the Indian* (1981), quote at 290. David Hackett Fischer examines the change and continuity in transplanted English dialects in *Albion's Seed* (1989). Edward H. Spicer discusses Yaqui-Spanish linguistic blending in *The Yaquis* (1980), and Franciscan missionary linguistic encounters as well as broader issues of linguistic change in his *Cycles of Conquest: The Impact of Spain, Mexico, and the United States on the Indians of the Southwest, 1533–1960* (1960). Jay Gitlin considers trade jargons and other elements of cultural exchange in Clyde A. Milner II, Carol A. O'Conner, and Martha A. Sandweiss, eds., *The Oxford History of the American West* (1994), chap. 3. Andrew L. Knaut quotes Ginés de Herrera Horta in *The Pueblo Revolt of 1680* (1995).

Chapter 9
New Peoples and New Societies

On racial mixing and the new peoples who developed, see Woodrah Borah, "The Mixing of Populations," in Fredi Chiappelli, ed., *First Images of America*, 2 vols. (1976), 2: 707–22. Andrew L. Knaut considers the acculturative processes at work in New Mexico, including the extreme amount of miscegenation, in *The Pueblo Revolt of 1680* (1995). D. W. Meinig explores the multiethnic nature of colonial Carolinian society in *The Shaping of America*, Vol. 1, *Atlantic America, 1492–1800* (1986). On the Métis, see Jacqueline Peterson and Jennifer S. H. Brown, eds., *The New Peoples: Being and Becoming Métis in North America* (1985). Denys Delâge, *Bitter Feast* (1993), discusses the Métis as well as the contrasting nature of French and Indian societies. Dennis F. K. Madill provides a guide to the historical literature on the Métis in "Riel, Red River, and Beyond: New Developments in Métis History," in Colin G. Calloway, ed., *New Directions in American Indian History* (1988), chap. 3. On French policies of racial mixing, see Olive Patricia Dickason, "From 'One Nation' in the Northeast to 'New Nation' in the Northwest: A Look at the Emergence of the Métis," *American Indian Culture and Research Journal* 6: 2 (1982): 1–21, and Cornelius J. Jaenen, *Friend and Foe: Aspects of French-Amerindian Cultural Contact in the Sixteenth and Seventeenth Centuries* (1976), 161–65. Henry Dobyns examines the multiethnic character of Tucson in *Spanish Colonial Tucson* (1976). On the Lumbees, see Karen I. Blu, *The Lumbee Problem: The Making of an American Indian People* (1980), and Gerald M. Sider, *Lumbee Indian Histories: Race, Ethnicity, and Indian Identity in the Southeastern United States* (1993). John Lawson's recommendations are in Hugh Talmage Lefler, ed., *A New Voyage to Carolina* (1967); Jefferson's speech to the Indians is in Saul K. Padover, ed., *The*

Complete Jefferson (1943), 503; his ideas are discussed in Bernard W. Sheehan, *Seeds of Extinction: Jeffersonian Philanthropy and the American Indian* (1973).

On Garcilaso de la Vega, see Lawrence A. Clayton, Vernon James Knight Jr., and Edward C. Moore, eds., *The De Soto Chronicles* (1993), quote at xxii. Kathleen Deagan's observations on St. Augustine are in her "Accommodation and Resistance: The Process and Impact of Spanish Colonization in the Southeast," in David Hurst Thomas, ed., *Columbian Consequences*, vol. 2 (1990), 297–314, and her "Spanish-Indian Interaction in Sixteenth-Century Florida," in William W. Fitzhugh, ed., *Cultures in Contact: The Impact of European Contacts on Native American Cultural Institutions, A.D. 1000–1800* (1985), 281–318. On the various "categories" of people produced by ethnic intermixing in the Spanish southwest, see Ramon A. Gutiérrez, *When Jesus Came, the Corn Mothers Went Away* (1991), as well as David J. Weber, *The Spanish Frontier in North America* (1992) and Jack Weatherford, *Native Roots* (1991), who provides the information on "certificates of whiteness." Helen C. Rountree traces the decline in status of Virginia's Indian population in *Pocahontas's People* (1990).

On tribe formation and identity, and the creation of new societies, see Charles Hudson and Carmen Chaves Tesser, eds., *The Forgotten Centuries* (1994); James H. Merrell, *The Indians' New World* (1989); Patricia Galloway, *Choctaw Genesis 1500–1700* (1995); and John H. Moore, *The Cheyenne Nation: A Social and Demographic History* (1987). Jerald T. Milanich describes the impression of the chiefdoms on the Spaniards in "The European Entrada into La Florida," in David Hurst Thomas, ed., *Columbian Consequences*, vol. 2 (1990).

Susanna Johnson's impressions of Charlestown are reprinted in Colin G. Calloway, ed., *Dawnland Encounters* (1991). Thomas E. Burke Jr., *Mohawk Frontier: The Dutch Community of Schenectady, New York, 1661–1710* (1991), examines the cultural composition of one frontier town. Cornelius J. Jaenen discusses the founding of Detroit and French reactions to Indian liberty and sharing in *The French Relationship with the Native Peoples of New France and Acadia* (1984). William E. Foley and C. David Rice trace the careers of the "Founding Family" in *The First Chouteaus: River Barons of Early St. Louis* (1983). Paul Philip's comment on Pueblo, Colorado, is from *The Fur Trade*, 2 vols. (1961).

The debate on the Iroquois and the Constitution, and the broader influences of Indians on American democracy, is presented in Bruce E. Johansen, *Forgotten Founders* (1982); Donald A. Grinde Jr., *The Iroquois and the Founding of the American Nation* (1977); Donald A. Grinde Jr. and Bruce E. Johansen, eds., *Exemplar of Liberty: Native America and the Evolution of Democracy* (1991); Elisabeth Tooker, "The United States Constitution and the Iroquois League," *Ethnohistory* 35 (1988): 305–36; Bruce E. Johansen and Elisabeth Tooker, "Commentary on the Iroquois and the U.S. Constitution," *Ethnohistory* 37 (1990): 279–90. Oren R. Lyons and John C. Mohawk's comments on Indians and democracy are contained in Lyons et al., *Exiled in the Land of the Free: Democracy, Indian Nations, and the U.S. Constitution* (1992).

German Arciniegas, *America in Europe: A History of the New World in Reverse* (1986), Jack Weatherford, *Indian Givers* (1988), and William Brandon, *New Worlds for Old* (1986), consider Indian contributions to European social thought. Georges E. Sioui's views are expanded in *For an Amerindian Autohistory* (1992). Robert F. Berkhofer Jr., *The White Man's Indian* (1988), discusses images of the Indian from Columbus to the twentieth century. Alfred Goldsworthy Bailey included discussion of Indian impact on the French in *The Conflict of European and Eastern Algonkian Cultures, 1504–1700* (1937). Bougainville's complaint about the corruption of French soldiers is in Edward P. Hamilton, ed., *Adventure in the Wilderness* (1964, 1990). John Winthrop's sermon is quoted in David Hackett Fischer, *Albion's Seed* (1989), 174. Gary Nash considers European views and suppression of Indian social values in *Red, White and Black*, 3d ed. (1992). Cabeza de Vaca's observation on treatment of children is in Cyclone Covey, trans. and ed., *Cabeza de Vaca's Adventures in the Unknown Interior of America* (1990). The concerns of Cotton and Increase Mather about indulgence of children are quoted in John Canup, *Out of the Wilderness* (1990), and James Axtell, *The European and the Indian* (1981), respectively. Canup also quotes William Hubbard on frontier settlements.

Conclusion

The story of Sir William Johnson's dream is given in John Long, *Voyages and Travels of an Indian Interpreter and Trader* (1791), reprinted in Reuben G. Thwaites, ed., *Early Western Travels, 1748–1846*, vol. 2 (1904), 125–26. Dean Snow recounts one of the versions involving Hendrick in "Theyanoquin," in Robert S. Grumet, ed., *Northeastern Indian Lives* (1996), 217. Richard Slotkin examines the power of frontier mythology in a trilogy: *Regeneration through Violence: The Mythology of the American Frontier* (1973); *The Fatal Environment: The Myth of the Frontier in the Age of Industrialization, 1800–1890* (1985); and *Gunfighter Nation: The Myth of the Frontier in 20th-Century America* (1992). James Axtell's assessments of the impact of Indians on English identity are in *The European and the Indian* (1981) and "Colonial America without the Indians," in *After Columbus* (1988). Michael Zuckerman offers more cautious thoughts in "Identity in British America: Unease in Eden," in Nicholas Canny and Anthony Pagden, eds., *Colonial Identity in the Atlantic World, 1500–1800* (1987). R. David Edmunds discusses emerging pan-Indian identity in "Native Americans, New Voices: American Indian History, 1895–1995," *American Historical Review* 100 (1995): 717–40.

Index

Blackfeet Indians, encounter with mounted Shoshones, 113
Blackfish (Shawnee), 161
Blue Jacket (Shawnee), forms Indian confederacy, 111
Book of Common Prayer, in English and Mohawk, 86–87
Boone, Daniel: hosts Indians in his home, 167; as Shawnee captive, 161
Boonesborough, siege of, 167
Bossu, Jean-Bernard: on Indian treatment of wounds, 30; quoting Indian on pre-European America, 9; on sweat baths, 32
Boston Tea Party, and colonial identity, 7
Bouquet, Henry, 130; required return of captives, 159, *160*
Bowles, William Augustus, leads Indian delegation to England, 166
Braddock, Edward, *106;* defeat, 107
Bradford, William, 39; on Indian deaths from disease, 35; on Indian desire for firearms, 96; misinterprets Indian gift, 127; on Morton's village, 185; on Pequot War, 98
Brafferton Hall, built for Indians, 170
Brainerd, David (missionary), 89
Brandon, William, on Indian ideas on liberty, 189
Brant, Joseph (Mohawk): forms Indian confederacy, 111; as landlord, 170; portrait painted, 166; relocates, 149; translates Bible into Mohawk language, 84, 171; visits London, 166
Brant, Molly, 154
Braudel, Fernand, on Indians as guides, 136
Breen, T. H., on creative adaptations, 6
Brims (Creek), diplomacy of, 120
Brothertown, New York, 146
Brulé, Etienne, cultural conversion of, 162
Buffalo, spread of cattle disease to, 14
Burnaby, Rev. Andrew: on Indian employment, 168–69; on Virginia Indian clothing, 67
Burning, as war tactic, 109

Cadillac, Sieur de la Mothe, founder of Detroit, 186
Cahokia, rise and decline of, 59
Caldwell, Sir John, *65*
California missions, 80–81; Indian conversions at, 80
Calumet, spread of, 128
Calusa Indians, speak Spanish, 176
Cameron, Alexander, 131; marries Cherokee woman, 154
Canada, as exile home for Indians, 149
Canandaigua, treaty of, 128
Canasatego (Onondaga spokesman), 131; on English education, 170; speech, 188; on written documents, 132
Canoes: of Indian birchbark, 49–50; as making

wide-ranging travel possible, 135; properties of, 50
Canonicus (Narragansett), sends gift to Bradford, 127
Cape Girardeau, Shawnees move to area of, 145
Captive taking, 155–57; of Indians by Europeans, 165; as slave raids, 99, 102
Captives: living with Indians, 155; preference not to return home by, 156, 161; ransomed, 155; relations with captors after release, 161; returned to Bouquet, 159, *160*
Captivity narratives, 155
Capuchin, Don Tomes Vélez, on diplomacy, 116
Cartier, Jacques: disease among crew of, 24; interpreter for, 125; return of captives taken by, 165; route of, 24–25; trading, 43
Castiglioni, Luigi: on Indian clothes, 67; on Indian habits, 154; inventories plants, 28–29; on plants as medicine, 31
Catawba Indians: English name applied to all Indians, 143; smallpox epidemics among, 36; survival of, 121
Catechism, Indians reciting in Spanish, 172
Catholicism: conversion to, 157; Indian, 146; Mohawk conversion to, 147
Catlin, George, on Delaware migrations, 145
Caughnawaga: mission, 70; as new town, 147
Ceramics, Indian styles of, 43. *See also* Pottery, Native
Ceremonial objects, beads as, 47
"Certificates of whiteness," 183
Champlain, Samuel de, 43–44; Indian battles, 92; notes disappearance of Indians, 25; sends French boys to live with Indians, 162
Charbonneau, Toussaint (interpreter), 126
Chauchetière, Father Claude, on Indian community cooperation, 190
Cherokee Indians: British invade lands of, 109; Cameron living with, 154; delegations of, sent to London, 166; divided and relocated, 149; smallpox among, 36; towns of, 61, 122
Cheyenne Indians, migration of, 150
Chickamauga Indians, origins of, 149
Chickasaw Indians, 109
Chiefs: authority of, 111; power bases, 123; powerful, 184–85; responsibilities of, 123
Children: captive, *158;* European, as smallpox carriers, 35; Indian treatment of, 192; "Indianification" of, 156; of mixed marriages, 182
Choctaw Indians: as allies, 109; and depletion of deer herds, 16; diplomatic relations of, with Europeans, 120–21
Chota, political authority centered at, 122
Chouteau, Auguste and Pierre, St. Louis founders, 186
Christian Indians: of Florida, 168; of Stockbridge, 185
Christianity: compared to native religion, 72;

French: allies of Indians and, 118; army recruits Indians, 104–5
French-Iroquoian dictionary, 125
Frontier: defined, 7; hero, 196; human influences on, 3; merging and crossing, 152–77; Turner on, 3
Fur trade, 14–15; Indians as key figures in, 167

Gaelic, spoken by Scots in North Carolina, 174
Garcés, Francisco, mission in southwest, 89–90
Gender relations, changes in, 191
Generational struggles, Indian, 123
Génizaros: baptized, 169; as laborers, 169
Geography, fitting America into concepts of, 10–11
German-speaking settlers, 139–40
Gift giving, 44; as symbolic language, 127
Gilbert, Sir Humphrey, counters guerrilla tactics, 97
Gill, Joseph Louis, adopted by Abenakis, 157
Ginseng, curative use of, 28–29
Girty, Simon: allegiance of, to Senecas, 162; as interpreter, 125–26
Glass beads, origin in trade of, 45
Glen, James, 121
Gnadenhütten, massacre at, 81
Gonzalez, Manuel, becomes San Jose alcalde, 167
Good Peter (Oneida), translates Psalms, 83
Gookin, Daniel: on Indian democracy, 190; on Indian housing, 60
Gosnold, Bartholomew, on Indian clothing, 66
Governor Kiefft's War, 98
Grass, European, introduction of, 14
Great Migration, beginnings of, 140
Great Philadelphia Wagon Road, 141
Great Swamp Fight, 98; Tefft's role in, 164
Great Tree of Peace, 147
Great Warriors' Path, 135
Green Corn Ceremony, 85, 91
Greenville, treaty of, 159
Guale Indians, rebel against mission, 78
Guerrilla war, 96, 99, 107–8
Guides, French kidnapping of Indians for use as, 136
Guns: furnished to Indians by Europeans, 105; influence on Indian warfare of, 92–93. See also Firearms
Gutiérrez, Ramon, on intermarriage, 182

Hagler (Catawba), diplomacy of, 121
Hamilton, Alexander: on Indian clothing, 66, 67; on sitting in church with Indians, 81
Hamilton, Henry, scalp buying by, 103
Hamlin, Hannibal, cured by Molly Ockett, 31
Hancock, John, on Indians, 1
Handsome Fellow (Creek), on European goods, 46–47
Handsome Lake (Seneca), promotes religion, 91

Hariot, Thomas, on Indian disease, 34
Harley, Brian, on Indian renaming, 12
Hartwell, Ephraim and Elizabeth, death of children of, 40
Harvard College: chartered to educate English and Indians, 170; Indian college at, 83; medical school, 41
Hawikuh: battle of, 93; Spanish troops occupy, 94
Hawkeye *(Last of the Mohicans),* as frontier hero, 196
Heckewelder, John: on alcohol, 37; on Indian healing, 30; on Indian medicine, 27; on interpreters, 123; as missionary, 81; on sweat baths, 32–33
Hellebore, as emetic, 28
Hendrick (Mohawk), *64;* death of, 107; in story of Johnson's dream, 195; visits England, 166
Highland Scots, emigration of, 142
Honeybees, European, introduction of, in America, 13
Hopi Indians: adopt European plants and food, 57; conversion of, 80; livestock of, 57–58; religion of, 79–80
Horses: change pattern of warfare, 111–14; mobility increased by use of, 150–51; spread of, 13, 58, 112
Horta, Ginés de Herrera, on Indians speaking Spanish, 174
Hospitals: in New Spain, 40; in Philadelphia, 40–41
Housing, European: adaptations of Indian styles, 61; Indian attitudes about, 60
Housing, Indian: building materials, 59; European-style, 59; Iroquois, 61
Hubbard, William, on freedom, 192–93
Hudson's Bay Company, reliance of, on Indian middlemen, 144
Hunt, Thomas (Squanto's kidnapper), 124
Hunting, 55; of buffalo on horseback, 58; as ceremonial activity, 72; discouraged by missionaries, 55; European adaptations to native, 56; prayers for, 73; wasteful, 56
Huron Indians: accommodate Christianity, 73; destroyed by Iroquois, 74, 144; disease among, 36; and smallpox, 36; trade with whites, 43–44; warrior attire of, *100*
Hutchinson, Anne, daughter's capture by Indians, 156

Identification, of Indians by Europeans, 142–43
Identities, Indian-white, 196–97
Illinois Indians, disease among, 38
Immigrants, hardships of, 139
"Inca, the." *See* de la Vega, Garcilaso
Indentured servants, Indians as, 167–68
Indian captives: European views about, 155; as guides, 165–66
"Indian English," 176. *See also* Language

Narragansett Indians: converted, 84; taught stone masonry, 169
Narvaez, Pánfilo de, Ortiz as expedition member with, 152–53
Nash, Gary: on conglomeration of cultural entities, 3; on suppression of admired values, 193
Natick: census, 105; decline of, 77; as Eliot praying town, 76; Indians of, support English in war, 77
Neutrality: effectiveness of, 120; Indian, in American Revolution, 1; native, 117
New Sweden, immigrant hunters in, 55
"New World," in European imagination, 9
Niles, Samuel, minister to Narragansetts, 84–85
Nootka Indians, famine among, 22
Norridgewock, raid on, 89
Nutrition, changes in Indian, 58. See also Diet; Food

Occom, Samson (Mohegan): becomes missionary, 171; career of, 83–84; on diversity of language, 175; hymns by, 84; visits England, 166
Ockett, Molly, "the Great Indian Doctress," 31
Oconostota (Cherokee), joins Scottish Society of St. Andrews, 167
Odanak, burning of, 109
Oglethorpe, James, takes Creek chief to England, 166
Ojibwa Indians, evict Sioux from Minnesota, 113
Omaha Indians, disease among, 38
Oneida Indians, after American Revolution, 149
Onondaga Indians: resisting English education, 170–71; wampum belts deposited by, 129
Opata Indians, at Tucson, 104
Oquaga, Iroquois village, 81–82
Oral culture, importance of, 132
Ortiz, Juan (DeSoto's interpreter), 153; found by DeSoto, 152
Oswegatchie, founding of, 149
Otsiquette, Peter, accompanies Lafayette to France, 166

Paine, Thomas, on absence of misery in Indian societies, 191
Pandemics, 33. See also Disease
Papago Indians, 104
Passenger pigeons, extinction of, 17
Paths, extensive use of, 136
Pawnee Indians, sold as slaves, 102
Peace pipe. See Calumet
Pecos, trade fairs at, 153
Pellegra, 53
Penn, William, on ethnic diversity, 172; on Indian democracy, 190; on Indian sharing, 191; invites German immigrants into Pennsylvania, 140

Pennsylvania Dutch, 140
Pequot War, 97–98
Petroleum, used as medicine, 29
Philadelphia, as gateway for Scotch-Irish, 141
Philips, Paul C., on origins of Pueblo, Colorado, 186
Pigs, effect of, on environment, 14
Pilgrims: English-speaking Indians and, 124; find non-Indians buried in Indian mounds, 153; theft of Indian corn by, 52
Pima Indians: allied with Spain, 104; dislike of speaking Spanish, 173
Plants: American, introduction of European diseases to, 21; Indian use of, in cures, 27; inventories of medicinal, 28; trading of therapeutic, 27
Playing cards, Indian use of, 47, 48
Plowing, destruction of, 20–21
Pocahontas, sails to Europe, 165
Point Pleasant, battle of, renegades in, 164
Pontiac, as multitribal movement leader, 197
Pontiac's Revolt, 110
Popé (Tewa medicine man), 79
Population: categories, 182; of colonial Tucson, 182; growth, 139; growth of Pennsylvania, 141; growth of U.S. and Indian, 40; role of disease in decline of, 34
Potatoes: importance of, 50; use of, 53, 54
Pottery, Native: of Blackfeet, 47; design changes in, 47
Pouchet, Pierre, on Indian clothing, 66
Powhatan: as capable diplomat, 117; captures John Smith, 127; hired to kill wolves, 168
Powhatan Indians: acquire firearms, 96; battle rituals of, 95; beliefs of, 81
Prayer, as replacement for old customs, 73
Praying towns: Eliot's, 76; established, 170
Profane words, absence in Indian languages of, 175–76. See also Language
Protestant Irish, immigration of, 142
Pueblo, Colorado, origins of, 186
Pueblo Indians: adopt European plants and foods, 57; allied with Spanish, 104; and Coronado, 137; migration of, 151; population decline of, 34; revolt of, 78–79; smallpox among, 34; town building by, 61
Pueblo Revolt, 79, 104; Apache raids as precipitating, 112
Puritans, 140; and conversion, 74; on fears of alteration to English culture from Indians, 7; missionary teachings of, 74

Quakers, 140
Quapaw Indians: smallpox among, 34; village of, 128
Quebec: capture of, 109; French defeat at, 109
Quivira, search for, 137

Racial intermarriage, 180; advocates for, 179
Rasles, Sebastian: on Abenaki faith, 88; career of, 88–89; life among Abenakis, 89; on thinking like an Indian, 154
Rats, European, introduction of, in America, 13
Reading, status of learning, 77
Reconquista, 94
Red Jacket (Seneca), on education, 171
Red Shoe (Choctaw), 121
Redeemed Captive Returning to Zion, 157
Religions, Indian: beliefs as viewed by Europeans, 68; characteristics of, 76–77; complexity of, 68–69; Spanish attacks on, 78
Renegades, characterization of whites living with Indians as, 164
Resistance movements, Indian, 110–11
Revolutionary War: Indians drawn into, 110; splits Iroquois league, 149
Rituals, Indian, prohibitions against, 85
Rivers, renamed by Europeans, 12
Roanoke colony, 34
Rock carvings, as trail markers, 135
Rogel, Father Juan, 77
Rogers, Robert, 108; Rogers' Rangers, 108–9
Rolfe, John: imports tobacco, 54; marriage and death of, 165
Rolfe, Thomas, son of Pocahontas, 165
Ronda, James, on combining Christianity and Indian religions, 75
Root powder, as medicine, 30

Sacagawea (Shoshone): as translator, 126; in Upper Missouri villages, 151
Sacred places, Indian, 12–13
Sagard, Gabriel: on becoming savages, 153; on Huron sense of community, 190–91; on sweat baths, 32
Sailors, Indians as, 147, 169
St. Augustine, Florida: Indians in area of, 143; intermarriage at, 180–81, *181*
St. Clair, Arthur, ambushed, 111
Saint Denis, Louis Jucheron de, 125
St. Louis, founded, 186
St. Regis, founded, 147
Salish, language of Flatheads, 126
Samoset (Abeñaki), speaks English, 124
Sassafras, as a drug, 28
Sattelihu (Andrew Montour), 125
Saukamappee (Cree), on mounted Shoshones, 113
Savery, William, on negotiations, 128
Savignon, taken to Europe by Cartier, 165
Scalping, 103–4
Scarouady (Oneida), on Braddock's defeat, 107
Schenectady, New York, origins of, 186
Schoepf, Johann David: on Indian medicine, 28; on white-Indian similarities, 4
Scotch-Irish, emigration history of, 141

Scottish Highlanders: settle in Cape Fear Valley, 174; speak Gaelic, 174
Scouts, Indian, 104–5
Scurvy: Cartier crew contracts, 24; limes as cure for, 24
Sea otter pelts: in China trade, 48–49; effect on Indians of trade in, 22; ethnic groups in trade of, 179
Seal of Massachusetts Bay Colony, 69
Second Mesa, 79
Seminole Indians: speak Spanish, 176; travels to Cuba by, 143–44
Seneca Indians: employment of, 169; return home after Revolutionary War, 149; support French, 120; use of European tools by, 46
Serra, Junípero, in California, 80
Settlement patterns, Indian, changes in, 21–22
Settlements: Indian, abandoned, 11; European, as reflections of Europe, 11
Seven Years' War, as first world war, 105
Sexual encounters, Indian-white, 153
Shamans: as healers, 27–28; opposition to missionaries by, 71
Sharing, as Indian obligation, 191
Shawnee Indians: captives of, 161; divisions of, 145; migrations, 144–45
Sheep, raised by Indians, 57, 58
Shickellamy (Oneida), 195; as interpreter, 126
Shoshone Indians: change in fortunes of, 113; horses and trade advantages of, 112–13; migration of, 150
Shuffleton, Frank, defines ethnicity, 3–4
Sioui, Georges, on Indian influence on world, 189
Sioux Indians: dominance of, 113; evicted from Minnesota, 113
Six Nations Reserve, 149
Slaves: African, 23, 142; Indians as, 169; Indians compared to, 81; sale of New England Indians as, 147; taken in war, 99, 102
Slotkin, Richard, on frontier hero, 196
Smallpox: epidemics, 34–37; in Florida, 33; in New England, 35–36; powerlessness of defenses against, 38
Smith, James, on Indians cursing, 176
Smith, John: finds corn fields, 52; on fishing, 55; as subchief to Powhatan, 127
Smith, Richard, 88; visits Iroquois town, 81–82
Smith, William, on response of captives to liberation, 161
Smoking, 154
Snake bites, Indian treatments for, 29
Snowshoes, 104
Spanish: adopting from Indian culture, 4–5; conquest of Iberia by, 94; exchanges of, with Indians, 5; on resemblance of white Americans to Indians, 2; as trade language, 175; use of Indian medicine by, 31

Spokan Indians, prophecies attributed to, xv
Spotswood, Governor, opens Indian school, 170
Squanto (Patuxet): abducted by Spanish, 166; corn introduced by, 52; as interpreter for Pilgrims, 124; kidnapped, 124
Steele, Ian, on Indian-European allies, 107
Stevens, Phineas, as former captive turned middleman, 161–62
Stockbridge, Massachusetts: established as model mission, 185; evolution of, 185–86
Stone masonry, Indians taught, 169
Sullivan, John: invasion of Iroquois country by, 110; reliance of, on corn, 53
Swedish immigrants, exchanges with Indians by, 5

Talon, Pierre (interpreter), 125
Talon, Robert (interpreter), 125
Taos Pueblo, on place and people, 9
Tapp (Taptico), William, 42
Tecumseh, as multitribal movement leader, 197
Tefft, Joshua, as renegade, 164
Tekakwitha, Kateri (Mohawk), converts to Christianity, 70
Tennent, Dr. John, discovers Indian medicine, 30
Thomas, Gabriel, on Indians as doctors, 26
Timucuan Indians: population decline of, 34; rebellion by, 78
Tobacco, 54–55
Tocqueville, Alexis de, 140–41
Tokkohwomput, Daniel, succeeds Eliot, 83
Tonyn, Patrick, on Indians in Florida, 185
Toothaches, Indian treatment of, 29
Totem poles, 49
Towns: Cherokee, 61; location of European on previous Indian, 11–12; use of Indian labor in building, 61
Towns, Indian: population of, 59; rebuilding of, after migration, 145
Trade: ceremonial aspects of, 43–44; competition in, 144; growth of towns on routes of, 186; jargons used, 175; reasons for, 43; spread of disease through, 33
Trade fairs, Spanish at Indian, 153
Trade goods, dispersal of, 48
Trade network, extent of, 43, 44
Transients, Indians as New England, 147
Translations, multiple, 126–27
Treaties: effect of European on Indians, 122; negotiation of Indian-white, 119–20, 131
Tribal origins, legends of, 134
Truteau, Jean Baptiste, on Indian skin maps, 137
Tucson, Arizona: categories of residents of, 182; intermarriage at, 181–82
Tufts, Henry, cured of thigh wound, 31
"Turk, the," 137
Turkeys, destruction of, 17

Turner, Frederick Jackson, on Indian influence on Americans, 2–3
Tuscarora Indians, join with Five Nations, 147
Typhus, brought by Drake's crew, 33–34

Underhill, John, night attack by, 98
Uniforms, British, as clear targets, 109

Van der Donck, Adrian: on Indian cures, 26; on smallpox, 36
Vancouver, George, on Indian smallpox, 37
Venereal disease, curing, 29
Vermin, European, introduction of, in America, 13
Vermont, impact of Europeans on forest resources in, 19–20
Verrazzano, Giovanni da: on Indian houses, 60; trading with Indians, 45
Vespucci, Amerigo, 11
Vincennes, siege of, 103
Vocabulary, Indian words added to English, 173. *See also* English Language; Language

Waban, leads faction, 85
Wage earners, Indians as, 169
Wallace, Paul, on Indian trails, 135, 136
Wampanoag Indians, Mayhew preaches to, 74
Wampum: belt, 130; designs of, 128–29; and diplomacy, 129
Wanalancet (Pennacook), conversion of, 70–71
War: adoption of Indian war tactics, 107–8; changing Indian tactics in, 93; as continuing process, 103; contrast between European and American methods of, 114; de la Vega describes, 94; deaths from, 105; disruptive aspects of, 111; emphasis by Plains tribes on, 114; European tactics of, 103; importance of Indian tactics in American Revolution, 110; Indian methods of, 92, 103–4; introduction of European, in America, 97; joint strategies, 107; merger of European and Indian, 104; ritualized, 106; as source of status, 114; tactics, 94–95
Ward, John, captive as renegade, 164
Washington, George: investment in western lands by, 110; war tactics of, 110
Watermelons, introduction of, 56
Wayne, Anthony: and Shawnees, 145; victory by, 111; Wells as scout for, 162
Weather, effect of clearing land on, 20
Weatherford, Jack: on Americanization, 56; on Americanization of English language, 173; on cultural mixture, 3
Weber, David: on mental adjustments to New World, 10; on Spanish concessions to Indian culture, 4–5
Weeds, European, introduction of, in America, 14

Library of Congress Cataloging-in-Publication Data

Calloway, Colin G. (Colin Gordon), 1953–
    New worlds for all : Indians, Europeans, and the remaking of early
America / Colin G. Calloway.
        p.   cm.—(The American moment)
    Includes bibliographical references and index.
    ISBN 0-8018-5448-2 (hardcover : alk. paper).
    1. North America—History—Colonial period , ca. 1600–1775.
    2. Conquerors—North America—History.   3. Indians of North America—
First contact with Europeans.   4. Indians of North America—
History—Colonial period, ca. 1600–1775.   I. Title.   II. Series.
    E45.C34   1997
    970.02—dc20   96-20625
                                                            CIP

    ISBN 0-8018-5959-X (pbk.)